The Encrypted State

The Encrypted State

Delusion and Displacement in the Peruvian Andes

David Nugent

Stanford University Press

Stanford, California

Stanford University Press
Stanford, California

Printed in the United States of America on acid-free, archival-quality paper

Library of Congress Cataloging-in-Publication Data

Names: Nugent, David, author.
Title: The encrypted state : delusion and displacement in the Peruvian Andes /
    David Nugent.
Description: Stanford, California : Stanford University Press, 2019. | Includes
    bibliographical references and index.
Identifiers: LCCN 2018053500 | ISBN 9781503609037 (cloth : alk. paper) |
    ISBN 9781503609723 (epub)
Subjects: LCSH: Political stability—Peru—History—20th century. | Legitimacy
    of governments—Peru—History—20th century. | Dictatorship—Peru—
    History—20th century. | Odría, Manuel A. (Manuel Arturo), 1897–1974. |
    Partido Aprista Peruano—History—20th century. | Amazonas (Peru)—
    Politics and government—20th century. | Peru—Politics and
    government—1919–1968.
Classification: LCC F3448 .N836 2019 | DDC 985.06/3—dc23
LC record available at https://lccn.loc.gov/2018053500

Cover design: Rob Ehle

Typeset by Newgen in 11/13.5 Adobe Garamond

For Joan Vincent and Eric R. Wolf, Teachers and Mentors

Contents

Acknowledgments

This volume is the culmination of many years of investigation into the dynamics of state formation, and of political rule more generally, in the Andes and beyond. A great many people and organizations have contributed to the culmination of the project. It is not possible to thank them all, but I would like to express my deep appreciation to Gabriel Aguilar Gallardo, Ananth Aiyer, Jennifer Alvey, Florence Babb, Tom Biolsi, Yolanda Burga Díaz, Asunta Burga Mas, Carlo Caduff, Kim Clark, Don Donham, Paulo Drinot, Ben Fallaw, Tim Finan, Carol Greenhouse, Akhil Gupta, Angelique Haugerud, Steven Hirsch, Angela Hobart, Bruce Knauft, Chris Krupa, Roberto Lazo Quepuy, Leah Nugent, Jeff Maskovsky, Chandana Mathur, David Napier, Gyan Pandey, Richard Rechtman, Mariano Rubio Pizarro, Olga Santillán Campojoo, Víctor Santillán Gutierrez, Derek Sayer, Gerald Sider, Karen Spalding, Shreyas Sreenath, Adeem Suhail, Ida Susser, Carlos Torres Mas, and Thomas Wilson.

Talks presented at the following institutions provided especially useful feedback regarding the arguments in *The Encrypted State*: the University of Arizona Department of Anthropology; the British Museum; the Bellagio Center Conference on "Fear of the Foreign: Pandemics and Xenophobia"; the Fernand Braudel Center for the Study of Economies, Historical Systems and Civilizations; the University of California at Los Angeles Department of Anthropology; the Colonial and Postcolonial Studies Program at Emory University; the conference on "Off-Centered States: State Formation and Deformation in the Andes," cosponsored by the Carnegie Corporation and FLACSO-Ecuador and held in Quito,

Ecuador; the University of Florida Department of Anthropology; the National University of Ireland, Maynooth Department of Anthropology; the Princeton University Department of Anthropology; the Wenner-Gren Foundation Conference on "The Anthropology of Corruption" held in Sintra, Portugal; and the Wenner-Gren Foundation Conference on "Tax Matters" held at Emory University.

I am equally indebted to the organizations that provided support for research and writing. These include the Centro Incontri Umani Ascona, the Colby College Social Science Council, the Institute for Comparative and International Studies of Emory University, the National Endowment for the Humanities, the National Endowment for the Humanities Summer Stipend Program; the School for Advanced Research (Santa Fe, NM), and Emory University. I owe these organizations a debt that cannot be repaid.

Finally, I owe a special debt of gratitude to my publisher. It has been a great pleasure to work with Stanford University Press. The anonymous reviewers provided excellent critical feedback and allowed me to make major improvements to the volume. And Michelle Lipinski, senior editor for the press, has been marvelous, as has all of her staff! May all scholars be so fortunate as to have an editor (and a press) as capable, insightful, and supportive as she.

I am beholden in a very different way to Weisu Zhu Nugent, my partner, and to James and Leah Nugent, my children. During the many long years that I have worked on this project they have given me the kind of personal support, love, and care that only the most fortunate of people ever experience.

Note on Sources

The Encrypted State is based on a comprehensive, in-depth review of regional archives. I have been doing fieldwork in Chachapoyas since 1982, and during the intervening thirty-five years have formed close relationships with the officials in the National Cultural Institute (Instituto Nacional de Cultura), the Prefecture, the National Police (the Guardia Civil), the National Bank, the Subprefecture, the Municipality, and the Catholic Church. These ties have made it possible for me to access all the major archives of region. In my manuscript, many of the sources are listed as being housed in Archive of the Subprefecture of Chachapoyas. In the not-so-distant past, however, these documents were housed in the Archive of the Prefecture of the Department of Amazonas—along with the documentary record of the Prefecture, and archival materials for the period in question that pertain to the region's other provinces (Luya, Bongará, and Rodriguez de Mendoza) and a number of its districts. One of the peculiarities of working in the Chachapoyas region is that archiving practices are unstable. As a result, the documents that are housed in one archive at one point in time are commonly moved to a different archive thereafter. Furthermore, the documents that are to be found in the archive of the Prefecture, for example, are not limited to documents that are relevant to the Prefecture (or the Subprefecture). Rather, documents from a wide range of jurisdictions are often thrown together. During the thirty-five or so years I have been doing fieldwork in Chachapoyas, however, I have been able to review the vast majority of archival sources. The irregularity in archiving practices, I would argue, reflects a deeper irregularity in state practices more generally—a point that is central to the argument I make about state formation.

The Encrypted State

Part I

State Formation as Antiepistemology

Introduction

The Routine and the Remarkable in State Formation

States, if the pun be forgiven, *state*; the arcane rituals of a court of law, the formulae of royal assent to an Act of Parliament, visits of school inspectors are all statements. They define, in great detail, acceptable forms and images of social activity and individual and collective identity; they regulate, in empirically specifiable ways . . . very much . . . of social life. Indeed, in this sense "the State" never stops talking.
—Corrigan and Sayer, *The Great Arch* (1985)

CIRCA 1950 the military government of Peru, under the leadership of General Manuel Odría, undertook a project of truly massive proportions. Mobilizing the collective resources of virtually the entire state apparatus, the regime mounted a campaign of vicious persecution against APRA, Peru's most important political party, which was regarded as a dangerously subversive threat.[1] In the Chachapoyas region of northern Peru the campaign failed, precipitating a (temporary) crisis of rule. Officials came to believe that they were incapable of carrying out even the most basic of government functions, especially those concerning surveillance, conscription, and taxation. Furthermore, officials came to believe that their efforts to govern the region were being thwarted by APRA, the party they themselves had forced underground, by means of the most brutal repression. In accounting for the failure of their own efforts to govern, officials attributed to APRA a subterranean party apparatus with all the powers of state that their own regime lacked—and then some. Indeed, the political authorities came to view their administration as a pale imitation of a sophisticated, complex state structure located somewhere deeply underground. They could not actually see the subterranean party state to which they attributed such power and influence. They were certain it was there. But because APRA insisted on remaining hidden from view—on remaining precisely where government officials had left it—the authorities could not actually find APRA. As a result, they were left to imagine the contours of their invisible enemy.

The plague of fantasies (Žižek 1997) that swept through the Chachapoyas region at the beginning of the Odría regime is reminiscent of other "panics" that have seized hold of the Peruvian population. The most recent of these was during the early 1990s, when the Shining Path—which appeared to be on the verge of seizing control of the national government—warned that it had "a thousand eyes and ears" that watched and listened (Mayer 1991).[2] Like the Sendero episode, the earlier one that involved APRA generated the most extreme of responses on the part of the authorities. As time passed government officials became increasingly fearful of those around them. Initially, their concerns were limited to groups already considered of dubious loyalty—radical teachers, outspoken youth, rural Indian cultivators. As the plague of fear spread, however, government officials came to have doubts about the most unlikely of suspects—children in elementary school, members of girls' volleyball teams, even staunchly conservative elements of the landed elite. As officials became increasingly paranoid, the "radius of doubt" with which they operated became ever broader and grew to include more and more of the population. The circle of people who could be trusted became ever narrower, to such an extent that government officials came to question the loyalty of other government officials. Indeed, the authorities went to great lengths in what proved to be a futile effort to purge the government apparatus and society writ large of the nefarious influence of APRA.

At the very height of the epidemic of fear, government officials came to feel deeply threatened by the Party of the People (as APRA referred to itself). They also came to suspect that the Apristas were closing in around them. In response, the authorities sought to build an unbreachable cordon of security around themselves that would guarantee their safety and autonomy in the face of an all-pervasive danger. The creation of such a zone of safety, however, was no easy matter, because the Party of the People appeared to be everywhere. So "close" did the authorities consider the party to be that in order to protect themselves, they took an unprecedented step. They abandoned the outer domain of the state to the party and attempted to inscribe a new inner frontier between state and subversive. They did so by encrypting the state. A select group of high-ranking officials, who (initially!) regarded one another as completely trustworthy, took to communicating amongst themselves in coded messages. Their goal in doing so was to ensure that the prying eyes of APRA did not penetrate into the inner sanctum of rule.

But as those within the security cordon came to distrust one another, even this precaution proved insufficient to protect the state from the party. When it became clear that measures designed to ensure absolute secrecy and security were of little use against APRA, government officials came to feel ever more exposed, ever more vulnerable. They also became increasingly distrustful of those around them. No one was above suspicion.[3]

Ultimately, the authorities came to fear those they relied upon most—their own police force (the Guardia Civil). As the boundary between state and subversive dissolved, officials came to believe that the police had been thoroughly infiltrated by the Apristas. So distrustful of the Guardia Civil did government officials become that, as a general policy, they recommended to the central government that all police be transferred out of region every two years, lest they be "contaminated" by the highly odious nature of local political sentiments (i.e., by APRA). But the authorities went further still: they refused to take the constabulary's repeated assurances of loyalty at face value—even though government officials insisted that such assurances be made.

So fearful did the authorities become that they concluded that the assurances offered by the police were the very opposite of what they seemed. Government officials concluded that the Guardia Civil were merely disguising their secret underground activities behind a mask of commitment to the preservation of the social order. The authorities also concluded that the police were only biding their time, were waiting for the opportune moment to strike, so that they could seize control of the region on behalf of the subversives. In light of this very dangerous state of affairs, the authorities in Chachapoyas appealed to their superiors in Lima for armed reinforcements. No one was to be trusted, they asserted. Everyone was an Aprista.[4]

The "State" of Theory

This work draws upon these paranoid and delusional dimensions of rule in Chachapoyas to rethink the dynamics of state formation. Existing state theory is ill equipped to explain developments such as those outlined above, in which government officials experience a crisis of rule. State theory is similarly ill disposed to explain the official response to Chachapoyas's midcentury crisis of rule—in which the authorities project into being a dark and dangerous counterstate that could not be seen with the naked eye. This is because the central question that guides much of state theory (and much of state practice!) is that of *order*. How, scholars have asked, has it been possible for states to establish and reproduce order, regularity, and routine (or the illusion thereof) in social and political life? This is regarded as an especially puzzling problem in light of the enormous inequalities that are found in virtually all parts of the contemporary world, and the role of state processes in reproducing them.

The scholarly community has addressed this problem in several different ways. Many scholars have sought to explain the persistence of order (or the illusion thereof) in highly stratified societies by drawing upon Enlightenment-based understandings of power as a repressive force. They have stressed either the monopoly on coercion that states are said to exercise (which is at times [Agamben 1998] framed as "sovereignty"), or some combination of coercion and consent. Others scholars have sought answers to the question of order by drawing on post-Enlightenment perspectives (especially those of Foucault) on power as a productive force and emphasize processes that may be broadly termed "governmental." Whether the focus is on the repressive or productive dimensions of power, however, the existing scholarship's preoccupation with problems of order and regularity in political life makes it ill prepared to understand the chaotic, contradictory, delusional, disorganized, and irrational dimensions to the dynamics of rule—the kinds of developments that are the focus of the present work.

Were disorder, delusion, contradiction, and irrationality exceptional, there would be little reason to pay them any mind. However, they are anything but: they are both normal to and inseparable from official efforts to order political life. The pervasiveness of disorder, delusion, and contradiction is especially significant because these forces are generally understood as exceptional—as if they were aberrations from a purportedly normal state of affairs. This tendency to label disorder and delusion as exceptional and inherently foreign to the activities of the state is shared by scholars and politicians alike.[5]

One of my purposes in the present work is to explore the implications of the fact that those who claim the right to rule—and many of those who study this process—represent disorder and delusion as exceptional, as inherently foreign to the activities of the state. *The Encrypted State* views the ordering claims of state as themselves delusional. The "delusion" extends beyond familiar assertions that the right to rule is based on understandings that are exaggerated, highly distorted, or grossly misconceived.

For one, state claims about order are founded on a contradiction between the interested, violent, and coercive activities that state processes so often support, and official representations of these processes as peaceful, noncoercive, and disinterested. Second, these claims are founded on denying and concealing the contradictions upon which they are based, even—or especially—from those making the claims. As a result, there is a kind of cultural duplicity at work at the very heart of state formation—one that leads to a pervasive "structural blindness." Because of the disjuncture between the nature of many state activities and how government officials must represent these activities, this duplicity is unacknowledged, and unacknowledgeable.[6]

The ubiquity of the irrational, the contradictory, and the chaotic in processes of state formation raises another important point. Not only do government authorities treat disorder, delusion, and contradiction as exceptional to what states ordinarily do and are; much the same can be said of the scholarly community that has sought to understand the dynamics of state formation. As I have written elsewhere (Nugent 2010), while many authors acknowledge the fragility of rule and the contingency of state forms (Roseberry 1994; Sayer 1994), most analysts of the state concern themselves with contexts in which organized political subjection has in some sense been achieved (Agamben 1998; Bourdieu 1999; Corrigan and Sayer 1985; Ferguson and Gupta 2002; Gupta 2012; Hansen and Stepputat 2001, 2005; Joseph and Nugent 1994; Scott 1998). Their main concern is with the formation and the operation of "functioning" polities.[7]

In recent decades, scholars in multiple disciplines have devoted their energies to understanding the peculiar nature of that collective illusion known as "the state."[8] The emphasis of much of this work has been on understanding how states work their "magic" (Coronil 1997; Taussig 1997)—on understanding the processes by which states come to be accepted as real, powerful, and all-pervasive elements of the social world. *The Great Arch: English State Formation as Cultural Revolution*, by historical sociologists Philip Corrigan and Derek Sayer (1985), is among the most sophisticated and influential of works to grapple with this problem. As did Weber before them (1980), Corrigan and Sayer emphasize that the state is not a thing but rather a *claim*—a claim to authority, to legitimacy (Corrigan and Sayer 1985, 7). It is not only a means by which one group of people subjugates another but also a process by which groups misrepresent what they seek to do. This process, Corrigan and Sayer argue, is deeply cultural in that it relies upon moral regulation: "a project of normalizing, rendering natural, taken for granted, in a word 'obvious,' what are in fact ontological and epistemological premises of a particular . . . form of social order" (Corrigan and Sayer 1985, 4; see also Corrigan 1981).

State claims to authority and legitimacy are grounded in culture, but they are violent claims nonetheless. Only by systematically undermining and delegitimating alternative constructions of morality and society can states aspire to make their own assertions collectively shared (or at least tolerated). Corrigan and Sayer invoke Durkheim's notion of a collective conscience, but they anchor his conception in politics—in struggles over conflicting moral visions of sociocultural order (Corrigan and Sayer 1985, 6).

Although the control of the means of physical violence plays a crucial role in state formation, Corrigan and Sayer emphasize "the immense material weight given to . . . cultural forms by the . . . routines and rituals of state" (Corrigan and Sayer 1985, 5). In other words, the ability to regulate the moral domain is critically dependent on the *iterative* dimension to state activities. States are engaged in endlessly repeated, highly ritualized, and carefully routinized assertions about acceptable forms of social activity and collective identity. To paraphrase Corrigan and Sayer, states *state*. Indeed, they never stop talking (see chapter epigraph).

Through its capacity to state, the state seeks to establish itself as the sole, legitimate authority and ultimate arbiter regarding what may be considered true, proper, acceptable, and desirable (Corrigan and Sayer 1985, 10, see also Bourdieu 1999). To the extent that they become authoritative, Corrigan and Sayer suggest, the state's unending iterative productions—its everyday bureaucratic routines, its formulaic documentary practices, and its magnificent public rituals—establish for it a seemingly neutral, objective vantage point that stands "above" or "outside" the social order, watching, preserving, safeguarding (1985, 10).

In *The Great Arch*, Corrigan and Sayer seek to understand long-term continuities in the forms and rituals of rule—to grasp how (peculiarly English) state forms endure over a period of centuries. Other scholars have shown an equally strong interest in the cultural dimensions to political legitimation in state contexts. They too have investigated the role of iterative practices—from the implementation of routine, bureaucratic procedures (Herzfeld 1992), to the production and circulation of official government discourse (Hull 2012; Navaro-Yashin 2007; Trouillot 2001), to the staging of elaborate political performance (Kapferer 1988; Taylor 1997)—in establishing the authority of the state, and in generating state effects (Mitchell 1999). Anthropologists in particular have tended to focus on ethnographically observable dimensions to the processes by which states come to be accepted as real.

Ferguson and Gupta offer a fascinating analysis of hitherto unappreciated aspects of state formation. Arguing that the scholarly literature has not attended sufficiently to the ways that states come to be imagined, they examine the "images, metaphors, and representational practices [through which] the state comes to be understood as a concrete, overarching, spatially encompassing reality," arguing that "through specific sets of metaphors and practices, states represent themselves as reified entities" (2002, 981–82).

Among the most important of these metaphors, the authors suggest, are "verticality," the idea that the state is above society, and "encompassment," the notion that the state encompasses many localities.[9] To convey how the state comes to be imagined as above and beyond, Ferguson and Gupta present a fine-grained, thick description and analysis of everyday bureaucratic routine—the "mundane practices [that] often slip below the threshold of discursivity, but profoundly alter how bodies are oriented, how lives are lived, and how subjects are formed" (2002, 984). They show how verticality and encompassment are reproduced in the course of people's ordinary encounters with state administration. Like Corrigan and Sayer, they are ultimately concerned with how the processes they identify contribute to the legitimation of rule—how these processes help states "secure their legitimacy . . . naturalize their authority . . . and represent themselves as superior to, and encompassing of, other institutions and centers of power (2002, 982).

Other scholars concerned with how states come to be imagined as natural and real parts of the social environment have focused more directly on the role of discursive practices. A case in point is Yael Navaro-Nashin (2007), who builds upon Corrigan and Sayer's notion of moral regulation to consider the ways in which states structure affect (Laszczkowski and

Reeves 2017; Stoler 2002). Noting that "state-like structures make themselves evident to the persons who inhabit their domains in the form of materialities" (2007, 94)—and that "[d]ocuments are among the primary paraphernalia of modern states . . . are its material culture" (2007, 84)—Navaro-Yashin explores the role of official documentary practices in statecraft.[10] "[T]he document (or letter)," she observes, "is an emblematic site for the operation of . . . statecraft" (2007, 84).

So powerful is the aura of authenticity and the implicit demand for accountability embodied in these documents that they have the ability to generate the most intense forms of affect, especially among those living in the margins of the state (Das and Poole 2004). Official state documents, Navaro-Yashin argues, act as state fetishes.[11] They "are phantasmatic objects with affective energies which are experienced as real" (2007, 81). How important are official documentary practices to the crafting of states? "If documents seem more benign than the police, I would argue that from the point of view of the affects they generate amongst those who deal with them, especially from marginal positions, they are not" (2007, 83).

Other scholars have focused more systematically on the role of fantasy and performance in constructing states as real, powerful, and all-pervasive elements of the social world. Among the most influential to explore these realms has been Diana Taylor, in her book *Disappearing Acts: Spectacles of Gender and Nationalism in Argentina's Dirty War* (1997). Taylor's original and penetrating analysis draws on performance theory to show how the armed forces transformed Argentina into a vast "theater of operations" for the cleansing of the social body and the formation of the state.

Taylor focuses in particular on the military's violent reorganization of the visible and invisible realms of Argentine society. The assault on the former sought to establish the armed forces' mastery of the visible domain—to make public and private space available for inspection, as it were, to make it wholly transparent to the military gaze. The armed forces employed strategies intended to convey to the general population the existence of a general state of surveillance from which they could not escape—much like Jeremy Bentham's *Panopticon* (Taylor 1997, 96). From this all-seeing vantage point, the military sought to rid society of the various social ills that plagued it.

The armed forces also sought to demonstrate their mastery over the invisible realm—said to have been peopled by dangerous subversives who posed a dire threat to the social body. "Members of the armed forces wore disguises, carried volumes by Marx and Freud [to masquerade as intellectuals], and 'penetrated' the hidden spaces associated with subversion" (Taylor 1997, 97). The military did more, however, than simply penetrate the underground. They also *appropriated* it. The armed forces established an entire series of "secret" detention centers and concentration camps where the most horrific forms of torture were carried out. These centers came to be inhabited by those detained in carefully staged public exhibitions of power—neighborhood sweeps, house-to-house searches, and spectacular public kidnappings. Detainees subsequently reappeared in public—in the form of horribly mutilated corpses—leaving no doubt as to the armed forces' total mastery of the visible and invisible realms alike.

Taylor brilliantly shows how fear is made to "emanate through the public sphere, rippling through newspaper headlines, magazine covers, films, ads and TV spots" (1997, x). In her analysis it is terror—and its ability to produce observed and felt *effects*—that connects widely separated and disparate events, scenes, and discourses, integrating them into a single, overarching presence. Terror is thus the force that animates the state, the force that makes it seem (monstrously) real and foreboding. While clearly not accepted as legitimate, the state is nonetheless regarded as frighteningly and irrationally present.[12]

In a now-famous article, Philip Abrams argues that the "state is not the reality which stands behind the mask of political practice. It is itself the mask which prevents our seeing political practice as it is" (1988, 58). The path-breaking scholarship discussed above may be thought of as revealing the complex processes by which that mask is made and remade. Important though this work is, in the chapters that follow I explore a different issue. I examine what transpires when the mask of the state is *unmade*. My interest is in the processes responsible for the dissipation of the magic of the state (Coronil 1997; Taussig 1997): for the erosion in the authenticity (Navaro-Yashin 2007) of its discursive products, the emptiness of its performances and the hollowness of its proclamations (Taylor 1997). My concern is with the state's failure to separate itself from society, with its inability to maintain clear and discrete hierarchical levels (Ferguson 2004; Mitchell 1999), with the breakdown of verticality and encompassment (Ferguson and Gupta 2002), with its inability to show mastery over the visible or invisible domains (Taylor 1997), with the failure of state representatives to generate affect in their everyday interactions with vulnerable populations (Laszczkowski and Reeves 2017).

Closer in spirit to the present study is the work of Begoña Aretxaga. In an important and insightful analysis, Aretxaga (2000) has argued that "the state [does not] lose its mystifying power when it is unmasked as being an effect of power rather than the unified agent it appeared to be (2000, 43). Bringing to light "the 'interiority' of the state," she says, "does not necessarily dispel its 'magical' power" (2000, 43). To the contrary, she says. Such revelations seem to augment the magic of the state "by triggering an endless proliferation of discourses about the state in the most diverse areas of social life" (2000, 43).

Revelations concerning the misdeeds, the corruption, the malfeasance of government officials rarely demystify the state (Masco 2010). This is hardly surprising when one considers that the magic that the state performs does not operate at the level of reflection and understanding. The state is not a creature of thought but rather of experience and affect (Aretxaga 2003; Laszczkowski and Reeves 2017; Stoler 2002). As Corrigan and Sayer (1985) argue, and as Ferguson and Gupta (2002) reiterate, people "learn" (or unlearn) the state through endless mundane encounters with its institutions and personnel, with the form and content of official discourses, with carefully scripted public performances, both great and small. Since these are the domains in which the state is made, they must also be the realms in which it is unmade.

As will become apparent in the chapters that follow, I have benefited enormously from the above-mentioned body of work. Even so, I argue that there is also much to be learned about state formation by examining contexts such as mid-twentieth-century Peru, in which political rule falters or fails. For this is a case in which the state *is* unmasked and *does* lose its mystifying aura. During these moments, the lineaments of power and control that otherwise remain concealed are revealed. This work seizes upon these moments of unintended transparency to *see* the state differently—and to do so by examining failed efforts to order and legitimate political rule.

The chapters that follow focus on two interrelated problems. The first concerns the importance—and also the difficulty—of recognizing the pervasiveness of the delusional in political life. The second concerns the stakes involved, and the interests at stake, in this failure to recognize. By analyzing the formation of states through the lens of crisis, I seek to show that disorder, delusion, and contradiction are integral to the workings of the state. I also highlight the significance of this recognition—why it matters whether we view these forces as typical or exceptional with regard to the state.

Encountering the Encrypted State

I first became aware of Chachapoyas's midcentury crisis of rule during the summers of 2000 through 2005. At this time, I was in Chachapoyas doing research on the history of APRA. My work included a review of government archives, among them the Archivo Subprefectural de Chachapoyas. The subprefecture had been kind enough to lend me the services of Sr. Gallardo, the custodian of the archive, to assist me.[13] Sr. Gallardo proved to be crucial to my research efforts.

The archive went through cycles of care and neglect. There were periods when the documents were carefully organized (chronologically), and when the archive itself was housed in a secure, safe location, away from the elements. Much to the dismay of those charged with maintaining the institution, however, there were periods when the subprefecture was denied the funds it needed to maintain the archive. During such times it was common for other government offices to colonize the space formerly controlled by the subprefecture. This meant that it was necessary to move the documents to a new location, often on short notice, where they could be housed for little or nothing.[14]

Such spaces were few and far between. Furthermore, in transferring the archive to a new locale, files from different years could be thrown together, in a state of complete disarray. Finally, the sites were not always suitable for housing an archive. As a result, the documentary record was often in a state of disorganization and could also be damaged by the elements. Unfortunately, when I was trying to finish my research on APRA, the archive was in one of its disorganized periods. As a result, Sr. Gallardo and I found ourselves going through document files piled from floor to ceiling, in a column approximately ten feet in diameter at its base. The files in this enormous pile were in a state of complete disarray and were housed in an old adobe building that was used to store cement and fertilizer. The building had a leaky roof and an unfinished plank floor. While most of the documents were resting on wood, some had spilled onto the dirt beyond it.

As we made our way through this huge pile, we stumbled across document files that were to have a lasting effect on my understanding of the state. The first file (or, *legajo*) was called "Oficios Remitidos. Personal y Secretos. Años 1947–48–49–50–51–52 y 53." This file contained detailed correspondence from a range of government officials about their efforts to know and control APRA. Although I did not know it at the time, this *legajo* revealed much about the state of anxiety and paranoia that gripped government officials.

Of equal significance was a second *legajo*, which was tied to "Oficios Remitidos" with a length of thin rope. It was called, simply, "Continuación." Upon opening this file, I was completely bewildered, for it was filled with official communications written entirely in numbers (see Figure 2.1). It quickly became clear, however, what the messages were. Pinned to several were "translations" into Spanish (see Figure 2.2). Comparing these communiqués, it became clear that the "Continuación" file was filled with messages that had been encrypted. They had been encrypted to prevent APRA from being able to read them. Thereafter, Sr. Gallardo and I found a number of files from the period that revealed an obsession with the Party of the People. It was these documents that led me to see the state in a whole new light.

When I first became aware of the paranoia and hysteria associated with Chachapoyas's crisis of rule, I regarded these developments as presenting the opportunity to approach state formation from a novel perspective. The focus on order that dominates so much of the scholarly literature seemed especially inappropriate to make sense of the chaotic and paranoid developments in Chachapoyas circa 1950. What was striking about state formation in Chachapoyas was not order but disorder. How might we come to see the state differently by examining a context in which the government's efforts at domination had faltered or failed, and the state descended into a kind of madness?[15] For, in such moments, which are filled with delusion and systemic doubt, dimensions of power and control that are masked in more normal circumstances become visible. Thus, examining what is usually assumed to be a problem of order through a lens of disorder appeared to have much potential to offer new insights into state formation.[16]

As the book project continued, however, my perspective began to shift. I continued to see the value of studying contexts where political rule falters or fails—of examining situations in which the state is "not itself" in order better to understand what it actually is. But I was puzzled by the *origins* of the hysterical state. In the period immediately prior to the state's descent into madness, everyday administration had seemed utterly normal and routine. What was it about the ordinary state that allowed it to become extraordinary—to become something fundamentally different from itself? And if the state had not been as normal as it seemed, why were there no signs or symptoms of any underlying malady? To continue with the same metaphor, why did the symptoms of distress flare up so suddenly, dramatically, and unexpectedly?

If the state did indeed "go crazy," how are we to understand the fact that it had seemed entirely sane just a short time before? What are the theoretical implications of this development—in which we are confronted in very short order with two qualitatively different and contradictory faces of the state (Navaro-Yashin 2002)? Was the state's descent into madness simply an aberration? Was the plague of fantasies that swept through Chachapoyas at midcentury a momentary blip of paranoid fear in an otherwise dull, repetitive, and secular history of state administration? Was the rational state the norm and the irrational state the deviation?

Having been confronted in the most forceful of manners with the state in its irrational guise and having no way of understanding where such a state had come from, I felt the need to come to terms with these questions. Toward that end, I was led to reexamine my ethnographic and documentary materials for the period leading up to the midcentury crisis of rule. The materials I had managed to gather were rich and varied. They included an extensive set of interviews with former government officials, individuals from all social classes and all walks of life, and members of APRA. They included as well an extensive corpus of archival materials pertaining to everyday state administration.[17]

Although I pored over these materials, I saw nothing to indicate how or why the rational state had become a paranoid one. There were a series of problems that appeared time and again in the official record, but these were much like those faced by government regimes across the colonial and postcolonial worlds. I was struck by one problem in particular. The documentary record was in many respects an unending litany of the frustrations of government functionaries in attempting to conscript rural cultivators for modernization projects. These projects were considered essential to the nation's future, and efforts to implement them had absorbed much in the way of official time and energy.

Struggles to conscript labor were also a constant theme that ran through my interviews, whether with hacendados, peasant cultivators, government officials, or Apristas. From scholarship I was familiar with from other parts of Latin America, however, and other parts of the world, I knew that this was anything but unusual. In fact, the dilemmas involved in trying to coerce labor from subaltern groups were very common in such contexts.

More to the point, the inability to coerce labor said nothing per se about the irrationality of the state. The ability to tax and conscript is regarded as one of hallmarks of the modern, rational bureaucratic state (Centeno 2002; Lopez-Alvez 2000; Tilly 1985). The fact that conscription was a challenge for state officials might therefore be seen as indicating a "weak" state (Marten 2012; Migdal 1988; Rice, Graff, and Pascual 2010) but still a rational rather than a paranoid one.[18]

It was in scrutinizing the documents produced in the course of everyday government efforts to conscript labor that I was finally able to see continuities between the rational and the hysterical guises of the state. Two sets of documents proved crucial in this regard. The first set described a conflict between the Office of Highways and the Office of Military Conscription, which sought to conscript the same group of rural cultivators, at the same time, to contribute to different modernization projects. This set of documents included overall estimates of the number of conscripts demanded by these offices. The second set of documents consisted of estimates of the number of able-bodied men who were available to be conscripted, based on the national census of 1940 (MHC 1942).

The attempt of different offices of government to simultaneously conscript the same group of rural cultivators piqued my interest. From the perspective of a rational state apparatus, the conflict made little sense and suggested that the state was incompetent and disorganized. It was clear that, initially, neither government office had been aware of what the other was doing and both were surprised to discover that there was any conflict at all. It was as if the different branches of government were operating in complete ignorance of one another. This was hardly suggestive of an efficient and rational system of administration—one that had been designed to advance a common goal. To the contrary: the conflict showed that there was no overarching mechanism in place to coordinate or regulate government activities. It seemed to me that the simultaneous attempt to recruit the same group of people toward different ends bordered on the irrational.

If the conflict between these two government offices appeared lacking in sense, the response to it seemed even more so, as it proved unusually difficult to resolve the matter. The problem had not been caused by a temporary breakdown of an otherwise orderly and efficient system of conscription; there was no such system. Nor had there ever been one.

The Office of Highways and the Office of Military Conscription refused to work together to try to solve what appeared to be a technical problem—how to divide the rural workforce. Instead, they engaged in a pitched battle, in which each was determined to prevail over the other, which was treated as if it were an enemy camp. The two offices of government eventually arrived at an impasse, but not without grave accusations leveled on both sides.

The head of the Office of Military Conscription claimed that, by interfering with his conscription efforts, the Office of Highways had usurped the authority of the central state and had undermined the efforts of the military to strengthen the armed forces and thus the nation. He demanded that the guilty parties be imprisoned. The head of the Office of Highways countered with the same accusation. He argued that the Office of Military Conscription was interfering with projects deemed essential to the future of the nation. He too insisted that the responsible parties be jailed.

Both offices thus invoked the authority of the state and the needs of the nation. Ultimately, the departmental prefect—the highest-ranking government official in the region, and the direct representative of the central government—was forced to step in.[19] He managed to establish an uneasy peace between the two government offices. Even so, struggles between them over the control of labor continued unabated.

Several aspects of this conflict puzzled me. What would account for the fact that these two government agencies were so determined to prevail? Why would the offices feel compelled to push so far—to the point of accusing the other of having broken the law and having betrayed the national trust? Their behavior bordered on the irrational and suggested that the stakes for both were unusually high.

It was not just the intensity of the conflict, however, that was puzzling. So was the fact that the conflict was never really resolved. During this time, there was a running battle between Highways and the Military, but it was not just these two branches of government that were fighting with one another. Rather, *all* government offices that relied upon forced labor for their everyday functioning—which included virtually all government offices—were doing much the same.

The documentary record revealed that something of a war of all against all was being waged in Chachapoyas. Contra Hobbes (1964), however, this was not a war fought within society at large, which the offices of the state were seeking to control. Instead, the war was being fought within Leviathan—between the various offices of government, each of which made its own autonomous claim to the rural labor supply. As was true of the conflict between Highways and the Military, these battles were quite pitched ones, in which neither side was willing to give quarter and all seemed determined to fight to (and for!) the last man. These struggles had been so endemic, and so integral to government administration, that they created a highly disordering impact on the everyday operation of the state apparatus.

These insights posed a direct challenge to "institutional" understandings (Tilly 1985) of the state. For in the case at hand, the state was not a disinterested body that used its monopoly on armed force to impose social peace on society writ large. It was not a terrain of order and security but rather one of violence and insecurity. The various agencies of government that were engaged in such fierce struggles with one another were always careful to represent their efforts by drawing upon the legitimating language of the modern nation-state. But these competing claims to the right to exercise force on behalf of the nation to compel the rural population against its wishes were thinly disguised efforts on the part of each state agency to prevail over adversarial state agencies.

From the Mundane to the Remarkable

The fact that something of a war of all against all had been waged within the apparatus of government suggested that the state had been highly disordered. But this understanding did not really help me grasp how a seemingly rational state had so quickly become a paranoid one. The fact that battles like the one fought between Highways and the Military had been so common, however, convinced me that I needed to understand these struggles in more detail. I was struck by the fact that struggles over *labor* had been the source of so much conflict. I was also struck by how deeply invested the various offices of government had become in their struggles over the workforce. I was equally struck by the fact that the labor problem had never been resolved. In light of these aspects of intrastate struggle, it seemed likely that the real issue was an overall shortage of labor.

Upon first becoming aware of the conflict between Highways and the Military, I had been surprised by how heavy their labor demands were.

In order to explore the possibility that a scarcity of conscripts was pit-
ting government offices against one another, I decided to investigate the
possible role of labor shortage in the conflict between Highways and the
Military. My decision to begin with this conflict was largely a matter of
expedience. The information was readily at hand, so it was easy to calculate the total number of workers these two offices sought to conscript
(in 1940).[20] I did so and discovered that they had sought several thousand
workers. This figure reinforced my impression that official labor demands
were very high. While this figure suggested a state form that was highly
abusive, coercive, and disorganized, it did not indicate that the state was
paranoid or hysterical.

In order to gauge how coercive the state had been, I needed a
measure—one that would indicate the kind of strain a labor tax of several
thousand men would have put on the rural cultivating population. I decided to calculate the percentage of the adult male population these two
offices had sought to conscript. Using the census data on the total number
of adult men available to be conscripted, I calculated the percentage of
the population being sought by Highways and the Military. Suddenly and
unexpectedly it became abundantly clear that the state apparatus was not
simply violent, abusive, and conflict ridden. In comparing the census materials and the conscription figures the utter irrationality of state practice
leapt off the page with startling clarity, belying the seeming objectivity and
rationality of the written record.

Calculating the percentage of the population being sought by
Highways and the Military produced results that were nothing short of
bewildering. So confused was I by these calculations that I assumed I had
made an error, and redid them, first once, then again, and then many
times. After ending up with the same result, however, I satisfied myself
that the calculations were correct. What made it so difficult to accept
about these figures were their implications about the state. Indeed, so odd
were these numbers that they led me to view state formation in an entirely
new light.

It wasn't just that Highways and the Military had been exceptionally
greedy with respect to labor. The polities of the Andes have a long history of
imposing heavy labor demands on inhabitants (Rowe 1957; Spalding 1984;
Wightman 1990). In terms of historical precedent, such a finding would
have been interesting, but hardly surprising. There was something different,
however, about twentieth-century labor exactions. What I found was not

unbridled greed but rather delusion. These two offices had not been content to conscript most or even all of the labor supply. Rather, they had demanded a workforce that was roughly double the size of the actual population.

What kind of a strain would a labor tax of several thousand men have placed on the rural peasantry? If Highways and the Military had prevailed in their efforts, there would not have been a single able-bodied man left among the entire rural population! The thousands upon thousands of fields that dotted the landscape, and that were the basis of peasant livelihoods, would have been empty. The regional food supply would have disappeared. Rather than being hard at work in their *chacras* (fields), all men would have been away building highways or building (*sic!*) their national characters (as soldiers).

But the expectations of these two state offices were in fact even less rational and more remarkable than this quite delusional set of demands implies. If Highways and the Military had been left to their own devices, there would been a significant deficit of men. Official labor demands were such that these branches of government were operating in the realm of negative numbers. They were engaged in a form of "deficit spending."

There were additional dimensions of delusion concealed beneath the apparent rationality and neutrality of bureaucratic procedure. I came to realize that my initial calculations had in fact been incorrect. What was revealing, however, was the direction in which they would have to be revised. I discovered that my initial calculations had not been too liberal but rather too conservative. It was not just that these offices were operating in the realm of negative numbers. In fact, this deficit increased steadily through time, as more and more of the population would have been off-limits for conscription.

I was astonished that government offices had engaged in such delusional practices (and kept redoing my calculations to be sure I had not made a mistake). Equally remarkable was that they seemed oblivious to the fact that they were seeking to modernize the region by drawing on a fictive labor force—one that they had projected into being.

At this point in my investigations, it became abundantly clear that I had entered the realm of the irrational and fantastic. It became equally clear, however, that these state fantasies appeared in the documentary record in the guise of rational projects and plans. The story did not end here. These two state agencies were far from being the only branches of government that relied upon forced labor to carry out important tasks. The same was true of a broad range of governmental offices: the district, provincial, and departmental branches of the executive, the judiciary, and the military; the district and provincial offices of municipal government and the government ministries and even the Catholic Church (whose lands, chapels, and churches were scattered about the regional space).[21]

It was the norm for *all* of these bodies to use coerced peasant labor for their functioning. Furthermore, this had been normal practice for a very long time. Taking into consideration all government demands, state agencies had imagined into being a vast field of peasant labor, the size of which dwarfed the actual population. But the fantasies of state officials did not end here: they also assumed that this (imaginary) population was largely idle and waiting to be put to work to help redeem the nation.[22]

These findings said a great deal about the relationship between the routine and the remarkable, the rational and the irrational in state formation. By insisting on mobilizing a large body of imaginary laborers, the agencies of the state had to studiously ignore information readily at hand (the population figures in the national census) that showed just how delusional their assumptions were. They did this over and over again for decades. Small wonder, then, that these agencies were constantly at war with one another for control of the work force. Small wonder, as well, that government functionaries had been continually frustrated in their efforts to mobilize a workforce to support state modernization projects. For the labor supply they sought out with such diligence and determination was not a thing of fact, but of fiction.

I came to realize that what appeared as the most rational of projects and plans—and the most mundane and ordinary of government practices—were based on assumptions about the rural populace that were nothing short of delusional. I also came to see that the apparent rationality of the state was based on magical processes that had been dressed in the guise of everyday bureaucratic procedures. These procedures had generated two different kinds of effects, both of which are essential to understanding the dynamics of state formation at midcentury.

The first of these effects concerns the objects of government regulation: the labor force, which government officials were so determined to conscript. The bureaucratic procedures associated with the modernization process had made it possible for government officials to manufacture an imaginary labor force out of thin air—and without having any awareness that they had done so.

The second effect generated by the government's bureaucratic procedures concerned the subjects of state regulation: the government officials who were responsible for implementing modernization. So convinced were these officials of the reality of their own practices that, despite overwhelming evidence to the contrary, they insisted that this nonexistent labor force was a thing of flesh and blood. Indeed, they were initially baffled, later became deeply alarmed, and ultimately turned profoundly paranoid when it proved impossible to mobilize this (fictive) workforce.[23] They refused to recognize the imaginary nature of the labor supply no matter how many times they failed to locate it.

Instead, they attributed their failures to interference from powerful nonstate forces, which were thought to be creating problems that were actually of the state's own making. Government officials invested a great deal of energy in seeking to control three nonstate forces. The first of these was official corruption: State functionaries who had most direct access to the labor supply were said to be betraying central government aims by diverting the labor supply away from modernization projects for their own private gain. The second force was the political subversion of APRA: The Party of the People was said to be undermining government conscription efforts by encouraging rural cultivators to refuse to cooperate. The final obstacle was the peasant population itself. The supposedly innocent and childlike nature of the Indian peasantry was said to render them incapable of understanding their duty to contribute to important national causes. The naiveté of the rural peasant population was also said to make them unusually susceptible to the subversive message of the region's Apristas.

State offices *did* find that the functionaries who were responsible for delivering workers often diverted labor elsewhere or refused to provide the labor demanded of them. This was not because they were "corrupt," but because they could not but do otherwise. The problem was not greedy individuals but delusional government plans. The authorities had conjured into being a labor force several times the size of the actual population. As a result, there was simply not enough labor to go around. Each time any government functionary complied with the wholly legitimate labor requests of one government office, he was necessarily undermining his ability to comply with the equally legitimate requests of other government offices. In so doing, he opened himself to accusations of illegality from offices that did not receive the labor they desired.

Much the same can be said of the government's views of the rural cultivating population and the members of the APRA. The peasantry did indeed do everything in their power to avoid corvée labor, but not because they were childlike or unable to understand important national causes. It was because conscription was so damaging to their well-being. The Apristas were indeed encouraging the rural population to refuse to provide labor. But despite their considerable efforts (see Nugent n.d.) their ability to influence the peasantry was limited.

The problems to which government officials attributed their difficulties were not complete fabrications but rather "quasi-phantoms." They were both there and not there. It was the fact that these quasi-phantoms were not complete fabrications that made them so compelling and made it so easy to return to them time and again, as the source of the government's difficulties.[24]

Two aspects of the way that the authorities constructed their quasi-phantoms are of special significance to understanding the dynamics of state formation in Chachapoyas. First, because they saw modernization as entirely rational, government officials could not help but view those who sought to interfere with it projects as irrational (whether greedy, fanatical, or naive). Second, on this basis the authorities attributed to its quasi-phantoms truly extraordinary powers.

The role of delusion in confusing and confounding the authorities is indicated by the following: if there had been no corrupt functionaries, no childlike Indians, and no subversive Apristas, there still would have been a massive shortage of labor. The real source of the government's difficulties lay with the government and its insistence on conscripting such large numbers of people against their will. Being unable to acknowledge its role in creating the problems it sought to solve, the government "displaced" responsibility for those problems onto the shoulders of others. By engaging in displacement, the authorities breathed life and agency into imagined entities.[25] The more the government failed in its modernization efforts, the more irrational and powerful the authorities were compelled to regard these quasi-phantoms.

Once I came to see that the workforce needed for modernization was a figment of official imaginations, it was a simple matter to recognize that the forces said to be interfering with government efforts were as imaginary as were the (fictive) laborers themselves. Officials were so out of touch with the realities of the countryside, and so determined to "modernize" the region, that they failed to recognize the utter futility of their entire endeavor. Indeed, so convinced were officials that the source of their problems lay beyond the state that they passed new laws, established new forms of surveillance, and put into place new procedures and routines (see Chapter 8) that were intended to control these dangerous and malevolent forces. Nevertheless, shortages of (imaginary) labor continued to plague the region. As a result, those who were responsible for mobilizing labor found themselves having to explain away their inability to produce what did not exist.

Before Displacement

I received a powerful shock to the system upon recognizing the delusional nature of post-1930 state activity—and the ways that delusion was concealed behind a veneer of the ordinary, the rational, and the everyday. But this was not the last shock I was to receive. My understanding of regional political dynamics benefited from yet another blow, which further transformed my understanding of "the state."

Decades before the 1950 episode of state paranoia, during the 1920s, the national regime of Augusto Leguía engaged in a program of massive deficit spending to modernize Peru. Much of the regime's efforts were focused on doing away with the remote, "feudal-like" social structures that were believed to dominate the highlands (see Chapter 3). Eliminating the many throwbacks to an earlier age that were scattered about highland areas, it was believed, would help the country to overcome backwardness and realize its vast potential for growth and prosperity. The Leguía regime was thus intensely preoccupied with introducing forces that would bathe the highlands in the redemptive waters of modernity.

The Leguía regime underwrote an entire series of reforms in an effort to modernize Peru (see Chapter 4). The most important focused on highway construction. The government invested huge sums of money in a program designed to extend Peru's network of highways across the nation. The additional shock to the system that I received came in the course of investigating how labor was recruited for this program.

The funds to build the roadways considered crucial to Peru's future came from US banks. The labor, however, came from the Peruvian populace. Under the provisions of the 1920 Ley de Conscripción Vial, the Law of Highway Conscription, all male citizens between the ages of eighteen and sixty were required to provide between six and twelve days of labor per year to advance the cause of highway construction. The 1920 law thus construed the challenge of building the highway network as a national challenge, one in which the national citizenry as a whole would participate.[26]

If the government was to have any hope of overcoming backwardness, and of realizing the region's potential for growth and prosperity, it would have to organize labor conscription on a heretofore unprecedented scale. Prior to 1930 government officials relied upon a great many of the same conscription processes that they would employ after 1930. But whereas they utterly failed in the 1930s and 1940s, they succeeded during the 1920s.

Surprisingly, during the 1920s state officials had not only succeeded in conscripting an extensive workforce. They had also managed to do so without virtually any difficulty. While the reproduction of rule during this period was contingent upon its own forms of delusion (see Chapter 3 and 4), the very kinds of normal, mundane activities that would prove to be impossible in the 1930s and 1940s were entirely unremarkable in the 1920s.

Government officials were able to generate the most detailed and accurate of information about the regional workforce. They were also able to draw upon that information to conscript workers in an orderly and regular fashion. The delusion and displacement that accompanied conscription efforts after 1930 was entirely absent prior to 1930. There were no tendencies to conjure into being an imaginary workforce, as there would come to be later. Nor was there any reason to invoke interference from phantom forces when that workforce was not forthcoming.

In short, none of the problems that so plagued government officials were of any significance prior to 1930. During the 1920s the government apparatus in Chachapoyas was able to "see like a state" (Scott 1998). It was also able to "be like a state"—to compel the regional population to do its bidding.

The discovery that state processes had been more conventional during the 1920s did not detract from the importance of investigating the forces that were responsible for unmasking the state. But it did raise new questions. The material from the 1920s focused attention on the conditions of possibility of the ordinary and the mundane.

The fact that state processes had gone from (seemingly) conventional to highly unconventional was interesting for other reasons. In contrast to what one would expect based on institutional understandings of state formation, this breakdown of "state capacity" occurred in the context of the centralization of state power. After 1930 the elite power structure of Chachapoyas collapsed, and the obstacles to centralization that the Leguía regime had been so determined to eliminate were no longer present. This should have cleared the way for the region to be modernized. Ironically, it was in these very circumstances that the government apparatus found itself unable to see or be like a state. It was during this very period that government officials found themselves unable to conscript a workforce. It was in these very conditions that representatives of the state engaged so extensively in delusional practices, which they represented as rational and routine. It was in these circumstances that government officials experienced a crisis of rule and indulged in dark fantasies about the threat represented by dangerous forces that could not be seen with the naked eye.

Conclusion

The developments that unfolded in the Chachapoyas region between 1920 and 1950 confronted me with a series of paradoxes that challenge conventional views of the state and state formation. Contrary to institutional conceptualizations, which find inspiration in the writings of Max Weber, the state was at its most efficient and its most coercive prior to 1930, when it had virtually no armed force at its disposal. Conditions in Chachapoyas thus represent an inversion of Weberian understandings. In Chachapoyas, the ability of the state to coerce and compel was contingent not upon the elimination of nonstate political forms (elite-led political coalitions) but on their preservation. Indeed, when the central government succeeded in doing away with the region's traditional political forms, the government lost its ability to govern the region.

Once the central government had finally established a monopoly on the use of legitimate force, state officials found it increasingly difficult to see or be like a state. In this context, seemingly rational bureaucratic practices were centrally involved in creating a fictive workforce that was more than double the size of the actual population—one that government officials struggled in vain to produce. It was from this point onward that government officials conjured into being phantom forces that were said to be interfering with state efforts to advance the cause of nation building. In other words, it was during the era of "modern" state organization that irrationality and delusion took on lives of their own and came to haunt those who acted in the name of the state.

In the chapters that follow I reconstruct the history of this process. I begin (in the remaining chapters of Part One) with the post-1930 period, when delusions and dark fantasies were concealed beneath a veneer of the rational and the routine. In Part Two, I consider the period prior to 1930, when the government apparatus was able to see and be like a state despite controlling little in the way of armed force, and despite having to contend with regionally autonomous political organizations that were fully capable of defying central decrees. In Part Three, I return to the post-1930 period, and offer a more in-depth analysis of the government's failure to embed the remarkable in the routine. Throughout the book, I explore an approach to the state that views rationality and paranoia as alternative expressions of a single project of rule.[27]

1

Sacropolitics

I have endeavored to break the great chain of forces that has enslaved us to the past . . . so that Peru can escape from the rut of its own misfortunes and strike out valiantly on the road toward the future.
—President Augusto Leguía, May 24, 1929

Sacropolitics, Necropolitics, and the State of Exception

How are we to conceptualize the seemingly odd state of affairs in which delusion—in the form of the relentless pursuit of a nonexistent work force—masquerades as rationality? How are we to understand government officials' inability to grasp why their efforts to recruit that workforce inevitably failed—and why they attributed their failures to interference from ghostlike entities who haunted official efforts to rule? Below, I draw on influential writings on sovereignty (Giorgio Agamben 1998; Achille Mbembe 2003) and spectrality (Blanco and Peeren 2013; Gordon 2008) to extend some of the theoretical questions raised in the Introduction.

Among the most influential of recent thinkers on the dynamics of political rule is Giorgio Agamben. As Agamben (following Carl Schmitt) famously argued in his 1998 work, the sovereign is the person who can declare a state of exception. The latter, he explains, is a peculiar state—exemplified by World War II's concentration camps (and other camp-like contexts)—in which the sovereign uses law to declare specific groups beyond the law (Birmingham 2014). In the process, the sovereign reduces these groups to a condition of "bare life." That is, they are transformed from rights-bearing citizens into mere biological bodies that are stripped of social and political personhood.

In the process of reducing people to bare life, Agamben argues, the sovereign makes them into entities that can be killed with impunity—whose death represents no sacrifice to the broader political community. Indeed, sovereigns often declare states of exception in an effort to safe-guard, consolidate, or stabilize the position of the political community, which may be regarded as under threat. As the example of the concentra-tion camps implies, the state of exception is often a highly reactionary measure. It is intended to define the margins or limits of political com-munity. We see this boundary-marking, exclusionary dimension to states of exception not only in concentration camps but in a range of other, more familiar settings, where the normal rules of political life are (temporarily?) suspended.[1] The proliferation of such sites leads Agamben to argue that the state of exception is at the very core of contemporary political life. As he puts it (2000: 36), "the [concentration] camp is the nomos of the modern."

Agamben's work has been extensively (if critically) employed across multiple academic disciplines. His writings have been especially influen-tial among scholars who explore contexts where violence (or the threat thereof) is used by state (or state-like) representatives in their everyday dealings with vulnerable populations. Indeed, many regard Agamben's work on sovereignty, violence, bare life, and the exception as an important corrective to Foucault's work on biopolitics, with its emphasis on the man-agement of life rather than death.[2]

I offer this brief summary of Agamben's work not to criticize or assess—a task admirably performed by other scholars.[3] Instead, I draw on his framings of law, bare life, and the state of exception as a heuristic that can be employed to identify a very different form of "sovereignty."[4] For it is striking just how little application or relevance Agamben's formulation has to the developments considered in this book. Indeed, the period of Peruvian history discussed in the present volume represents almost a com-plete inversion of Agamben's formulation. Sovereigns in Peru did not seek to safeguard or consolidate an already existing state of affairs, as is so often true of contexts where states of exception are declared. Rather, Peruvian sovereigns sought to bring into being an entirely new state of affairs. They attempted to bring about the wholesale transformation rather than the preservation of key dimensions of the social order.

I use the term *sacropolitics*—politics based on group sacrifice—to refer to the cultural and political logic that informed the transformations
these sovereigns sought to effect.[5] I bring out the distinctive features of
sacropolitics by discussing its similarities to and differences from other
forms of sovereign claims to rule. We may begin, however, with the following general observation: Sacropolitics differs from biopolitics (Foucault
2003) in the sense that it is not about the management of life. It differs
from *necropolitics* (Mbembe 2003) in that it is not about the subjugation
of life to death. Sacropolitics is about neither managing nor taking life but
rather *animating* it. Sacropolitics is about bringing to life dead, dying, or
moribund populations and social formations.

In what sense was Peru dead, dying, or moribund during the period
considered in this book? To address this question, we must identify the
peculiar norm that Peruvian sovereigns utilized to reach that conclusion.
As was the case in the European contexts explored by Foucault in his discussion of biopolitics, sovereigns in Peru did employ a kind of norm to
assess the state of affairs that existed in their country. Unlike biopolitics,
however, the standard utilized in sacropolitics was not established on the
basis of precise statistical calculations that sought to characterize the normative state of the national population. Neither did sacropolitics seek to
identify threats to the national population (threats that Foucault [2003:
243–44] called "the endemics"), nor to take steps to protect the population from those threats. The norm employed in sacropolitics was less
precise and more ineffable than the careful statistical calculations upon
which biopolitics is based. It was also transnational rather than national.
It focused on the well-being of Peru relative to other nation-states in the
global arena.

The conclusion that Peruvian sovereigns reached by applying a transnational standard of relative well-being to their country was a discouraging
one. It was also one reached by sovereigns across the postcolonial world
about their own national domains. When judged by the standards of the
day, it was clear that Peru was in a profoundly moribund, stagnant state.
Indeed, it had failed even to approach the global norm established by the
prosperous countries of the Euro-American world. Despite the great riches
it possessed, Peru lagged tragically behind these more advanced nation-
states. This was because Peru's present was in many ways its past—a "feudal," premodern present/past from which the country had been unable to
break free. The enormous dead weight of the past-in-the-present made it

impossible for the country to achieve the kind of progress it should have been able to achieve.

This state of affairs had made Peru a historical exception to a global norm—an exception to what should and could have been. Unlike the state of exception discussed by Agamben, however, this one had not been formed intentionally, by sovereign fiat.[6] Nor was it a state that the country's sovereigns wished to preserve. The exceptional state in which Peru found itself—being beholden still to feudal social structures—was, rather, regarded as a tragic historical accident. And while this exceptional state had not been produced by the exercise of sovereign power, the country's sovereigns sought to use their power to overcome the country's exceptionality. Toward that end, beginning circa 1920, high-ranking government officials engaged in a concerted effort to bring the country out of the feudal past and into the modern present. They sought to animate or bring to life what they regarded as a stagnant social formation.

Perhaps the most important mechanism they employed toward that end was the law. Unlike what Agamben (1998) describes for the state of exception, however, Peruvian sovereigns did not narrow the boundaries of the political community by excluding groups from it. Instead, they expanded the boundaries of the political community by including new groups within it. In other words, Peruvian sovereigns did not use the legal apparatus to create subordinate categories that could be killed with no sacrifice. Instead, they used the law to broaden the political community, to ensure that *everyone* could be called upon to sacrifice.[7]

In the opening decades of the twentieth century (especially from 1920 onward) Peruvian sovereigns used the law in an attempt to mobilize the entire national population. They did so in order to promote projects of broad social transformation that would redeem the country—that would allow Peru to free itself from the dead weight of the past. The "state of redemption" that the authorities declared had superficial similarities to the states of exception discussed in the scholarly literature.[8] In Peru, however, a state of redemption was not declared as an exception to a broader normative sociopolitical order. It was called to do away with the exceptional state of the entire social order.

This difference between a state of redemption and a state of exception is reflected in the following: Peru's sovereigns did not seek to establish special camps or sites that were set off from the rest of society, where the normal rules of political life would not apply. Instead, they sought to convert the *entire country* into a kind of modernization or development camp in which entirely new rules would apply. In Peru, the concentration camp was not the nomos of an already existing modern, which was safeguarded by excluding groups whose death represented no sacrifice to the political community. Rather, in the case discussed in this book the "nation-as-development-camp" was the nomos of a not-yet-modern, which had to be created rather than defended—through inclusion and sacrifice on the part of all.[9]

In the pages that follow I use the term *sacropolitics*—the politics of public, mass sacrifice—to refer to the cultural and political logic employed by sovereigns in their attempt to redeem the nation. In addition to its preoccupation with reviving dead, dying, or moribund social formations, several features of the logic of sacropolitics bear emphasis in the present discussion. Sacropolitics is based on a politics of generalized obligation on the part of an undifferentiated national citizenry. It operates by expanding the boundaries of political community, and by decreeing that the entire national community is to be involved in practices of group sacrifice.

Sacropolitics is based on a different temporality than that implied in the state of exception. Sacropolitics rejects what *is* as a betrayal of what *should and could be*: it seeks out the wholesale transformation and animation of what exists. Sacropolitics is oriented toward the future rather than the present and seeks to distance itself from what is/was. The state of exception, on the other hand, embraces what is (or recently has been) as a reflection of what should be, and seeks to preserve (or recover) it at all costs.[10] It is oriented toward the present/past rather than the future and seeks to arrest rather than promote change.

It is not only the temporality of sacropolitics that differs from other forms of sovereignty but also its geography. This is reflected in the following: Agamben's state of exception is generally declared in a few limited social or spatial locations that are considered marginal to the political community and are regarded (by definition) as an exception to a norm. A state of redemption, however, is declared in virtually *all* social locations and seeks to establish a new norm. This is because the nation-state as a whole is regarded as the terrain of redemption.

As suggested earlier, sacropolitics makes extensive use of the politics of sacrifice. The form and meaning of sacrifice in sacropolitics has elements in common with what is described in traditional anthropological literatures on this subject (especially in the work of Bataille [1985]). Sacrifice as employed in sacropolitics also has elements in common with what Achille Mbembe describes in his pathbreaking work on necropolitics (2003).

Like Bataille before him, Mbembe emphasizes the importance of excess and exuberance, of living in defiance of the limits of death, and of overcoming the taboo against taking life, in establishing sovereignty. Since the rise of modernity, however—and its associated processes of colonialism and imperial expansion—excess and exuberance have been employed in contexts and toward ends that have little in common with what is described in studies of "primitive" societies.[11] The contexts in which sacrifice acquires meaning and in which sovereignty is established in the contemporary world, Mbembe suggests, involve "the subjugation of life to the power of death" (2003, 39–40). They are contexts in which "weapons are deployed in the interest of maximum destruction of persons and the creation of death-worlds" (40).

The proliferation of zones of exception, Mbembe argues, has generated "new and unique forms of social existence in which vast populations are subjected to conditions of life conferring upon them the status of *living dead*" (2003, 40). In such contexts (and in their precursors—the colony, the slave plantation, etc.)—those who have been reduced to the dehumanizing conditions of bare life are often driven to sacrifice *themselves*. That is, they choose behaviors such as resistance, protest, suicide, martyrdom, etc. These actions are intended to recuperate what is denied to all people who live within the death worlds associated with contemporary zones of exception—some degree of control, autonomy, agency, humanity. In other words, in such circumstances the sacrifice of self is intended to revalue lives that have been declared without value and make their sacrifice matter. As Mbembe puts it, "under conditions of necropower, the lines between resistance and suicide, sacrifice and redemption, martyrdom and freedom are blurred" (40).

What is true of necropolitics is also true of sacropolitics: sacrifice and redemption, martyrdom and freedom are intimately interrelated. In sacropolitics, however, individuals do not engage in isolated acts of self-sacrifice to protest the dehumanizing conditions of bare life encountered in zones of exception. Rather, the citizenry as a whole engages in public performances of officially endorsed *mass* self-sacrifice to free the country from the dead weight of the past. The intolerable state of affairs from which the nation-state seeks redemption has not been imposed by a sovereign in zones of exception, but by a historical accident. Today we use the term *underdevelopment* to refer to these conditions. Only mass sacrifice and generalized martyrdom can overcome these conditions. And the sovereign takes steps to animate the entire national population in order to do so.

According to the logic of sacropolitics, in such circumstances it is essential that *everyone* sacrifice. The way that people sacrifice themselves in sacropolitics, however, has little in common with necropolitics. They do so not by surrendering their lives but rather by "enhancing" them. People are asked to become new kinds of subjects and in the process go beyond the ordinary to contribute to the transformation of the worlds of which they are a part—to participate in the creation of new life worlds. The lives, the participation, the commitment of each person is of the most profound significance to the success of the broad social transformation called for by a state of redemption. So much so that those who refuse to join in—who will not give of themselves selflessly for the greater good—are guilty of the worst of crimes. They threaten to undermine the society-wide effort to redeem the country—to bring it to life, to help it out of its moribund state. As we will see, they ultimately come to be regarded as the ghosts that haunt the transformational aspirations of sacropolitical regimes.

Early scholars of sacrifice argued that this practice is intended to mediate between the realms of the sacred and the profane (Frazer 1922; Hubert and Mauss 1899; Smith 1927; Tylor 1871). Indeed, in classical writings sacrifice is thought of as a rite in which an offering is made to create, continue, or restore a proper relationship with the sacred. Such an understanding of sacrifice has clear relevance to the case at hand. The state of historical exception in which Peru found itself was regarded as very much a profane condition. And the state of redemption declared by Peruvian sovereigns—to which the public was to give itself through mass sacrifice— was intended to do away with that profane condition.

Sacropolitics thus seeks to mobilize extensive social forces in order to effect broad processes of animation, transformation, and redemption. It is not just the scale of these transformations, however, that distinguishes sacropolitics from other forms of sovereignty. Of equal importance is the pace of the changes that sacropolitics envisions. The *urgency* of the transformations sought out in a state of redemption is not to be underestimated. Only by undertaking the immediate transformation of the past-in-the-present can sacropolitics do away with conditions that have had such tragic consequences for the country as a whole.

Regimes that draw upon the logic of sacropolitics thus commit themselves to the urgent, immediate transformation of the past-in-the-present. Indeed, the latter stands out as a glaring indictment of everything the country has failed thus far to do. As a result, efforts to transform rarely proceed on the basis of careful or prolonged study of what already exists. Instead, the emphasis is on acting in an effort to create what should and could exist. This means that, while sacropolitics is not averse to quantification and management (see Chapter 4) its spirit lies elsewhere. The spirit of sacropolitics is to be found in the politics of "excess," in going beyond existing limits and conditions.

This difference between sacropolitics and other forms of sovereignty can be seen by comparing the way biopolitics and sacropolitics approach the phenomenon of population. While biopolitics seeks to know and protect the population, sacropolitics seeks to mobilize and transform it—in a sense to create it. Sacropolitics seeks to do so by bringing the population to life, as it were—by liberating it from the shackles that have long kept it bound to place, inert, frozen in archaic social structures. As this implies, the point of a state of redemption is not to plan based on what is, but to imagine based on what might be. Redemption means going beyond what already exists. It also means employing life-enhancing, public mass sacrifice to do so.[12] In a state of redemption no one really knows what the parameters of the population might be. Nor does anyone know what the population might be capable of. For it is emergent and imminent rather than already existing—a phenomenon that has yet to fully reveal itself.

In light of sacropolitics' peculiar temporality, it is not surprising that its assault on what is takes on the features of a mission or a crusade—one whose immediacy cannot be ignored even for a moment. In a sense, the more extravagant the vision of a redeemed future, the more grandiose the schemes for redeeming it, and the more immediate and pressing the plans for doing so, the more the vision honors the spirit of sacropolitics. As is true of sacrifice in "premodern" and necropolitical settings, excess and exuberance are centrally involved in sacropolitics. But the integral role of excess and exuberance—of going beyond existing conditions and limits—unfolds in conditions and focuses on goals that have little in common with discussions of sacrifice in other contexts.

As generative as the abovementioned scholarship on bare life and necropolitics has been, it has limitations. These limitations are relevant to the other main problem engaged in this book—the role of fantasy and delusion in structuring seemingly ordinary processes of rule. In *Cruel Optimism*, Lauren Berlant (2011, 96–97) offers a brief but trenchant critique of the notion of sovereignty as developed by writers such as Carl Schmitt, Giorgio Agamben, Georges Bataille, and Achille Mbembe. She argues, in essence, that sovereignty as used by these writers is not an objective state, as they suggest, but rather "a fantasy [of control] misrecognized as an objective state" (97). Akhil Gupta argues similarly in *Red Tape*, where he develops his own critique of Agamben—showing that Agamben "assumes that a decision to declare a state of exception is tantamount to its de facto existence" (2012, 45).

Two points from these critiques are especially germane to the arguments presented in this book. The first concerns the assumptions about power that are implicit in conflating a declaration of a state of exception with its existence. In the case of the midcentury Chachapoyas episode discussed in this book, state officials issued an entire series of sovereign decrees—both sacropolitical and "exceptional" (in Agamben's sense of the term). Most were completely or partially ignored. Others were enthusiastically embraced—to such a degree that key social actors decided to continue the bans even after the "sovereign" had ordered them lifted (an action that called into question the power and position of the sovereign). What is important is not only the declaration of the ban or decree, but the conditions that variously enabled or disabled efforts to enforce it.[13]

The second critical point is that conflating the declaration of a sovereign ban with its existence involves more than just misrecognition. As Berlant points out, it involves a *fantasy* of misrecognition, a kind of delusion of omnipotence. While Berlant is concerned with the implications of this fantasy for social theory, I shift her focus to explore fantasies of control on the part of those who seek to govern. I also extend Berlant's discussion to argue that a key dimension of this fantasy is that it cannot be represented or acknowledged as such. Rather, it must be glossed and understood as entirely ordinary and unremarkable—as a description rather than a construction of political life. I also explore the mechanisms that seek and ultimately fail to sustain this delusion of ordinary, mundane omnipotence.

The delusion that sovereignty is an objective state clearly informed the activities and attitudes of government officials in Chachapoyas. As alluded to earlier, it took a great deal of work to sustain this delusion. Officials had to systematically misrepresent and misapprehend what was going on around them. They also had to filter out the multiple dimensions of the everyday social environment that contradicted that fantasy. This required the use of a particular optic—one that distorted what government officials were able to see and left them blind to the actually existing state of affairs. The fact that the government viewed everyday life through this distorted lens meant that delusion informed not only officials' fantasies of sovereign control but also their understanding of the forces that threatened their control.

Only by recognizing the (carefully concealed) role of fantasy and delusion in seemingly mundane, ordinary political processes can we understand the intermittent emergence of the "spectral" aspects of rule (Blanco and Peeren 2013). My analysis emphasizes both the contingent nature of the conditions that allowed sovereign decrees to be established as well as the (disguised) role of fantasy in sustaining the illusion of sovereignty. In addition to analyzing how this fantasy was sustained, I also attend to the reasons that officials' delusion of control eventually broke down. I suggest that it was only after government officials had failed to impose an entire series of sovereign bans that they were unable to sustain the illusion that they were sovereign. Key in this regard were their unsuccessful efforts to control a series of ghost-like entities that haunted everyday efforts to rule (Gordon 2008).

This process of breakdown was associated with a major shift in the affective regime (Banerjee and Bercuson 2015; Chouliaraki 2010).[14] Once officials' fantasy of sovereign control collapsed, the affective regime that had helped sustain that fantasy—a regime of "nonaffect" (see below, this chapter)—was replaced by an affective regime of anxiety and paranoia. The emergence of this new affective regime brought into stark relief what had earlier been so difficult to see—the role of nonaffect in sustaining conventional rule.[15] Government officials went to great lengths to sustain the illusion of mundane omnipotence, and employed a variety of techniques toward that end.

Antiepistemology

In "Removing Knowledge," Peter Galison's (2004) fascinating discussion of the classification of state secrets, the author focuses on a process that has received relatively little in the way of scholarly attention: "antiepistemology," that is, how knowledge may be covered and obscured. Galison examines antiepistemology in the rarified world of official state secrets. He does not, however, explore the possible relevance of antiepistemology to understanding domains of political experience that are at less of a remove from the mundane details of everyday life.

The importance of Galison's argument extends far beyond the realm of state secrecy. What Galison calls the arts of nontransmission are at work not only in extraordinary circumstances of the kind he examines but are equally if not more important in defining the parameters of "ordinary" political life (if such a concept is not a contradiction in terms). Antiepistemological forces are both ubiquitous to and constitutive of the normal. Despite their ubiquity, however, it proves unusually difficult to recognize the role of the arts of nontransmission in organizing mundane political worlds. This is because in such arenas the kinds of processes noted by Galison work not only to conceal knowledge but also to conceal the fact that they are doing so. In the worlds of the ordinary and the routine, the antiepistemological processes that obscure and cover knowledge cover their tracks, as it were. They systematically misconstrue themselves. They take on guises that conceal the very labors of nontransmission they perform.

It is no coincidence that the antiepistemologies of the everyday involve a double process of concealment. By concealing the fact that they conceal, these processes of nontransmission draw attention away from the highly constructed and contested nature of the mundane political relations they seek to organize and mediate (in the case at hand, sacropolitical relations). In the process, they seek to render those relations as wholly unremarkable and ordinary.

In the present work I identify different forms of antiepistemology, each of which performs the art of nontransmission in its own distinctive manner. Some of these forms of antiepistemology, especially those that are at work during the extraordinary moments associated with state crisis, are highly "transparent," and openly declare themselves as antiepistemological (see Chapter 2). However, other forms of antiepistemology, particularly those employed during more ordinary times (when the process of governing seems largely unproblematic) tend toward the opaque, remaining silent about the fact that they obscure (see Chapter 6 and 7).

Removing Knowledge, Erasing Affect

As noted in the Introduction, my efforts to understand how a seemingly rational state went mad led me to the realization that the state had always been both rational and delusional. What changed from moment to moment was which of these two disguises the state had donned as its public face. What I did not understand, however, was why the state adopts its different guises when and where it does—so that it appears as eminently reasonable and rational in some contexts but hysterical, angry, vengeful, and out of control in others. To understand why states undergo such transformations, and what is involved in the process of transformation, I focus on the mechanisms by which states produce an appearance of rationality and inevitability that can bely their inevitably delusional tendencies.

One of these mechanisms, *displacement*, refers to the process by which governing regimes seek to shift responsibility for problems and dilemmas that are caused or abetted by government officials and government activities onto quasi-phantom nonstate sources—sources that are variously depicted as dangerous, irrational, immature, irresponsible, etc.[16] The impetus to engage in displacement stems from a contradiction built into the very heart of state activity. Those who act in the name of the state are frequently involved in the arbitrary use of force to pursue highly specific interests, and to support particular constituencies. The fact that they are so engaged, of course, is in direct contradiction with the state's raison d'être. The state's stated reason for being is to eliminate the arbitrary use of force, and to oppose special interests. The state is to establish conditions of general social peace, so as to insure the disinterested use of force to advance the common good.

In this sense, at the very core of seemingly ordinary, mundane practices of governance are rites of purification (Douglas 1966)—procedures that state representatives employ in a (futile) effort to purge the process of rule of what it is not allowed to be (see Nugent and Suhail 2018). Interestingly, these rites are neither declared nor recognized as such. Rather than being set apart from the everyday, and producing a separate, transcendent dimension of sociality (Durkheim 1995 [1912]), state rites of purification *become* the everyday (of the state). In the process, they seek to transform state activity as a whole into a transcendent realm. But unlike conventional rituals of the sacred, state rites are disguised as "anti-rites"— activities so seemingly ordinary and unremarkable that there is no reason to pay them any mind. Indeed, these rites of state take the form of an endless round of dull, repetitive, mundane activities.

Documentary practices are among the most important of these anti-rites. Not coincidentally, documentary practices are also integral to the process of cleansing, by means of which those who act in the name of the state seek to purge the state of what it is not supposed to be. In many circumstances, these practices serve as essential means by which regimes represent themselves to themselves as well as to those they would govern. The fact that these regimes employ a language of the ordinary, the mundane, and the unremarkable—and in the process construct an entire regime of nonaffective affect (Banerjee and Bercuson 2015; Chouliaraki 2010)—is central to the process of purification by which states seek to transform themselves into what they are not. It is also central to the process by which states conceal the fact that they are involved in this transformative process. The use of such (non-)affective language to characterize "routine" state activity is as much an encryption as are the transparent, numerical coded communications of the Odría era (see Chapter 2). So too is the very notion of routine state activity.

As Philip Corrigan and Derek Sayer (1985, 3) have famously argued, states state. Indeed, they never stop talking. Amid all this endless chatter, surely it is significant not only that states talk but also how they talk.[17] Indeed, one might extend Corrigan and Sayer's point to suggest not only that "states state" but that they *over*-state. It is the specific way in which they do so that is especially relevant to the present discussion.

Among the most striking features of government communication in midcentury Chachapoyas is a peculiar kind of "overstatement"—the official obsession with a language of the ordinary, the rational, and the routine, and its complimentary (non-)affective regime. This is an obsession that overstates in an important yet subtle manner, so that one hardly notices that the state is stating at all. Indeed, the state chatters on endlessly about itself as an inevitable yet unremarkable feature of life, as a constant that is simply there.

In so doing, the state draws attention away from the fact that the seemingly ordinary statements it is making concern issues of the most extraordinary significance. Indeed, although one would never know it from the state's (over-)statements, the issues in question are among the most consequential that can be imagined. They concern life, death, work, well-being, identity, marriage, etc. Through its relentlessly understated overstatement about these highly consequential matters, the state does much to insure the systematic erasure of affect, imagination, and delusion from the entire realm of government activity. So broad and ubiquitous is this official self-representation that it proves exceptionally difficult to see behind it—to not mistake the veil of the routine, the unremarkable, and the non-affective in which state activities shroud themselves for the state itself.

If the seemingly ordinary is in fact highly extraordinary, and if there is a battery of forces at work that make this so difficult to see, then what is presented to us as the everyday is not to be taken for granted. Indeed, the fact that the remarkable is routinely masked as the routine suggests that there is much at stake in what comes to be considered as ordinary and routine. Much is also at stake in whether we consider taking "second glances" at the official documentary record. Assertions about what is and is not worth paying any mind, I suggest, are best understood as highly interested political claims rather than unremarkable, disinterested inevitabilities. In seeking to impose their own definition of the ordinary and routine, however, state processes seek to transform the former (highly interested political claims) into the latter (mundane inevitabilities).

It is difficult to imagine a process that relies more on the "art of non-transmission" (Galison 2004, 237) than everyday processes of state formation, which are based so extensively on anti-rites of purification. Unlike the situation described by Galison, in the case of routine governance in Chachapoyas it is not only knowledge that is made to disappear. A similar kind of "disappearing act" (Taylor 1997) is performed on the entire domain of affect. The peculiar kind of overstatement in which government officials engage makes it appear that the affective has been erased from virtually all manifestations of state activity.

In other words, the state relies on mechanisms that suppress, bury, conceal, and misrepresent entire domains of experience and forms of knowledge. It is crucial that these remain proscribed, unutterable, unrepresentable, because they threaten to contaminate or sully what official anti-rites seek to maintain as pure. As is true of the classification of state secrets discussed by Galison (2004), the effectiveness of the everyday forms of state formation that are the focus of the present volume is contingent upon mechanisms that reinforce and safeguard the process of nontransmission. These are mechanisms that interfere with the recognition of proscribed domains of experience and impede the transmission of sensitive forms of knowledge. The classification of state secrets, however, differs from routine processes of state governance in an important way. In the former, a battery of forms of scientific knowledge and expertise, as well as sophisticated technologies of surveillance and regulation, are consciously brought to bear on the problem of blocking the transmission of knowledge. In other

words, there is little about the antiepistemological process that is accidental, informal, or unplanned.

In everyday processes of state formation, however, the opposite is
the case. The mechanisms that interfere with the recognition of proscribed
domains of experience and sensitive forms of knowledge cannot be consciously articulated or designed as such. Only in circumstances that governing regimes declare as exceptional—when the state adopts its hysterical,
delusional guise, and openly declares itself under threat—are such mechanisms consciously designed and openly articulated. This begs the question
of what such mechanisms might be, and how they might operate during
periods that state representatives deem ordinary and mundane. It also suggests that even the most ordinary of periods are usefully understood as
"states of security"—even if these are unacknowledged, and unacknowledgeable as such by the individuals who are involved in enforcing them.

In the next section of the chapter I explore the mechanisms that
are central to concealing proscribed domains of experience and forms of
knowledge during periods represented as ordinary as well as those deemed
extraordinary. I use the term *standard deviations* to refer to these mechanisms. Understanding ordinary and extraordinary forms of classification
as alternative expressions of the same underlying practice underscores the
continuities between the rational and irrational faces of the state.

Standard Deviations

(Anti-)rites of purification that seek to purge the state of what it is
not supposed to be are central to state formation. These (anti-)rites are an
inevitable, ongoing part of the dynamics of rule.[18] By employing a language of the mundane, the unremarkable, and the nonaffective over and
over again, in myriad social contexts, states overstate. In the process, they
make a powerful if illusory claim about what the state is and what it does.
They make equally powerful and equally illusory assertions about what the
state is not and what it does not do. And they make an equally powerful if
illusory claim that the state is.

These everyday exercises in purification are one of the mechanisms
that is constitutive of the state. By means of these (anti-)rites, and the dissimulation and concealment they help effect, the state seeks to transform
itself from what it is into what it can never be. Contradiction is thus built
into the very fabric of state, as is denial of contradiction. The denial of

contradiction in ordinary circumstances represents the public face of the state—itself constructed by means of a peculiar form of overstatement. The enormous overinvestment in overstatement speaks to the magnitude of what state activity seeks to conceal and deny.

Official rites of purification are far from being the only mechanisms upon which state formation depends. The veil of the state is constructed out of more than just the proactive dimensions to government activity—out of more than what the state insists that it is. That veil is in equal measure reactive. It is built up out of official claims about what others are—those who are said to interfere with or represent an obstacle to the plans of state. Claims about these others are articulated in the endless mundane accounts generated on a daily basis by the large number of government officials who are confronted with the task of explaining away resistance to state projects and plans—of accounting for their failure to realize official, and generally illusory, goals.

To the extent that state projects and plans are delusional, violent, and discriminatory, they tend to generate widespread resistance on the part of those who are coerced and compelled. In the case to be discussed in this volume, these projects and plans tend to be in a perpetual state of in-completion. Many of these projects prove to be impossible to implement. And many more are accompanied by delays, setbacks, and frustrations. As this suggests, an essential part of the process by which the state builds up its mask consists of how government officials contend with a quite specific and peculiar temporality. It consists of how they deal with the inevitable and ongoing problem of having "unfinished business"—how they repre-sent their efforts to manage failure, and the frustration, confusion, and anxiety that stem from it.

Because denial of the violent and coercive dimensions to state activi-ties is integral to state formation, displacement is an inescapable aspect of everyday processes of rule. But displacement is an internally differentiated process. Although it takes several different forms, displacement focuses on groups of people and kinds of activities deemed suspect or problem-atic: "awkward" groups and activities that challenge the normative political projects of those in power.[19]

I suggest that official representations of such "awkward" groups and activities in Chachapoyas tended to follow a standardized script. There were times when the authorities attempted to know in great detail the groups and activities deemed awkward. These were the periods during which an effort had been made to "see them like a state" (Scott 1998). It was equally common, however, for the forces of order to go through long periods when they studiously ignored all things awkward, when they passed up opportunities to gather information that would make it possible to better see and understand the groups and activities that posed a threat to the normative political projects of the ruling regime. There were still other times when those who spoke and acted in the name of the state collected systematic but limited information about such groups and activities.

In other words, what differed from one time to the next and one context to the next was the degree to which the authorities even bothered themselves about the awkward classes. In the situations in which they did, what differed from time to time and context to context was what the authorities did and did not regard as worth seeing, and the measures they took in an effort to see. What was clear, however, was that the rationale utilized by the state to collect information about problematic and suspect groups and activities did not follow a transparent, rational information-gathering logic. But what alternative logic were the authorities employing?

Making sense of patterns in what government officials sought to know about the awkward classes in different times and contexts suggests that officially articulated understandings of the ordinary, the routine, and the everyday—as reflected in endless instances of overstatement—act as the prism through which such groups come to be seen, understood, and recorded. It is not difficult to understand why this would be the case. Gathering and storing information about classes of people and kinds of activity considered awkward or suspect, and confirming their problematic or inappropriate nature, is an integral part of state formation. This process is integral to the (anti-)rites of purification that state actors employ in order to purge the state of what it is not supposed to be.

In other words, overstating again and again the utter ordinariness of the normal and routine is integral to the unending conversations regimes have with themselves and the populations they would administer about the legitimacy of rule. A characteristic feature of virtually all these conversations is their inversion of the prescriptive and the descriptive. Governing regimes are compelled to present highly interested and arbitrary claims about how national life should be lived as if they were neutral, disinterested descriptions of how it is lived. If such regimes are to transform "should into is," they must employ a clear and unambiguous definition of the normal and the everyday—of appropriate and inappropriate kinds of activities in which people may engage, and the kinds of people they may be (Corrigan and Sayer 1985, 4). It is equally important that they be in a position to identify, monitor, and, when necessary, eliminate deviations from the norm thus defined.

The commitment to the preservation of the ordinary and the routine is therefore anything but ordinary or routine. Rather, it is a matter of grave concern to the forces of order. Indeed, this concern necessarily colors official perceptions of virtually all groups and activities that do not conform to normative definitions of what should be. To the extent that the authorities become aware of such groups, what is important about them is the ways in which they diverge from normative prescription—the ways in which they trouble, unsettle, or challenge the regime's definition of the ordinary and the everyday.

It is their implicit challenge to routine that makes such groups and activities relevant to the forces of order. Consequently, the latter tend to see the awkward classes in very specific terms—and in ways that vary according to how, and how far, they appear to deviate from the norm. This also means that much of what the awkward, suspect, or out-of-place classes do and are is beyond state interest or recognition—that the official gaze remains blind to those aspects of awkwardness that raise no questions about the arbitrariness of the everyday.

Focusing on APRA, my findings suggest that official representations of the Party of the People alternated between three standard forms.[20] What characterized official views of the party as a First Order Standard Deviation was denial. For much of the twenty-five-plus years (1930–1956) that are the focus of my study, the proscribed status of APRA meant that it remained hidden, underground. Nonetheless, government officials were in possession of overwhelming evidence that the Party of the People was a *serious* threat to the established order.[21] As long as the party was content to remain invisible, however, the government repeatedly chose to minimize that threat or to ignore it completely—at times in ways that were delusional and that put the very survival of the government at risk. In other words, as a First Order Standard Deviation the forces of order considered APRA scarcely worthy of being seen or recorded at all.

It should come as no surprise that as long as the party remained out of the public eye, the government tended to minimize the threat represented by APRA. To openly acknowledge the influence exercised by the Party of the People—to acknowledge the existence of a large-scale social movement with a huge number of members that rejected the government's definition of the ordinary and routine—would be deeply problematic. It would call into question the taken-for-granted-ness, and thus the legitimacy of the entire political project to which the governing regime had committed itself. To the extent that APRA remained in the shadows, it is not surprising that the authorities' perceptions of the party were filtered through a lens of denial.

The government's insistence on minimizing or disregarding the party's influence led to a second standardized response to the deviation that was APRA. When it became clear that the Party of the People was testing the limits of official denial and was surreptitiously seeking to climb out of the shadows, what characterized official views of the APRA was fear. The authorities responded to their fears with a strategy of containment. The goal here was not so much to know the party as to monitor and control it—to ensure that APRA was not able to spread any further into the public sphere, or into the institutions of civil society (especially labor unions) or the government (especially the armed forces). In other words, how APRA came to be known, understood, seen, and recorded as a Second Order Standard Deviation was a function of official concerns with keeping it at a distance—with maintaining the boundary between order and disorder.

But officials also employed a third standardized script to represent and record information about APRA. During periods of political crisis—when the barriers erected to contain the Party of the People were overrun—the authorities became deeply paranoid about APRA (see Chapter 2). In this context the forces of order not only indulged in greatly exaggerated fears about the dangers posed by the party. They were also possessed of a burning desire to resolve their fears—to gather the intelligence necessary to convert anxiety into control. In times such as these officials suddenly became convinced of the relevance of wholly new kinds of knowledge about the party. Rather than limit themselves to surveillance intended to prevent the spread of party influence, they did everything in their power to expose party activity in every detail. They sought to collect information that would break through the wall of secrecy behind which APRA concealed itself, to make the party visible, transparent, and knowable.

Government reactions to the Party of the People as a Third Order Standard Deviation had much in common with the responses of other regimes reacting to groups regarded as a serious threat to order. The authorities responded to their fears about APRA by attempting to "see (the party) like a state" (Scott 1988). They sought to produce a series of what James C. Scott calls "simplifications" about the party that would allow them to fix it in time and space. The authorities sought to discover, for example, the identities of the APRA leadership and its rank and file. They also sought to ascertain how many party cells were in operation, when and where they met, and what transpired at these meetings. Faced with what appeared to be a complex organization that managed to coordinate its far-flung activities with great effectiveness, the forces of order also sought to penetrate the subversives' underground system of communication. Intelligence of this kind was considered essential to the government's efforts to eliminate APRA.

Had they succeeded in gathering this information, however, the authorities would still have been in the dark about what was most important for them to understand. Even the most detailed of information about the party structure would not have made Aprista "agency" comprehensible to the forces of order. It would not have explained to government officials why the Apristas insisted on doing what they did despite the most dire of consequences. It would not have explained, for example, why party members were so devoted to the cause—why they appeared willing to make virtually any sacrifice in its name. Nor would such information have revealed how a political movement that was proscribed by the central government could survive and even thrive in the face of systematic and quite brutal repression by the forces of order.

It was not just that the authorities failed to comprehend their adversaries. The forces of order rejected out of hand the notion that comprehension was even possible. Committed as they were to their own version of the rational, officials were compelled to regard APRA's opposition to their activities as wholly irrational—as motivated by fanaticism, extremism, and the desire to subvert. This understanding of the party and its members, however, carried with it alarming implications. On the one hand, it suggested that a great many people did not embrace government definitions of the normal and the everyday, despite official assertions to the contrary. On the other, it implied that much of the population was not to be trusted—that it was made up largely of fanatics or extremists. Indeed, the forces of order ultimately came to regard themselves as surrounded by a veritable sea of subversives.

The authorities reached this conclusion as they came to regard APRA as a Third Order Standard Deviation. It was not difficult for government officials to understand how a small group of committed fanatics could survive underground as long as the forces of order were content to leave them be (i.e., as long as the authorities had dealt with the party as a First or Second Order Standard Deviation). But the Apristas' ability to thrive in the face of an all-out campaign to eliminate them was inexplicable. In such a context, government officials came to believe, the fanaticism of its members would not have been enough to protect APRA. Rather, the subversives would need extensive support and protection from groups that were not openly Aprista. The authorities thus came to suspect that the party was not acting alone—that it was receiving crucial assistance from groups that claimed to be loyal to the government. The forces of order applied various litmus tests to assess the loyalty of these groups. Motivated as they were by paranoid fear, however, officials came to distrust the very tests they devised. Indeed, as we will see, the forces of order ultimately came to suspect that virtually everyone was an Aprista.

It is striking just how little the forces of order came to know about APRA despite the fact that they were in many ways obsessed with the party. What the authorities understood least of all, however, was how and why APRA could have such broad appeal to such large numbers of women and men. Government officials were unable to come to terms with this problem for a quite simple reason. Their deep commitment to a particular version of the ordinary and the routine compelled them to treat the party and everything associated with it as a dangerous and irrational aberration from the norm. From the perspective of the official powers, it was simply impossible that the Party of the People could represent aspirations that were valid or legitimate. As a result, there was little reason to try to understand APRA in these terms.

Conclusion

In the first half of the twentieth century successive political regimes sought to base their claims to rule on a form of sovereignty that was neither biopolitical nor necropolitical but rather sacropolitical. Sacropolitics differs from biopolitics (Foucault 2003) in the sense that it is not about the management of life. It differs from necropolitics (Mbembe 2003) in that it is not about the subjugation of life to death. Sacropolitics is neither about managing nor taking life but rather *animating* it. Sacropolitics is about bringing to life dead, dying, or moribund populations and social formations.

Peruvian sovereigns sought to use the law to expand the boundaries of the political community so as to mobilize the entire citizenry in broad projects of social transformation that would free Peru from the dead weight of the past—that would bring to life a moribund social formation. An integral part of the government's sacropolitical efforts consisted of calling on the population to engage in public performances of mass sacrifice. In so doing, Peruvian sovereigns sought to redeem the country from the profane condition into which it had fallen.

In declaring a state of redemption that encompassed Peru as a whole—in seeking to convert the entire country into a development camp—government officials were faced with a dilemma. Despite their appeal to everyone to sacrifice themselves in order to contribute to the creation of new life worlds, the sacropolitical programs the authorities sought to promote were based on brute force, which was employed to compel the population to labor against its will. In order to purge the state of what it was not allowed to be, officials employed a series of antiepistemological processes. These were intended to transform the remarkable into the routine. The next chapter analyzes a historical moment in which official efforts to transform the remarkable into the routine failed. It does so by focusing on the crisis of rule that shook Amazonas circa 1950, when the regime of General Manuel Odría was seized by the most paranoid of fears about APRA, and dealt with the Party of the People as a Third Order Standard Deviation. The chapters that follow trace the processes out of which this plague of fantasies emerged.

2

The Descent into Madness

The crisis consists precisely in the fact that the old is dying and the new cannot be born; in this interregnum a great variety of morbid symptoms appear.

—Antonio Gramsci, *Selections from the Prison Notebooks* (1971)

Introduction

This book focuses on official efforts to transform what were in reality the most delusional, violent, and coercive of practices into ordinary, mundane acts of administration. As I argued in the previous chapter, these efforts are usefully understood as an antiepistemology—as an attempt to bury, conceal, and misrepresent entire domains of experience (especially the affective) and forms of knowledge. The process by which the government sought to transform the extraordinary into the ordinary—to systematically misapprehend and misrepresent the social world—was an unusually subtle one. Because officials had to purge the state of what it was not allowed to be, even as they sought to mobilize the population to make the nation what it should have been, this process of transformation was also an ongoing, daily aspect of state activity. I have suggested that a particular kind of overstatement was integral to this process—one based on what Alexi Yurchak (2003, 2006) has called a "hegemony of form." Particularly important was officials' obsessive adoption of a hypernormalized form of expression that made extensive use language of the normal, the routine, and the everyday (Brenneis 2000). This discursive form created a disjuncture between the internal, self-referential world of government representation and the social realities that government communiques pretended and were intended to describe and engage.

In the process, official discourse represented the social world not "'as it was' but, rather, 'as it ought to [have been]'" (Boyer and Yurchak 2010, 205). Unlike the late socialist contexts explored by Yurchak, however, there was no acknowledgement of this disjuncture. Indeed, the process of purging upon which state formation depended relied crucially on the denial of any such disjuncture. Instead, government officials insisted on carrying on endlessly about the state and its social worlds in precisely the terms imagined in official discourse. So broad and systematic was this self-representation, I have argued, that it is exceptionally difficult to see through it—to not mistake the veil of the ordinary and the everyday in which official activities shrouded themselves with the state itself.

The previous chapter introduced the notion of "standard deviations" to shed light on the peculiar optic employed by government officials to (mis-)apprehend the world around them. In the remainder of this chapter we examine the forces that compelled the regime of Manuel Odría (1948–56) to treat APRA as a Third Order Standard Deviation. That is, we review the processes that forced the authorities to reveal the paranoia and the delusion upon which state projects and plans were based. The chapters that follow engage two broad themes. Chapters 3–5 analyze the conditions of divided elite rule out of which the paranoid fantasies of the Odría regime emerged. That is, having explored in the present chapter the kinds of "morbid symptoms" to which Gramsci refers in the epigraph, the following section of the book examines "the crisis [that unfolds when] the old is dying and the new cannot be born" (Gramsci 1971, 276). Chapters 6–8 examine state efforts to conscript labor to modernize the Chachapoyas region during periods when APRA is regarded as a First and a Second Order Standard Deviation—periods when everyday antiepistemological processes are intact, and state activities are able to maintain appearances to the contrary.[1]

Crisis and Paranoia

In April 1949 Sr. Manuel Alberto López, prefect of Amazonas, sent a series of frantic coded messages to his superiors in Lima, the national capital. Using the same crude numerical encryption technique to which he increasingly had recourse locally (to communicate safely with the few government officials he could still trust), the prefect pleaded with the national government for assistance. His regime was beset on all sides, he explained, by the followers of APRA (the Popular American Revolutionary Alliance)—the "terrorist" political party that sought to seize control of the government, nationalize land and industry, and establish workers' cooperatives in all branches of the economy.[2]

Sr. Lopez explained that his administration was in grave danger. APRA's terrorists, he claimed, were everywhere. The party's fanatics were to be found in large numbers in virtually all walks of private life. As a result, he was surrounded by a veritable sea of subversives. Equally alarming, however, was that the followers of the Party of the People (as APRA called itself) had lodged themselves deeply within the state apparatus. For example, in reporting to the central government about the presence of Apristas among the region's teachers, the prefect explained to his superiors the following:

I have confirmed that the teachers in service in the Province[s] of [Amazonas] are unquestioning propagandists of APRA, who work shamelessly against the present regime, blindly obeying the instructions of their superiors [in the party] . . . disobeying the regulations of the [Ministry] of Education . . . and betraying their sacred duty to form the next generation of patriotic citizens. . . . (ASC44, 2 April 1949)

But the prefect's suspicions about the loyalty of the region's public servants were not limited to teachers, who were scattered about the countryside in small, rural schools. He expressed equally grave doubts about the trustworthiness of virtually all the government functionaries who worked in the rural districts. These were not only teachers, but also governors, justices of the peace, and mayors—the personnel who were responsible for the day-to-day management of political life, and who interacted with the population on an ongoing basis. According to Sr. López, the majority of individuals who occupied all these posts belonged to the Party of the People.[3]

The prefect's doubts, however, extended far beyond the lower rungs of the government apparatus. He was equally convinced that a large but unknown number of higher-ranking government officials were secretly Apristas. These included provincial judges and members of the Superior Court. They included as well officials in the Bureau of Tax Collection and the Department of Public Works.[4] Sr. López' doubts about the loyalty of the department's public servants extended to key personnel in every government ministry in the region.[5]

By what means the Apristas had managed to infiltrate his administration so thoroughly the prefect could not say, for he had erected multiple defenses to protect the state from the party. Furthermore, his regime had been vigilant about maintaining these defenses. Despite this fact, however, APRA had overcome all the barriers he had placed in its path. As a result, he said, the Party of the People was poised to seize control of the region on a moment's notice. Even the forces of order—the Guardia Civil (the National Police)—were not to be trusted. They were only feigning loyalty to the government, Sr. López claimed, biding their time, waiting for the moment to strike:[6]

The political authorities [of Amazonas], who have the obligation to maintain order and preserve the prestige of the existing Government, cannot count on the assistance of the . . . police force. . . . The greater part of that force is made up of sympathizers or members of APRA, who for the time being simply disguise their membership [in the party], waiting for the moment to arrive when they can operate [openly] as opponents of the existing Regime. (ASC3, 17 March 1949)

It was clear from his messages that the prefect was in a state of panic about APRA. Indeed, it was for this reason that he appealed to Lima for reinforcements. And while he had failed to prevent the subversives from infiltrating his regime, Sr. López was determined to make up for his mistake; he was determined to identify all Apristas in the entire region and remove them from government employ and from society in general. He faced one major problem, however, in doing so. All party members went about their daily affairs in disguise, as it were, masquerading as normal, law-abiding citizens. It being so very difficult to distinguish friend from foe by ordinary means, the prefect had learned to distrust outward appearances. The truth about the party, he and other government authorities believed, was concealed from view. It would therefore be necessary to dig beneath the surface of things to root out APRA at its core—which Sr. López was deeply committed to doing. Indeed, the prefect and his administration were on high alert, in a state of extreme readiness. The difficulty was that they did not know exactly who or what they were looking for.

Although the Apristas found it prudent to conceal their true natures and their actual identities in their everyday interactions with society at large, the signs of APRA's importance were many, and the evidence of its profound influence incontrovertible—or so the authorities believed. Perhaps the clearest indication of the support the party enjoyed, and the power it exercised, was the following; after an initial round of success, the forces of order—the Prefecture, the Guardia Civil, and the PIP (the Secret Police)—had been stymied in most of their subsequent efforts to apprehend Apristas. Nor had they been able to control the party's underground activities. Nor, government officials had come to realize, had they even been able to gather accurate intelligence about APRA. It was as if the Party of the People was aware of the authorities' every move *before* they actually made it. Armed with this knowledge, it seemed, the terrorists were able to make themselves invisible whenever danger threatened. As a result, despite the government's long familiarity with APRA, and despite having struggled against it for almost two decades, the party remained something of an enigma—unknowable, unreachable, unfathomable.

On numerous occasions, for example, the authorities had sought to apprehend and arrest Apristas, and to disrupt party activities. One way they had sought to do so was by means of anti-APRA police raids. After meticulous planning, and acting on the most reliable of information, both the Guardia Civil and the PIP had attempted to surprise groups of subversives during the clandestine, nocturnal meetings that APRA was rumored to hold with great frequency. The forces of order had been frustrated, however, almost every time. With disturbing regularity, the Party of the People seemed to have known in advance of the authorities' intentions. With few exceptions, the Apristas had been able to avoid capture.[7]

While APRA had succeeded in remaining largely illegible to the authorities, the reverse was not the case. Indeed, the party seemed able to read the government like an open book. It was a common occurrence, for example, for the people of Chachapoyas (capital of the department of Amazonas) to awaken in the morning, take to the streets, and discover that APRA had been very busy the previous night. At times the populace would find freshly printed handbills, covered with party propaganda, slipped under doors throughout the city. At other times they would encounter APRA slogans ("APRA is Peace"; "APRA is Brotherhood") painted in large letters in prominent public places—locales that were in theory being patrolled by the police. On still other occasions they would learn that party propaganda sheets had been nailed to the very door of the Prefecture or the Guardia Civil headquarters—locations that were protected by armed guards around the clock.[8]

The degree of planning, preparation, and coordination necessary to carry out these tasks gave credence to the rumors that were circulating widely through Chachapoyas—that the party continued to hold its regular underground meetings in secret cells throughout the city.[9] Everyone knew, of course, that the authorities had been stymied in their efforts to discover when or where the meetings took place, or even who attended them. What was clear, however, was that the Apristas were able to roam through the streets, striking at will. It was equally clear that the police were powerless to catch the subversives.

It was not just the inability to apprehend Apristas, or to control their nighttime activities, however, that was troubling Sr. López. His regime was also finding it increasingly difficult to carry out even the most basic of governing functions—especially those concerning conscription, taxation, and the administration of justice. Behind all of these difficulties, the prefect was certain that he saw the hand of APRA.

Despite making repeated sweeps through the countryside, for example, the Guardia Civil were finding it impossible to locate enough military conscripts to serve in the army. The Guardia were having equal difficulty finding the labor conscripts they needed for the government's numerous public works projects. The party had long since stated its opposition to forced labor of all kinds, and the prefect had direct evidence, some going back years, that Apristas were seeking to interfere with the government's efforts to conscript the rural population.[10]

Similarly, the personnel of the Caja de Depósitos y Consignaciones (the forerunner of the National Bank), who were responsible for collecting rural excise taxes (the department's single most important source of tax revenue), were complaining bitterly about their inability to control the growing problem of contraband trade. Here as well APRA appeared to be the cause of the government's problems. The party had long declared excise taxes to be an abuse of all the laboring poor and had encouraged people to trade on the black market. The prefect had reports that Apristas were actually offering people advice about how they could avoid the personnel of the Caja and could thus avoid paying their taxes.[11] The prefect also had doubts about the loyalty of those who worked for the Caja.

Even the governors of the rural districts (who were the prefect's personal appointees), and the mayors and justices of the peace who worked alongside them, were finding their normal administrative duties more and more difficult to carry out.[12] Governors and justices of the peace, for example, often found themselves unable to locate the witnesses and suspects called to appear in large numbers before the Superior Court of Amazonas. Similarly, governors and mayors found that their efforts to call out the district population to repair roads and bridges were met with growing (if passive) resistance. People never defied the authorities. They were simply not at home. Or such large numbers would resist—and would offer the same, unimpeachable excuse for not complying (they had to sow or harvest their crops, for example)—that the authorities found it impossible to force them. The prefect received a steady stream of correspondence from his district-level subordinates explaining why they were unable to comply with their administrative tasks. It was not uncommon for these personnel to claim that, according to what they had been told, APRA was inciting the local populace to resist government authority.[13] The fact that the prefect had doubts about the political leanings of his district-level appointees further complicated his efforts to assess the significance of this correspondence.

Even so, such reports were anything but difficult to believe. The Party of the People had declared itself adamantly opposed to the multiple ways that district-level functionaries like the governor coerced the people under their jurisdiction and had characterized all of these "obligations" as thinly disguised forms of exploitation and abuse. APRA argued that the indigenous population—who bore the brunt of these policies—was saddled with all the duties of citizenship but none of its rights. The basic injustice of this state of affairs, the party said, was intolerable. It was this situation that the Apristas had vowed to change.

The authorities were deeply alarmed by the party's ability to survive and even thrive in conditions of such extreme repression. Government officials were equally concerned about APRA's success in undermining so many key government functions. It seemed nothing short of miraculous that party members, forced to operate in secret, beyond the gaze of the authorities, could defy every effort to apprehend them. It seemed equally miraculous that a persecuted political movement, driven underground, proscribed for decades by the national government, could be so effective in thwarting the authorities' efforts to govern. Especially alarming was the fact that the party seemed able to confound the government in so many different administrative domains, in town and country alike, at the same time. Indeed, the prefect would often find himself confronted with evidence of APRA's subversion coming in from all over the department, on the very same day! From one rural community he would receive a report that APRA slogans had appeared overnight on the public buildings surrounding the central plaza. From another he would learn that the Guardia Civil had located only a fraction of the number of labor conscripts needed for public works. From yet another he would hear that witnesses called to testify before the Superior Court could not be located. And in Chachapoyas itself, he would discover that APRA had once again littered the streets with propaganda.[14]

Government officials thus found themselves confronted on a continual basis with the most alarming evidence of the party's powers. At the same time, they had been frustrated in their efforts to gather the intelligence that would reveal to them how APRA was managing to do all of this. Indeed, the authorities were confronted with major gaps in their understanding of the party and its members—gaps that they considered crippling. Believing that the very survival of their regime was at stake, they had struggled mightily to fill in these gaps. But they had failed.

It was this failure that was generative of (an attempt at) order. In the absence of reliable information that would have answered the many weighty questions they had about APRA, the authorities were compelled to provide answers of their own. In other words, government officials were left to make *inferences* about APRA—inferences that would explain why the authorities were unable to do away with or even rein in the subversive movement despite its disturbingly radical and extremist nature. The less the authorities actually knew, the more they were compelled to imagine. And imagine they did. Faced with mounting evidence of their own impotence, and of the terrorists' seeming ability to thwart the government's every plan and to achieve the party's every goal, the authorities let their imaginations run wild. They began to indulge in the darkest of fantasies about APRA.

Sr. López and the region's other high-ranking officials concluded that APRA's seemingly miraculous abilities were enabled in large part by a party structure of exceptional complexity and sophistication—one that spanned the entire department and was able to organize and coordinate the subversives' activities in the most detailed of manners.[15] The authorities were also convinced, however, that such a party structure alone would not be enough to confound them. Only if it was staffed by a deeply fanatical membership, which had gone through an intensive process of indoctrination, would APRA be capable of such amazing feats. What was both confusing and alarming to consider, however, was *how* this political structure could orchestrate party affairs with such success, efficiency, and secrecy. It was equally alarming to consider how APRA could produce such fanaticism in its members. That is, it was unclear what the process of indoctrination would consist of, who would oversee it, where it would be carried out, who would submit themselves to it and why they would do so. High-ranking government officials speculated among themselves at length about these questions.[16] The difficulty was that they had only fragmentary and often contradictory bits of evidence to suggest answers.

Precisely because the Apristas did not expose themselves to visible scrutiny anywhere, government officials began to see evidence of the party's nefarious hand everywhere, even in the most seemingly innocent and innocuous of places—including elementary schools, church groups, volleyball teams.[17] The authorities also began to suspect everyone of being an Aprista. It was not just the usual suspects, like radical teachers and impoverished Indian cultivators, that came under suspicion, but also the most unlikely of candidates—including school children and single mothers, policemen and officers of the Superior Court. Even staunchly conservative, religiously devout members of the old landed elite came to be viewed as suspect by the forces of order.[18]

In their desperation to distinguish wholesome from dangerous social elements, officials first insisted that everyone offer proof of their loyalty to the military regime—that they sign loyalty oaths, that they swear (in writing, often before a notary public!) that they did not belong to the party, and that they constantly offer public affirmations of their commitment to the status quo. As people responded to these appeals, they would often employ the same discursive and affective distinctions—between the rational and the irrational, the normal and the exceptional—that government officials used to distinguish the state from the party:

March 23, 1949

Sr. Prefect of the Department

With the present communication I am honored to make you aware of the following facts: In 1945, a political movement [APRA] of great significance emerged in Peru, and believing that this movement represented the best hope for our country that had appeared until that time, I began my life as a citizen by joining that Party, and I did this with my heart filled with patriotism and with the fervor that is appropriate to all young people; this was my goal and my ideal, and by joining APRA I believed that I had complied faithfully with my duty as a citizen; but after years of struggle to make a living, I have come to see that politics has its mirages, and convinced of this truth, I wish you make known to your honorable Office that from this day forward I separate myself from the Party of the People [APRA], in order to dedicate myself to my own independent work, and that I will never again meddle in activities of a political nature.

Roberto Feijóo Ramos (ASC23, 23 March 1949)

After insisting that everyone declare precisely where they stood with respect to APRA—by means of public testimonials such as these— government officials then discounted the very declarations they had insisted people make. As a result, people who had already declared their loyalty to the military regime found it necessary to repeat themselves, as it were. Such was the case with Roberto Feijóo Ramos, author of the renunciation from APRA quoted immediately above. After having declared his commitment to the military government in March 1949, he found it necessary to reiterate his loyalty several months later, but to no avail:

May 21, 1949

Sr. Prefect

On March 23rd of this year I had the honor of informing you that I had renounced my membership in the Party of the People, guided as I was by the desire to dedicate myself in an honest and peaceful manner to my private affairs, nonetheless making it clear, of course, that I would collaborate with the Government in whatever modest way that I could.

Despite the frank and honest declaration that I made at that time, on the 4th of this month I was taken completely by surprise when I was told to come to the commissariat of the [Secret Police] where, along with a number of other people, I was detained for ten days. When I was finally released, I learned . . . that the order to detain me had come from Lima, which shows that my [earlier] renunciation has not been taken into account. It appears, therefore, that I am still considered a Party member, in spite of the fact that when I separated myself from APRA I did so of my own free will and conviction, and without any outside party having influenced me in any way.

Sr. Prefect, it is possible that my earlier renunciation was sent to the Dirección de Gobierno, the office to which your own answers. I therefore humbly ask that you contact that office, and add to my first renunciation the weight of this present one, which I intend to reinforce the first renunciation, so that I do not continue to find myself in situations like that which I have outlined above.

As you are no doubt aware, the newspapers in Lima constantly report about public employees who have rehabilitated themselves by renouncing their membership in the

Party of the People. This being the case, I find it odd that my own renunciation has served for nothing—not even to keep me out of jail.

For all of these reasons, Sr. Prefect, I ask that you please accept this new renunciation, and that you authorize its publication in whatever local newspaper you see fit, or in the dailies of Lima, so that my determination to leave the Party is taken into account.

Roberto Feijóo Ramos (ASC23, 21 May 1949)

Despite the apparent determination of people like Sr. Feijóo to leave the party, and to employ state-endorsed methods for doing so, the police were never satisfied that he (and others like him) was being truthful. Sr. Feijóo continued to be detained intermittently over the next several years—along with other (former?) party members—despite their multiple attempts to rehabilitate themselves. No matter how hard he and the others tried, they were unable to convince the authorities that they were being sincere. For the only means available for swearing to the truth had come to be seen as unreliable.

In other words, no matter how loyal one professed to be, no matter how proper one's behavior, no matter how law-abiding one appeared, the authorities were still left with doubts. Indeed, because the Apristas were seeking to deceive the government by masquerading as ordinary citizens, the authorities came to view as suspect the very act of presenting oneself as loyal—came to view anyone who presented themselves in these terms as potentially subversive. Furthermore, government officials came to question the truth-value of people's declarations of loyalty even though they insisted that everyone offer them, continuously—or else find themselves under suspicion of being an Aprista!

Faced with the inability to distinguish friend from foe, government officials came to see the state as being at risk of infiltration by the most dangerous of social elements. Initially, the prefect responded by charging the heads of government offices with the important responsibility of patrolling the (imaginary) frontier between state and society, in order to ensure that the state enjoyed as much "autonomy" as possible.[19] In order to do so, the prefect told the heads of these government offices that, in interacting with society at large, they were to take a less trusting attitude than they had in the past. In particular, they were to scrutinize with great care anyone who approached them concerning employment. In this way they could help insure that the state apparatus remained free of the influence of APRA. The prefect wrote to his subordinates with this explicit goal in mind:

My office has become aware of the fact that members of the Popular American Revolutionary Alliance (APRA) continue to attempt to find work in the Public Offices of this Department, taking advantage of diverse means in order to do so, without taking into consideration that membership in the Party has been declared illegal. And because [the Apristas'] only intention in doing so is to undermine the operation of the offices where they seek to work, as the supervisor of Public Administration in this Department, I find it necessary to direct your attention to this problem, and to ask that you be sure to take it into consideration whenever you appoint new personnel to work in the office at your command. (ASC44, 28 March 1949)

Unfortunately, however, this strategy to protect the state from APRA was fundamentally flawed. The prefect did indeed charge his subordinates with the task of patrolling the boundary between state and society. But he provided these officials with no guidance as to how they were to distinguish Apristas from non-Apristas in the process of doing so.

In this context, officials took to viewing everyone around them as a potential threat, including one another. As a result, they became ever more secretive about their deliberations and their decisions. Convinced that it was dangerous to send information by normal means, the authorities began using coded messages to communicate among themselves. Initially, the use of code was restricted to matters of major import. As time passed, and the authorities became increasingly suspicious of those around them, they used encryption to communicate about a broader range of issues.

As they sensed the party closing in around them, government officials changed the codes on a more frequent basis. They also experimented with different kinds of codes. They imposed extra surveillance on the personnel who hand-delivered coded messages between government offices in Chachapoyas, and on those who sent coded communiqués by wire from the capital to the rural districts. The authorities' decision to communicate in coded form, and to restrict the use of code to a select few, represents their suspicion that the broader arena of government activity and communication within which their inner circle was embedded was *not* autonomous of APRA influence, but rather had been infiltrated and contaminated by the party. The efforts of government officials to limit the flow of privileged information to an inner circle of government confidants reflects their fears about just how lacking in autonomy these officials considered the actually existing state to be. It also reflects their decision to surrender to APRA the outer domain of the state, as it were, and to reinscribe state boundaries further inward—to create a state within a state.

To the great misfortune of the authorities, however, this attempt to redefine the limits of the state (Mitchell 1991, 1999)—to "fix" state boundaries so that encompassed within them were individuals who were completely trustworthy and loyal—was deeply flawed. The reason was quite simple. High-ranking government officials could not be sure that some of the very individuals who had been entrusted to communicate in coded form about APRA and its activities were not themselves sympathetic to the party—or would not take actions that would protect Aprista clients, friends, or relatives.[20]

This problem was more than hypothetical. Consider, for example, the encrypted document shown in Figure 2.1 (and decrypted in Figure 2.2). In it, the prefect writes to a subprefect—one of a dozen or so individuals with whom the prefect communicated in code on a regular basis, and therefore

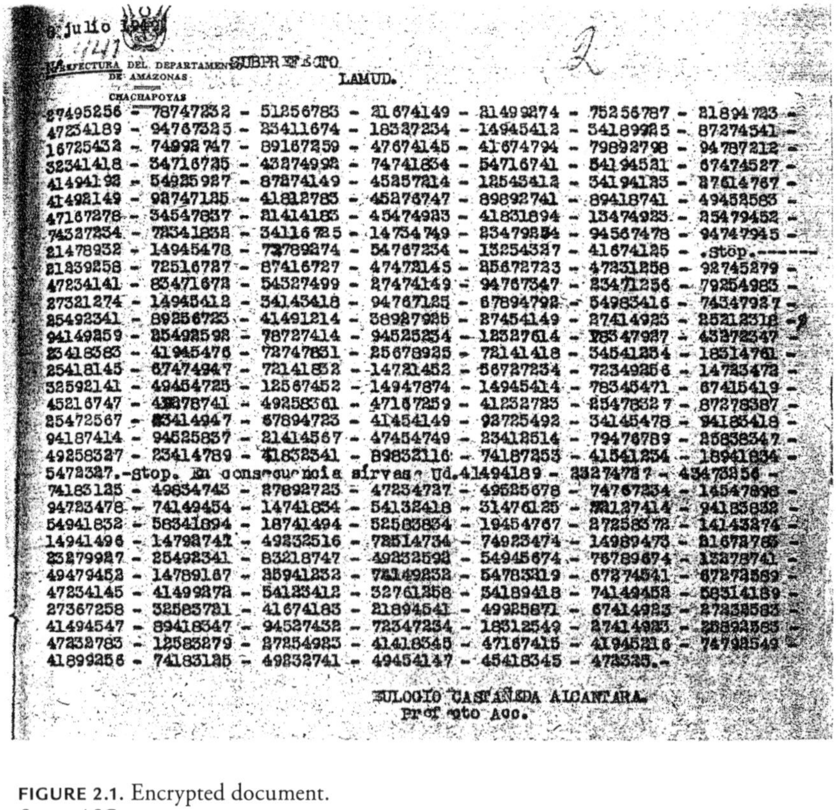

8 Julio 1942
1241
PREFECTURA DEL DEPARTAMENTO DE AMAZONAS CHACHAPOYAS
SUBPREFECTO LAMUD.
2

27495256 - 78747232 - 51256783 - 21674149 - 21499274 - 75256787 - 21894723 -
47234189 - 94767325 - 23411674 - 18327234 - 14945412 - 34189925 - 87274541 -
16725432 - 74992747 - 89167259 - 47674145 - 41674794 - 79892798 - 94787212 -
32341418 - 34716735 - 43274992 - 74741834 - 54716741 - 54194521 - 67474527 -
41494192 - 54925927 - 87274149 - 45257214 - 12543412 - 34194123 - 27614767 -
41492149 - 92747125 - 41812783 - 45276747 - 89892741 - 89418741 - 49452583 -
47167278 - 34547837 - 21414183 - 45474923 - 41831894 - 13474923 - 25479452 -
74327234 - 72341832 - 34116725 - 14734749 - 23479254 - 94567478 - 94747945 -
21478932 - 14945478 - 72789274 - 54767234 - 13254327 - 41674125 - .stop.------
21239258 - 72516787 - 87416727 - 47472145 - 25672723 - 47231258 - 92745279 -
47234141 - 83471672 - 54327499 - 27474149 - 94767347 - 23471256 - 79254983 -
27321274 - 14945412 - 34143418 - 94767125 - 67894792 - 54983416 - 74347927 -
25492341 - 89256723 - 41491214 - 38927925 - 27454149 - 27414923 - 25212318 -
94149259 - 25492598 - 78727414 - 94525234 - 12327614 - 78347927 - 43272347 -
23418383 - 41945476 - 72747831 - 25678925 - 72141418 - 34541234 - 18314761 -
25418145 - 67474947 - 72141832 - 14721452 - 56727234 - 72349256 - 14723472 -
32592141 - 49454725 - 12567452 - 14947874 - 14945414 - 78345471 - 67415419 -
45216747 - 43278741 - 49258361 - 47167259 - 41232723 - 25478327 - 87278387 -
25472567 - 23414947 - 67894723 - 41454149 - 92725492 - 34145478 - 94183418 -
94187414 - 94525837 - 21414567 - 47454749 - 23412514 - 79476789 - 25838347 -
49258327 - 23414789 - 41832541 - 89832116 - 74187253 - 41541234 - 18941834 -
5472327.-stop. En consecuencia sírvase Ud.41494189 - 23274727 - 43473856 -
74183125 - 49834743 - 27892723 - 47234727 - 49525678 - 74767234 - 14547898 -
94723478 - 74149454 - 14741834 - 54132418 - 31476125 - 72127414 - 94183832 -
54941832 - 58341894 - 18741494 - 52583834 - 19454767 - 27258372 - 14143274 -
14941496 - 14792742 - 49232516 - 72514734 - 74923474 - 14989473 - 21672783 -
23279927 - 25492341 - 83218747 - 49232592 - 54945674 - 75789674 - 13278741 -
49479452 - 14789187 - 25941232 - 72149232 - 54783219 - 67274541 - 67272589 -
47234145 - 41499272 - 54123412 - 32761258 - 54189418 - 74149458 - 58314189 -
27367258 - 32583781 - 41674183 - 21894541 - 49925871 - 67414923 - 27238583 -
41494547 - 89418347 - 94527432 - 72347234 - 18312549 - 27414923 - 25892583 -
47232783 - 12583279 - 27254923 - 41418345 - 47167415 - 41945216 - 74792549 -
41899256 - 74183125 - 49832741 - 49454147 - 45418345 - 472525.-

EULOGIO CASTAÑEDA ALCANTARA.
Prefecto Acc.

FIGURE 2.1. Encrypted document.
Source: ASC3.

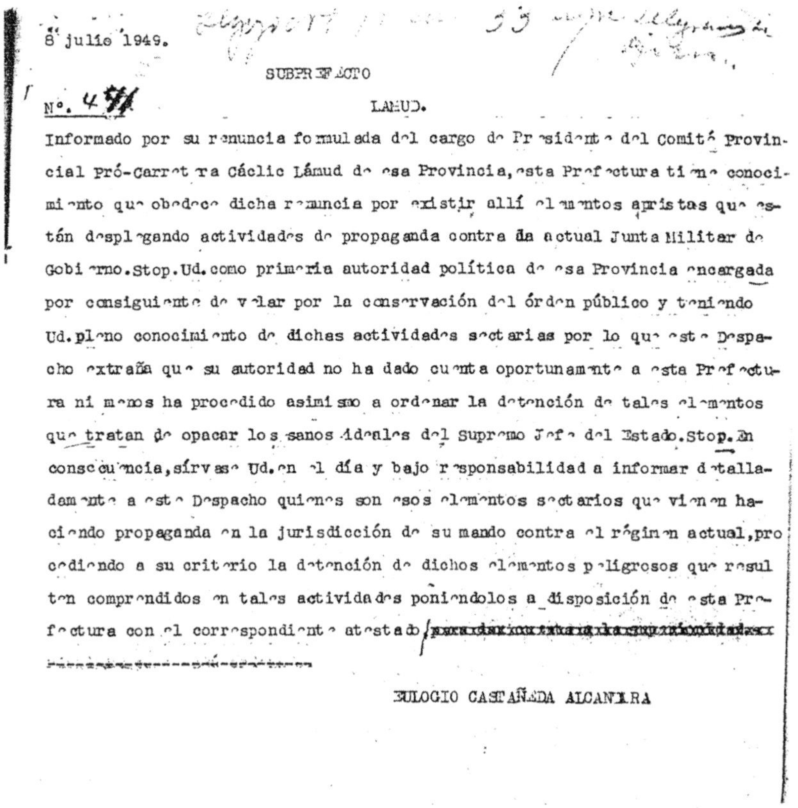
8 julio 1949.

SUBPREFECTO

No. 471

LAMUD.

Informado por su renuncia formulada del cargo de Presidente del Comité Provincial Pró-Carretera Cáclic Lámud de esa Provincia, esta Prefectura tiene conocimiento que obedece dicha renuncia por existir allí elementos apristas que están desplegando actividades de propaganda contra la actual Junta Militar de Gobierno. Stop. Ud. como primeria autoridad política de esa Provincia encargada por consiguiente de velar por la conservación del órden público y teniendo Ud. pleno conocimiento de dichas actividades sectarias por lo que este Despacho extraña que su autoridad no ha dado cuenta oportunamente a esta Prefectura ni menos ha procedido asimismo a ordenar la detención de tales elementos que tratan de opacar los sanos ideales del Supremo Jefe del Estado. Stop. En consecuencia, sírvase Ud. en el día y bajo responsabilidad a informar detalladamente a este Despacho quienes son esos elementos sectarios que vienen haciendo propaganda en la jurisdicción de su mando contra el régimen actual, procediendo a su criterio la detención de dichos elementos peligrosos que resulten comprendidos en tales actividades poniendolos a disposición de esta Prefectura con el correspondiente atestado

EULOGIO CASTAÑEDA ALCANTARA

FIGURE 2.2. Decrypted document.
Source: ASC3.

in theory someone completely trustworthy. The contents of the message reveal the difficulties involved in seeking to shore up the sagging boundaries of the state by means of encryption. Despite being written in code, the communiqué does not help government officials establish a secure space of privileged information from which they can more effectively prosecute the war against the subversives. To the contrary; the document shows the authorities' inability to accomplish these goals despite the attempted use of secrecy.

The document is as much an accusation as a communication. It reveals that the subprefect—one of relatively few state officials the prefect relied upon to help lead the fight against APRA—had not been using his position as the prefect intended. Rather than persecute the subversives, the subprefect had found it expedient to shelter a group of Apristas who were useful to him for political purposes.[21] All the while, he had communicated in coded form on a regular basis with the other members of the government's inner circle about the progress of the war against the Party of the People. But his behavior undermined government efforts to effect a clear separation between state and subversive.

Despite the use of encryption, the efforts of state officials to keep APRA from discovering government plans were to no avail. APRA remained opaque to the authorities, while it seemed that even the most secret of government plans somehow leaked out to the subversives. Indeed, government officials remained utterly confounded by the Party of the People and seemed unable to make any headway whatsoever against the enemy. The police continued to be ineffectual in apprehending Apristas in their nocturnal meetings. Party members grew ever more daring in leaving public evidence of their nighttime sojourns through the streets of Chachapoyas. And government officials continued to struggle with their administrative duties in the countryside. In desperation, the prefect appealed to the national government for assistance. No one was to be trusted, he reported. Everyone was an Aprista.

Power/Knowledge in Crisis

What were the processes that led government officials to indulge in such dark fantasies? By the middle of 1949 the government regime in Amazonas was in the midst of two interrelated crises that together undermined people's faith in the reality of the state—and that transferred some of that faith to APRA. One such crisis was of *power/knowledge*. Government officials went to elaborate lengths to "see (APRA) like a state" (Scott 1998)—to generate a comprehensive body of reliable information that would allow them to know the Party of the People (APRA's term for itself) in great detail. Having done so, the regime attempted to "be like a state"—attempted to translate this knowledge into power. Employing the intelligence it had gathered as a guide, the government used its control over the means of violence to attempt to eradicate APRA. Toward that end, government personnel surveilled, jailed, deported, and (in numerous cases) tortured. They closed meetinghouses, dissolved organizations, and banned publications. They eliminated all visible signs of the Party of the People. So broad and systematic was their assault on APRA, and so complete was the rout that the party appeared to have suffered, that the authorities concluded that they had destroyed the movement—a victory that the Odría regime was quick to announce to society at large. Indeed, the military government went so far as to claim to have been responsible for the demise of APRA:

Sr. Chief of Police.

I acknowledge receipt of your coded Oficio No. 4, [marked] 'Strictly Confidential' [in which] you ask this office to provide police headquarters with the Register of the members of the recently defunct Party of the People . . . I am pleased to attach this list . . . and to congratulate the forces [of order] of this locality ["plaza"] for their splendid work in eliminating this dangerous threat to the regime of . . . General Manuel A. Odría (ASC3, 13 January 1949)

The military government also began circulating a heroic "narrative of eradication" to explain how the government had prevailed over the Apristas—a narrative made up of exemplary acts of bravery, loyalty, and sacrifice (in the example below, a letter published in the Chachapoyas newspaper, and signed by 126 prominent citizens):

General Manuel A. Odría, President of the Military Junta, and Director of Lima's most important daily newspapers (*El Comercio, La Prensa, Vanguardia*).

We, the undersigned, filled with patriotic fervor, and with deep respect for our country's legally formed institutions, congratulate you with all sincerity for the brilliant position you have taken in favor of the Country [*Patria*], in refusing to grant safe conduct [out of Peru] to the Terrorist Leader of the Aprista Sect, Victor Raul Haya de la Torre. We declare our steadfast support for and solidarity with our government, and with the honorable Military Men who make up the Military Junta. (ASC44, 9 March 1949)

Within short order, however, it became clear that in their zeal to relegate the APRA problem to the past, in their rush to return to a more acceptable threat level, the authorities had allowed themselves to be deceived. It became clear that it was dangerously naive to regard the Apristas as a First Order Standard Deviation. The authorities were forced to acknowledge that the war with the subversives was far from over. Much to their dismay and embarrassment, government officials discovered that they had not destroyed the party but had simply driven it underground. In the face of intense repression, the Apristas had thought it prudent to conceal their identities, disguise their meeting places, and mask their communications. They temporarily suspended all party activities that would leave a public mark and made every effort to become indistinguishable from the rest of society. To the naïve observer, the Party of the People appeared to have disappeared from, or to have been driven from, the face of the earth.

It was at this moment, when the party had gone so far underground as to make itself invisible to the authorities, that the military declared definitive and final victory over the subversives. In the very wake of the government's celebratory announcements, however—while the authorities were still flush with success—the Apristas began to reemerge from the shadows, thus flatly contradicting the government's claims. In so doing, APRA did something far more damaging to the government than simply prove that the authorities had been mistaken. The party did far more than show that government officials were not fully aware of what was going on around them. APRA demonstrated that the Odría regime was totally in the dark about the one problem it had devoted virtually all its energies to resolving—the problem concerning which the very survival of the regime depended.

That question concerned the status of its war against the party. But it wasn't only that the authorities were in the dark. Making matters worse was that they hadn't even realized this fact. So completely deluded were they about what was actually going on in Peruvian society that they thought the war against the subversives was going splendidly! Once the party resurfaced, however, it became clear that while government officials had been busy congratulating themselves for finally vanquishing the enemy, APRA had been quietly rebuilding its strength.

APRA's demonstration that the government had been so deeply deluded about issues of such pressing concern undermined any pretensions the regime might have had to speak in an authoritative and credible manner. The Lazarus-like reappearance of APRA after the authorities had pronounced it dead made it clear that the government did *not* occupy a privileged position of knowledge and understanding from which it could manipulate and manage the social order. To the contrary; it became clear that the government was profoundly misinformed and dangerously ignorant about what was going on under its very nose. The state seemed to be hovering in a rarified space somewhere above society, at a great distance from it, rather than being in touch with it. From such a distance, it appeared, the state was incapable of perceiving just how out of touch it actually was.

The disclosure that the state knew so very little about a society that it claimed to know so well was deeply humiliating. For once it was clear that the party lived on despite official claims to the contrary, the many tales of prowess, perseverance, and courage that the authorities had circulated in constructing the state's narrative of eradication seemed ludicrous, pathetic, laughable—as did the government itself. With the revelation that APRA had deceived the authorities, the heroes of this narrative became fools, the triumphs became defeats, the victories turned into losses.

The failure of the government's campaign against APRA, the public humiliation the dictatorship suffered at the hands of the party, and the obviously delusional tendencies of the regime, made it appear that that there was a great absence at the center of Peruvian politics—just where there should have been a powerful presence. This was an absence not only of knowledge and understanding (about APRA, about society) but also of coordination and control (in government efforts to eradicate the party). It was an absence of unity and coherence (of the state apparatus itself), and of competence and commitment (on the part of government officials). The absence even extended to the effective use of violence; the authorities' efforts to use force against the subversives were ultimately in vain, not least, the government came to realize, because these efforts were often directed against the wrong people.

The authorities' inability to know, control, or effectively punish APRA made it seem that there was "no there there"; made it seem that there was no functioning machinery of government, no coherent, ordered structure that was coordinating the effort against the subversives. Instead, state activities appeared to be a chaotic and incoherent assemblage of sites, processes, and institutions. They seemed to be lacking any underlying, co-ordinating logic, and even to work at cross-purposes with one another.

Confronted with what seemed irrefutable proof that the party was alive and well despite their best efforts to destroy it, the authorities were forced to consider why their campaign against the subversives had failed. Government officials first developed doubts about the reliability of their intelligence. The fact that APRA continued to operate so effectively after the government had eliminated all *known* sources of subversion led the authorities to conclude that they actually knew very little about the Party of the People. It led government officials to believe that they could not state with confidence who was a party member and who was not. Nor could they be certain where the subversives held their meetings, what they decided at those meetings, how Apristas carried out their actions, how they managed to leave signs of their presence undetected by the authorities, and so on. In short, despite the authorities' best intelligence-gathering efforts, they came to regard the party as something of a black box, whose inner workings the government could not penetrate, and whose appeal to the general population the authorities could not comprehend.

As the months wore on, and the Odría regime failed to make significant progress against APRA, government officials came to question more than just their intelligence. It was difficult to understand how the government could continue to "miss" the subversives when its agents were everywhere, on the lookout for any telltale sign of party activity. Faced with one failed attempt after another, officials' "radius of doubt" began to expand beyond the realm of information alone. The authorities also came to question the loyalty and commitment of the state functionaries that gathered government intelligence, and of the state security forces that used it in their (unsuccessful) efforts to arrest the Apristas. As doubts about the loyalty of their subordinates loomed ever larger in the minds of government officials, the boundary between state and subversive began to blur. Lacking as they did reliable intelligence about who was and was not an Aprista, the authorities found it impossible to bring the boundary back into focus. Instead, their vision became blurred in general. They came to view everyone through suspect eyes—to regard themselves as menaced on all sides, by unknown and unknowable social elements, who threatened to subsume the governing regime.

In short, the crisis of power and knowledge that unfolded in the context of the failed campaign against the party unleashed upon the authorities a plague of fantasies (Žižek 1997).[22] Faced with the certain knowledge that they knew so little, government officials took to imagining much. They came to regard everyone as a potential subversive, came to see signs of APRA's presence everywhere, in the most unlikely of places.

Performance/Representation in Crisis

The government's campaign against the Party of the People was not limited to jailing, deporting, and torturing Apristas. The authorities also waged war with the subversives in the realms of meaning, discourse, and display. It was in these domains that the Odría regime experienced a second crisis, one that deepened its sense of danger, desperation, and paranoia with respect to APRA. This second crisis was one of *performance/representation*.

Upon seizing power government officials had sought to do battle with APRA to define what would be considered normal, legitimate forms of economic, sociocultural, and political order. Toward that end, they had imposed strict limits on what people could safely do and say, on what could be represented as important and worthwhile ways to live. In this way, the authorities sought to craft a new public sphere—one that was unambiguously and uniformly supportive of government visions of proper order.

At the same time, officials sought to make both public and private life wholly visible and transparent—so as to constantly reassure themselves that there were no hidden pockets of subversion where alternative notions of social life were being articulated. Precisely because of this fear, in the Odría regime's new public domain people were expected to perform their loyalty and commitment continuously, not only to government officials but also to one another. They were expected, for example, to turn out faithfully and to participate enthusiastically in all public political ritual. Failure to appear or to behave as expected by the authorities could raise suspicions, which in turn could have disastrous consequences.

More important than public political ritual, however, was the realm of the everyday. The government looked to the general populace to act out its loyalty not only during rare moments of political pomp and circumstance, but also on an ongoing, daily basis, in all walks of life. In short, the authorities made it clear that people were to do nothing in word, print, or behavior that would betray any sympathy whatsoever with the subversive cause.

The populace quickly learned that anyone—a friend, neighbor, enemy, even a complete stranger—could report "suspicious behavior" to the authorities, and that a single report was enough to launch an investigation by the forces of order. In these circumstances, the regional population began to police itself (Taussig 2003). Anyone who wished to avoid suspicion began to sanitize their behavior, to act at all times in ways that could only be regarded as wholly innocuous by any observer, hypothetical or real. People thus collectively conspired to hold one another in a set of ever-present, mutually interlocking gazes of conformity. In so doing, they went to great lengths to appear as transparent, loyal, and law abiding as possible.

In the aftermath of the Odría coup, social life thus quickly became akin to a vast drama (Taylor 1997), but one with no single director, no defined parts, and no set dialogue. In this drama everyone was a player, willing or not, and everyone felt compelled to improvise lines that they hoped would satisfy a director and audience they would never see, and whose reactions they could never be sure of. For there were no agreed-upon standards for judging the performances of the actors, and it was unclear who was evaluating the performances. In other words, the populace found itself performing everyday acts of allegiance to a hypothetical audience of fellow citizens and government officials whose fears people tried to anticipate and ameliorate.

In so performing for this hypothetical audience, local people brought into being a novel form of imagined [non-]community (Anderson 1991)—one that was a threat to their very existence. This was a form of collectivity that was rendered foreign or alien to its makers in the very act of its creation—a form of community to which they knew they did not belong. It was simultaneously, however, one in which they had to feign membership at all times. If they were to avoid arrest and possible torture, people had to maintain themselves in a state of constant alert about how others might regard them, and adjust their behavior and speech accordingly (Skidmore 2004). This process of [non-]community formation had a powerful individuating and alienating dynamic. Each time people strategized about how to avoid a bad "audience response" they did so on their own—as solitary individuals. It was not just that this new anticollective was a threat. It was a threat that isolated people, separated them from one another, turned each into a potential threat to all others—even as it purported to do and be the opposite.

In their zeal to establish a public sphere that would seem unambiguously supportive of the military regime, the authorities did not limit themselves to establishing strict limits on what people could do or say. They also used their extensive control over the media to bring into being new representational forms in which novel imaginings of the state, the subversives, and the public could be elaborated. As one might expect, during the dictatorship media of all kinds were purged of any positive reference to the Party of the People. But the government did not restrict itself to demonizing APRA in word and print. It also deployed a series of additional discursive weapons to give the dictatorship an air of authenticity it might otherwise have lacked.

Rather than go on endlessly about the virtues of their own regime, government officials introduced a series of new discursive forms that allowed "the people" to speak on the behalf of the dictatorship. These included signed and notarized loyalty oaths, open letters of support to General Odría, and exposés. They included as well letters written by the loyal public to the political authorities revealing the existence of "subversive" government officials who were seeking to mask their membership in the party:

Sr. Prefect of the Department:

We the undersigned citizens and residents of this district present ourselves to you with complete respect to ask [the following]:

That the present governor of this district . . . who is a person who only pretends to be concerned with the progress of this locale, be replaced. . . . [The governor] is a known member of the outlawed Party of the People, who uses his position to steal community lands . . . and [community] funds . . . and to propagandize for the Party, at the orders of his superiors. . . .

Sr. Prefect, we bring these facts to the attention of your office and ask that you take whatever steps are necessary to free us from the tyranny of [the governor].

What we seek is Justice. (ASC3, 28 January 1949)

The new discursive forms introduced by the military included as well formal renunciations from APRA (also signed before a notary), as well as a variety of testimonials (all carefully notarized), in which both individuals and groups swore their allegiance to the government:

Sr. Prefect of the Department:

I have the honor of addressing you in order to state the following: that in my condition as a teacher, Director of the Leimebamba School for Boys No. 133, fully conscious of the high purpose of forming the future citizens who are the hope of the Nation, my labors were, are and will be only and exclusively to carry out the mission that the State has given me and with my mission as a Catholic teacher, whose pedagogy is completely removed from any and all political tendencies, and is concerned only with the preparation of citizens of wholesome conscience who are capable of contributing to the true progress of our people. I also declare to you, Sr. Prefect . . . that never did I belong nor do I belong to any political party, and least of all the Aprista party . . . and that if someone has placed my name on the party list I take this opportunity to present to you my most energetic protest. . . . (ASC23, 18 March 1949)

The authorities literally filled the airwaves and the newspapers with these statements, in which the most diverse social elements were permitted to express to society at large their unconditional loyalty to the Odría regime.

Citizens' groups, labor unions, and social clubs were allowed to so testify, as were sports teams, primary schools, and mutual aid societies. Civil servants, Indian peasants, and aristocratic landowners were all permitted to do the same. As in the examples quoted earlier in the chapter, even former Apristas were given the opportunity to confess the error of their former ways, and to pledge their undying allegiance to the military government.

The effect of this barrage of testimonial and confession appeared to be overwhelming. By waging war in the realm of discourse, the authorities did much to create the image of a public that was united in its support of the military, and in its rejection of APRA. The implication was clear; in pursuing the destruction of the terrorists, the military was doing little more than obeying the will of the people.

The success of the Odría regime's campaign against APRA in the realms of performance and representation, however, proved to be as short lived, and as illusory as did its offensive in the realm of power and knowledge. Although individual behavior, social interaction, and discursive communication temporarily fell in line with official expectations, it soon became apparent that in producing such conformity government officials had done little more than construct a mask behind which even they could not see. Before long, evidence was forthcoming from all quarters that many individuals and groups who had sworn their allegiance were anything but loyal citizens. They were in fact subversives (or party sympathizers), who were so committed to APRA that they sought to trade on the image of the patriotic citizen to continue with their nefarious activities. In the process, they had perjured themselves before the government, and before society at large.

The discovery that many people who had sworn publicly to be part of the broad, anti-APRA consensus were actually committed to the overthrow of the Odría regime faced government officials with a real dilemma. Allowing such people to remain at liberty posed a significant threat to the government. At the same time, however, the authorities had no way of distinguishing those who truly were loyal from those who (mis-)represented themselves in these terms. Already in the grip of quite paranoid fears, government officials responded to this dilemma in a way that was very damaging to the image that the general population held of the regime. They unleashed a new round of persecution upon the very individuals and the very social groups that the authorities had formerly claimed were part of the anti-APRA consensus. In other words, after insisting that everyone declare precisely where they stood with respect to APRA, and after attesting publicly to the truth-value of these statements, government officials then discounted the very declarations they had insisted people make.[23] In this way what had initially seemed like evidence of state strength—the Odría regime's ability to compel the population to perform rituals of loyalty— ended up being regarded as a source of weakness.

As government officials reversed their position concerning the status of those who claimed to support the dictatorship, the general populace was witness to an odd admission on the part of the authorities: what officials had previously asserted to be true was in fact false. With this admission, government officials did more than simply acknowledge that they had been misled. They also acknowledged that both their methods for attesting to the truth, and what was asserted to be true on the basis of those methods, were wholly lacking in credibility.

As government officials came to realize that they could not tell friend from foe, they became increasingly suspicious and fearful of those around them. In this context, both government officials and the general population came to lose faith in the reliability of public truth claims made about people's relationship to the Party of the People. They came to lose faith in the multiple forms of swearing publicly to the truth of that relationship— representational forms that the military had elaborated in its efforts to craft a public sphere that was free of the influence of APRA (renunciations, oaths of loyalty, public letters of allegiance, etc.). Indeed, the authorities and the populace came to regard public truth claims as the *opposite* of what they appeared to be—as ways of concealing rather than revealing the truth. As first one and then another of these public truth claims came to be regarded as mechanisms for disguising rather than exposing the truth, the "loyal public" represented discursively by the military regime began to unravel, piece by piece. It was this loyal public upon which the government had staked its claim to represent an alternative to APRA that was endorsed by large numbers of people. In short, the local populace was witness to the state's inability to generate authoritative accounts of social life. In this context, the state apparatus experienced a deep and profound crisis of performance/representation.

The Drive to Resolve Uncertainty

It was the impossibility of truly knowing or even identifying the enemy that provoked such dark fantasies on the part of the authorities. It was impossible, government officials had learned, to distinguish subversive from loyal citizen on the basis of visual cues. It had proven equally difficult to identify the terrorists on the basis of their behavior. It was also futile to trust people's professed beliefs or their overtly expressed opinions about APRA, or about the military regime. On the basis of appearance, behavior, and belief, one would be forced to conclude that there were no terrorists anywhere. On the surface, everything appeared to be calm. And yet the authorities had what they considered overwhelming evidence that the subversives were *everywhere*, making a mockery of them before the general public, wreaking havoc with their efforts to govern the region.

In an effort to help his subalterns imagine the contours of their invisible enemy, in late April 1949 the prefect circulated a very important but rather dated document to a select group of government officials. These included the heads of the Guardia Civil and the PIP (the Secret Police), the president of the Superior Court, the subprefects and judges of the region's five provinces, and the governors of the department's many rural districts.[24] The prefect was at great pains to restrict access to the memo he was sending to these officials alone, so in addition to sending it in code he marked his communication "Secret" and "Confidential."

The dated document that the prefect circulated, which one of his subalterns had discovered in the archive of the prefecture only a short time before, was entitled, "Organización del Comité Provincial" (Organization of the Provincial Committee). It had been seized almost two decades prior, in 1931, from a party member who was carrying it from APRA's Central Committee in Lima to the party's local membership in Amazonas. It contained a description of the structure the local Apristas were to adhere to in establishing the party in Amazonas.

Regarded as being of only passing interest when it was first seized, "Organización del Comité Provincial" had been filed away in the archive of the prefecture, where it had languished ever since. Faced with political crisis in 1949, however, the prefect came to regard this document as an absolutely key piece of intelligence; for it appeared to answer many of the government's most pressing questions about APRA. Furthermore, it did so in a way that confirmed the authorities' worst fears about the enemy they faced.

"Organización del Comité Provincial" provided a detailed description of APRA's underground party apparatus, and the prefect asked that all those who received it review the document with care so that they would know what they were up against—and also what to look for as they did battle with the party. According to this document, APRA's structure was indeed extensive and elaborate. It took the form of a nested hierarchy of cells. In some senses, the structure of the party mimicked that of the state, for it reproduced the national territorial grid. Thus, there were (in theory) APRA cells or committees for each district, province, and department in Peru, and a national committee for the country as a whole. As "Organización del Comité Provincial" made clear, however, the actual make-up of these cells, their manner of operation, and the powers and responsibilities allotted to the members of each reflected a degree of specialization and differentiation that went far beyond that of the formal state apparatus.

APRA, it appeared, had organized itself into a series of secretariats, or ministries. In addition to a general secretariat, there were also ministries of the Interior, Defense, Organization, Information, Economy, Discipline, Social Assistance, and Peasant and Indigenous Affairs. Some of these were further divided into subsecretariats. The Ministry of Information, for example, was divided into subsecretariats of the Press, Mural Propaganda, Culture, and Sports.[25] As these names suggested, each ministry was responsible for attending to the affairs of particular subgroups and/or activities. Furthermore, the prerogatives and responsibilities of each secretariat were carefully spelled out. As "Organización del Comité Provincial" implied, this meant that party secretaries were to be on hand to provide people with key services that they otherwise lacked—medical care, legal help, occasional financial assistance, advice about how to deal with abusive political officials.

By drawing on this party structure, it seemed, APRA had sought to involve itself directly in the everyday lives of the population—despite the fact that the party was forced to operate in secret, beyond the gaze of the legally constituted authorities. Indeed, according to "Organización del Comité Provincial," the party was to establish secretaries for as many of its ministries as possible in every cell in the country, whether that of a remote rural district or a large urban center. This in turn suggested that the "bureaucracy" that the party had generated was considerably thicker than that of the formal state apparatus, whose representatives were sparsely scattered about the national territory.

"Organización del Comité Provincial" provided the authorities with something of which they were in desperate need—a kind of blueprint that allowed them to imagine the contours of their underground adversary. The fact that they felt compelled to rely on this document to provide them with such a blueprint reveals just how deep a crisis of knowledge that they were in. Between 1945 and 1948 the Party of the People had been entirely legal and had conducted most of its activities out in the open. During this period, the party's organizational structure had been visible for all to see. Just six months into General Odría's war on APRA, however, government authorities in Chachapoyas had come to believe that they could not trust what they thought they knew about the party, that APRA's public presentation of self was not to be taken at face value. Only a document like the "Organización del Comité Provincial"—a secret document, sent underground, from one group of Apristas to another—was regarded as a reliable source of information about the party's true structure.

But high-ranking government officials were not content to interpret this document in literal terms alone. Their worst fears about the complexity and sophistication of the party structure having been confirmed, the authorities could not resist the temptation, it would appear, to make additional inferences based on this document, and on others they had in their possession—inferences concerning APRA's followers. Government officials reasoned that only a membership of great size would be capable of maintaining such an extensive party structure, and of shielding it from official scrutiny—a conclusion that was reinforced by the authorities' growing doubts about the loyalty of much of the population. On the one hand, government officials were convinced that this membership was not only large in size but was also widely distributed through space, that Apristas were to be found even in the most remote corners of the department. The authorities were equally certain that APRA had supporters among all social classes and groups—among the rich and the poor, the young and the old, the uncouth and the cultivated, among women and men, peasants and hacendados, among Indians, mestizos, and whites.[26]

It was not just the size of APRA's following, however, that alarmed government officials. Of equal concern was that party members seemed willing to make virtually any sacrifice for the terrorist cause. For most of its existence APRA had been a proscribed political party, subject to vicious persecution by the forces of order. Its members had been hunted down, arrested, and jailed. Many had suffered torture at the hands of the authorities. Thousands had been killed. Despite the great personal risks involved, however, the Apristas seemed as committed to the subversive cause as ever. They appeared willing to stop at nothing to realize their plans for revolutionary change.

Government officials thus came to view themselves as increasingly under siege, by forces that were at once profoundly dangerous but also invisible to the naked eye. In the process, they came to regard the state apparatus of which they were a part in a different light. They came to see their own regime as less and less like a state—less and less like an ordered, principled mechanism that was capable of preserving public order and advancing the public good—and more and more as an incoherent, uncoordinated set of activities and processes with no common goal, that often worked at cross-purposes. Furthermore, the general public came to see the ruling regime in like terms. In other words, under pressure from the party, government officials found it increasingly difficult to sustain (to themselves or to others) the illusion of the state. What Timothy Mitchell (1999) has famously referred to as "the state effect" began to dissipate.

At the same time, however, the authorities came to view APRA as having all the attributes of "state-ness" (Nettle 1968) that their regime lacked—order, consistency and logic, unity, discipline and purpose. In the context of the crisis provoked by the Party of the People, government officials came to view their own administration as a pale imitation of a sophisticated, complex state structure that they could not actually *see*. They were confident that it was there. The problem was actually finding it.

In the aftermath of the failed coup of October 1948, the forces of order came to regard APRA as a Third Order Standard Deviation. That is, having become profoundly alarmed by what appeared to be the party's obsession with seizing power, and their fear that the Party of the People was just on the verge of doing so, the authorities became deeply paranoid about APRA. They responded by seeking to "see APRA like a state" (Scott 1998). Government officials sought to resolve their fears about the party by doing away with their uncertainty about APRA and its activities and turning that uncertainty into knowledge. The forces of order turned their most powerful optic on APRA, so that they could know the party in every detail.

Even if they had succeeded in gathering this information, however, the authorities would still have been in the dark about what was most important for them to understand. Even the most detailed of information about the party structure would not have made Aprista agency comprehensible to the forces of order. It would not have explained to government officials why the Apristas insisted on doing what they did despite the most severe of consequences. It would not have explained, for example, why party members were so devoted to the cause—why they appeared willing to make virtually any sacrifice in its name. Nor would such information have revealed how a political movement that was proscribed by the central government could survive and even thrive in the face of systematic and quite brutal repression by the forces of order.

The reason that the authorities remained in the dark about APRA was that they rejected out of hand the notion that comprehension was even possible. Committed as they were to their own version of the normal and the rational, officials were compelled to regard APRA's opposition to their activities as wholly irrational—as motivated by fanaticism, extremism, the desire to subvert. This understanding of the party and its members, however, carried with it alarming implications. On the one hand, it suggested that a great many people did not embrace government definitions of the normal and the everyday, despite official assertions to the contrary. On the other, it implied that much of the population was not to be trusted—that it was made up largely of fanatics or extremists. Little wonder, then, that the forces of order ultimately came to regard virtually everyone as a subversive.

Conclusion

With the crisis of rule that shook the Chachapoyas region at the beginning of the regime of Manuel Odría, government officials indulged in the darkest of fantasies about the Party of the People. Despite their delusional and paranoid nature, however, these reactions are not as remarkable as it might appear. Rather, as we will see, they are the culmination of a prior process of twentieth-century state formation in which the logic of sacropolitics was dominant. As discussed in the Introduction, this meant that what were actually delusional goals (bringing to life a moribund social formation; overcoming backwardness; animating the national population) were dressed in the guise of ordinary, rational state projects and plans. It also meant government officials set goals that were unattainable—that made it inevitable that the very notion of a rational state would come undone. The chapters that follow trace the process by which the remarkable emerged out of the routine. The story begins with a discussion of the regional social order of Chachapoyas, and the ways that sacropolitically informed government efforts to modernize the region transformed that social order.

Part II

The Rise and Demise of Elite Political Structures

3

The Consolidation of *Casta* Rule

[W]hat was involved was not that . . . there existed nuclei of a
homogenous ruling class whose irresistible tendency to unite
determined the formation of the new . . . national State. These nuclei
existed [in the form of *castas*] . . . but their tendency to unite was
extremely problematic. . . . These nuclei did not wish to "lead" anybody,
i.e., they did not wish to concord their interests and aspirations with
the interests and aspirations of other [elite] groups.
  —Antonio Gramsci, *Selections from the Prison Notebooks* (1971)

Introduction

In the quote above, from "Notes on Italian History," Antonio
Gramsci (1971, 104–5) draws attention to a phenomenon of great significance. Oddly, it is one with which scholars have shown relatively little concern. Although the scholarly community has shown great interest in the
conditions that variously promote or undermine the unity of the laboring
classes (Marx 1898; Moore 1966; Thompson 1963; Wolf 1969), they have
shown far less concern with the forces that affect the unity of elite groups.[1]
It is precisely this question that Gramsci engages in the epigraph. He does
so by drawing our attention to a social context in which an elite group (in
his case, the Piedmont bourgeoisie) fails to act as a unified class.

The question of elite unity is directly relevant to the problems explored in *The Encrypted State*. For the dark fantasies discussed in the previous chapter emerge out of a social context of the very kind that Gramsci

describes—in which the elite is deeply divided. Indeed, rather than having an "irresistible tendency to unite," the elite families of Chachapoyas demonstrate the irresistible urge to divide, to compete. While they act as nuclei, they show no tendency whatsoever to aggregate into a whole. Rather, each is determined to remain independent and autonomous, battling for existence with the remaining nuclei. Prior to 1930 the elite wage war with one another according to *casta* affiliation. After 1930 the elite becomes even more fragmented, as individual families struggle with one another.

Gramsci's discussion of the crisis-like conditions that characterize divided social contexts has direct bearing on the Chachapoyas region. As Gramsci observes (1971, 276), "the crisis consists precisely in the fact that the old is dying and the new cannot be born." By 1930, a crisis had indeed unfolded for the aristocratic elite. Circa 1900 the region's old families were involved in broad, stable alliance structures (called *castas*) that brought the members of each alliance great power and privilege, and that left them in firm control of regional affairs.

Within a few short decades, however, conditions had changed profoundly. By the 1930s the broad, stable coalitions of the past had dissolved, and had been replaced by short-term, shifting, ephemeral alliances. Furthermore, the elite families that were involved in these new alliances found themselves living in greatly reduced circumstances. Rather than exercising firm control over regional affairs, they had to enter into power-sharing arrangements with humble social groups. Not only were the elite accustomed to treating these groups as their social inferiors; they were also used to excluding them from virtually all positions of power.

To paraphrase Gramsci, the old was indeed dying. But the old nonetheless stubbornly hung on, and in the process prevented the new from being born. In their determination to retain some semblance of their former way of life, the new shifting factions of the elite that replaced the *castas* of old engaged in fierce competition. The object of their competition was positions in the government bureaucracy and also modernization projects. For it was only by controlling these positions and projects that the old aristocratic families could have any hope of retaining the elite powers and privileges to which they felt entitled by right of birth.

The problem was, however, that the available positions and projects could not support all the families of the elite. As many families converged upon a limited number of positions and projects, fierce competition ensued that would determine the fate of each. In these circumstances, elite families were not remotely interested in overcoming their differences. Indeed, something of a war of all against all broke out among the families of the elite.

As the foregoing suggests, understanding the breakdown of the *casta* structure—and the disintegration of elite unity that accompanies it—is central to the task of this volume. For the disintegration of the *casta* coalitions generates a new form of conflict among the elite. It transforms the apparatus of state into a terrain of conflict, where individual aristocratic families fight to retain whatever they can of their deteriorating elite status.

It is because the government apparatus has been converted into a terrain of conflict that the era's modernization projects have such a disordering effect on everyday administration. And it is this disorder that makes it increasingly difficult to embed the remarkable (a massive campaign of forced labor) in the routine (mundane, ordinary administration). For the modernization projects rely on the cooperation of large numbers of interdependent government officials. It is precisely this cooperation that is lacking after 1930.

As we will see, understanding why the region's aristocratic families compete rather than cooperate after 1930 is important for other reasons. Doing so makes it possible to comprehend the emergence of official fantasies about the rural labor supply—and the unending (and ultimately futile) struggles of government officials to locate that labor supply. Understanding why the *castas* come to be replaced by ephemeral, short-time alliances is equally important to making sense of the government's growing preoccupation with quasi-phantom threats like APRA. It was threats such as these—which the authorities conjured into being—onto which government officials displaced responsibility for their own inability to govern.

I begin by analyzing the organization of *casta*-based society on the eve of modernization. I continue with the breakdown of the *casta* order, and the elite factionalism that emerged in its wake. It was the fierce elite competition of the post-*casta* era that made it so difficult for government officials to carry out even routine acts of everyday administration. It was this that made it impossible to embed the remarkable in the routine.

Chachapoyas on the Eve of Modernization

During the opening decades of the twentieth century a peculiar relationship obtained between the principles of hierarchy and equality. Like many of the republics of Latin America, Peru had been founded in the 1820s on liberal principles of democracy, citizenship, private property, and individual rights. As was true throughout the continent, however, in Peru these precepts were rhetorical rather than actual. In keeping with the transnational language of political legitimacy that characterized the era as a whole (Mbembe 2003; Polanyi 1944), such principles were uniformly invoked in all political ritual and discourse. Social life, however, was organized according to principles diametrically opposed to these precepts of popular sovereignty.

Chachapoyas—located in the northern sierra, on the eastern slope of the Andes (see Map 1)—was one such region. The political landscape of Chachapoyas was dominated by a group of putatively white, aristocratic families who claimed descent from Spanish forbearers.

These families saw it as their birthright to rule over the region's multitudinous mestizo and Indian peasant groups. They rejected any and

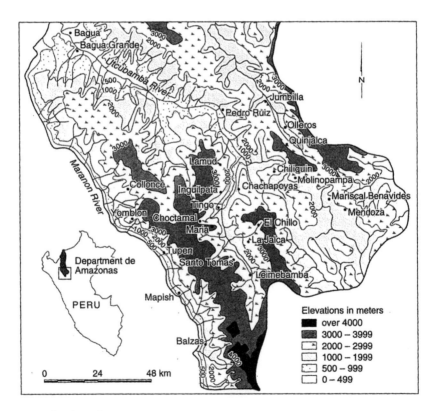

MAP 1. Southern Amazonas.
Source: Nugent 1997

all assertions of equality with such groups and regarded themselves as a separate aristocratic caste (the *casta española*) that was naturally entitled to power and privilege.

The problems of governing meant that the central regime was forced to ally with these families, who would rule in the name of the Lima government.[2] At any one point in time only select elements of the elite enjoyed the backing of the central regime. As a result, this class was far from unified. Indeed, all members of the elite saw themselves as having the inherited right to rule that no one could legitimately deny them. Furthermore, in order to exercise these rights, the elite believed it was their prerogative to use violence. There was a sense in which elite men regarded themselves as having no true peers, and certainly no masters. Rather, each believed he had the right to use power in defense of entitlements that were legitimately his by right of birth. Those who interfered with elite privilege therefore did so at their peril.

It was inevitable, however, that different factions of the elite continually interfered with one another's ability to exercise positions of power. The central regime was forced to choose select elite groups in each region to act in its name. In the process, the government denied other factions access to political power (Gorman 1979; Miller 1982, 1987). The result was endemic conflict, as factions struggled to control the apparatus of government. In their efforts to prevail, all factions of the elite were compelled to establish extensive clienteles among the humble social classes. The multiclass factions that emerged out of this process—each of which numbered in the hundreds and were referred to as *castas*—fought continuously for control of regional affairs.

The central government chose one particular elite faction to act in its name. This "ruling" *casta* used the broad powers of appointment it enjoyed as the state's privileged client to fill the entire government bureaucracy with elite allies and nonelite clients. This allowed the ruling faction to safeguard its own position, and to harass members of opposing factions—to remove them from office, prosecute them for supposed crimes, seize their goods, and do harm to their person and property. The backing of the ruling regime thus allowed the ruling *casta* to flaunt its ability to violate the rights of others.

The ability of the ruling *casta* to persecute the opposition, however, could not be sustained, because opposing *castas* mounted constant challenges to the ruling group. As a result, the period of strength and solidarity that characterized the initial phase of ruling *casta* control was followed by a period of growing weakness and eventual collapse.[3] Ultimately, no one faction could retain control of the regional political apparatus for any sustained period of time (typically, five years; occasionally, ten). Rather, as each new faction rose to power it went in pursuit of those who had recently been its persecutors, using its control over the police and the judiciary to do harm to its enemies in whatever way it could.

As a result of this state of affairs, the operation of the government apparatus and the imagined community of the nation were "compromised," in two senses. First, the region's landed elite took systematic steps to publicly contradict what the "state stated" (Corrigan and Sayer 1985). They used official powers and public institutions to subvert the very forms of egalitarian personhood and homogenous public imagined in national discourse. The elite did so for two reasons. First, national discourse emphasized equality, citizenship, and rights as the only legitimate basis for national life. These principles were in blatant contradiction with racial hierarchy, elite privilege, and with the violence employed by different factions of the elite as they struggled for regional control.

Second, state institutions were designed to support the public sphere imagined in national discourse—one consisting of a mass of formally identical (albeit male) citizens, each jurally indistinguishable from the next, all of whom were united behind the national cause of promoting "progress." This public sphere also offered an explicit critique of a social order in which local aristocratic elites used unlicensed violence on an endemic scale to defend their privileges.

To address the threat posed by the institutional and discursive presence of the nation-state, the ruling *casta* repeatedly demonstrated its ability to ridicule national injunctions about proper behavior. The ruling faction took great care to violate the constitutional protections of the opposing *casta*, and to show that it could do so with impunity. The ruling faction went to great lengths to compromise state institutions and national discourse, using both to further the aims of social groupings (their own faction), statuses (superordinate racial categories), and forms of interaction (violence and domination) that were unthinkable (or deemed "archaic") within the discourse of the nation-state.

The nation-state was further compromised, however, by the dysfunctional nature of "governance" that emerged in these conditions. To protect itself from the ruling *casta*, the opposing *casta* organized itself into a set of positions that replicated the state apparatus—a shadow state (see Nugent 1999). This alternative structure included individuals whose positions mirrored those of the prefect, subprefects, and governors—thus replicating the executive branch. It included as well individuals and corporate bodies (mayors and municipal councils) that replicated municipal government. It even included senators and deputies—although the manner in which they were chosen indicates just how conflictive this set of arrangements was.

Elections for senator and deputy were violent affairs, the first stage being decided when one *casta* defeated the other in an armed battle to control the voting booths (Basadre 1980; Nugent 1997; Taylor 1986). Despite this setback, the losing *casta* was rarely willing to concede defeat and would organize new elections for the same posts, in which its own candidates prevailed (in this new electoral contest only the clients of the defeated *casta* were allowed to vote).

As a result, the "elected" representatives of both *castas* attempted to take up their posts in Congress, both claiming to be the democratically elected senator or deputy. It was then up to Congress as a whole to decide who had actually won the election (see Basadre 1980). The process by which Congress did so, however, was anything but rapid or straightforward, because of which it often remained unclear for months at a time who was in the shadows and who as not. Even when Congress did reach a decision, the *casta* whose representatives had been disqualified was unlikely to concede defeat.

This meant that at any given point in time ruling and opposing faction both claimed to be the "legally constituted authorities." Neither of these factions, however, could hold on to the state apparatus for more than five to ten years before being deposed by the other. Furthermore, in that the rise of one faction inevitably meant persecution for the other, each faction fought viciously to protect its own interests.

Modernizing the Nation

Leguiísmo . . . is Peru's reaction against the feudal classes; it is the vocation of work in the face of ostentatious ineptitude; it is the seizure by the bourgeoisie of the posts formerly held by privilege; [it is] the financial salvation of the poor and the taxing of the rich; the people's aspiration to realize democracy and not to falsify it by allowing the oligarchy to predominate.

—President Augusto Leguía

(*El Comercio*, 26 de Marzo de 1927)

These conditions began to transform circa 1900, along with efforts to modernize the country as a whole. By this time "forward-looking" elites had reached the conclusion that the country's mountainous interior was backward and feudal. They regarded the highlands as controlled by despotic agrarian lords who owned vast tracts of land and dominated enormous populations of miserable Indian serfs. The persistence of these antiquated social structures, progressive elites believed, condemned the country to a permanent state of backwardness. The following article, from a progressive newspaper published in Chachapoyas, typifies these views:

The Martyrdom of a Town and Gamonalismo in Action

[T]he town of Colcamar does not enjoy its liberty, because its inhabitants [are] exploited in the most iniquitous manner by governors and local political bosses (*gamonales*). . . . In this oppressed pueblo the poor Indians are not owners of their liberty, their economic affairs, their animals, and at times . . . not even their women. They are obliged to work one week of every month on the haciendas of the political bosses, who pay them a miserable salary. . . . They are [also] sent by force to the haciendas of the Marañon Valley and to the salt mines of Yuromarca. . . .

That is to say, in the midst of our republic there are pueblos in Peru that live out lives of oppression, whose children, in the midst of the twentieth century, are still forced to endure the regimen of the *encomiendas*, from which their ancestors suffered so terribly during the colonial period. . . .

These abuses and . . . injustices must end forever . . . because the Indian . . . is a free being and as such, no one has the right to coerce him, to obligate him to work . . . no one has the right to exploit . . . his ignorance and his humility.

[A] moral imperative tells us that we must protect our aboriginal race, [and] remove it from the misery in which it struggles . . . so that the light may shine upon the dormant aptitudes [of] . . . these simple and hardworking Indians and, conscious of their rights and duties, they may become efficient elements for our nation . . . (*Amazonas* 2, no. 15 [March–April, 1928]).

The fact that the country's vast natural and human wealth was compromised by social structures and cultural patterns that were entirely out of place in the modern world was seen as having the most dire of consequences for Peru as a whole. The continuing existence of these abusive and backward social patterns was regarded as a major obstacle to the ability of the entire country to progress, to realize its true potential, to become a truly modern nation-state. Indeed, it was this problem that successive national administrations (beginning with the "New Nation" regime of Leguía, in

1919) sought to address. In order to "break the great chain of forces that ha[d] enslaved [Peru] to the past" (see section epigraph), these national governments introduced programs that were intended to modernize the highlands, to liberate it from its deeply entrenched and highly antiquated social structures and cultural patterns, to force it into the present.

The government's "will to improve" (Li 2007) in the sierra was reflected in efforts to implement a wide range of projects and plans. These included an extensive network of roads, bridges, and airfields, which were intended to facilitate the movement of goods, people, and commodities through the national space. They also included an equally extensive network of primary schools, where an army of teachers would steep highland children in national cultural values. Government programs of improvement also included new water, sewage, and sanitation facilities; improved marketplaces; and a series of small hydroelectric plants—to introduce the highlands to improved, modern living conditions. Official efforts to modernize the highlands also involved elaborating new bureaucratic infrastructures to enumerate the population and to monitor its well-being. These efforts also included establishing uniform and systematic procedures for recruiting the rural population into that most nationalizing of institutions—the armed forces.

The sacropolitical plans that government officials devised to bring moribund social formations to life were necessarily delusional in nature. The delusion inherent in the government's modernization efforts, however, was not visible to the naked eye. Rather, it was carefully dressed in the guise of order, rationality, and progress. But in seeking to implement programs that were intended to accomplish such a broad range of lofty and noble goals—do away with feudalism, overcome superstition, integrate the nation, form a citizenry, modernize the sierra, and eliminate inequality— government officials indulged in a broad range of fantasies indeed.

Prominent among these fantasies were those regarding the seemingly neutral and objective category of "population." In their zeal to carry out projects that would overcome the legacies of the country's unfortunate past, the authorities conjured into being a population of fictive proportions— the size of which was directly proportional to the delusional tasks of nation building progressive elites had set for themselves. But official delusions did not end here. Having performed this act of creative demography, officials went on to assume that their (imaginary) population was just waiting to be put to work for the redemption of the nation—whether they intended that population to be relocated in schools (as students), labor camps (building up a national infrastructure) or the armed forces (building up a national character).

Indeed, because these activities and sites of improvement were seen as crucial to the country's ability to redeem itself, they became more than just sites of improvement. They also became sites of excess, of overinvestment (Bataille 1985). By this term I refer not just to the material aspects of the processes under consideration but also to their moral and affective dimensions. Schools, work sites, military service, and so on all became invested with the greatest of hopes and expectations on the part of progressive elites. These sites also became the focus of enormous interest and preoccupation. They became fetishized sites (Pietz 1985), arenas that were regarded as having such vast potential for transformation that, within them, the country's most basic problems and contradictions would be overcome. As a result, elite groups subjected these domains to the most careful of scrutiny.

As we saw in earlier chapters, the inability of progressive elites to redeem the nation by animating regional societies that were regarded as dead or dying was a source of enormous frustration and concern. In order to explain their failure to modernize and improve, government officials in the Chachapoyas region displaced their fears, frustrations, and confusions onto a series of phantom forces: government corruption, the Indian peasantry, and political subversives. Because of their ability to obstruct and confound, these forces ultimately came to be seen as entities of great power and potency. They also came to be seen as unusually dangerous and threatening forces, which required systematic scrutiny, surveillance, and control.

But the authorities' tendency to engage in displacement did not stem only from their efforts to understand official failures. Displacement was equally involved in the authorities' efforts to imagine (future) "success." The hopes, desires, and expectations that the government projected onto its many sites of improvement were as delusional as were the authorities' fears of seemingly inexplicable and irrational forces like APRA. In this sense, the modernization projects in which the authorities were so deeply invested were as much phantoms as were the various forces that menaced the modernization process—forces that the government sought (vainly) to control. Indeed, schools, infrastructure projects, military service, and so on came to regarded as the basis upon which the future of the nation would rise or fall. In particular, it was the forms of *discipline* that were believed to be inherent in these numerous sites and activities that were seen as capable of redeeming the indigenous peasantry, who were believed to live in the most degraded and unfortunate of conditions imaginable (Matto de Turner 1948). Only by redeeming the peasantry would it be possible to redeem the nation.

The eleven-year regime of Augusto Leguía, who ruled Peru from 1919 to 1930 (a period referred to by historians of Peru as "the *oncenio*"), gave the clearest expression to these views. As we will see, Leguía's efforts to bathe Peru in the redeeming waters of the modern world did not seem delusional. Much to the contrary: just like the modernization projects that government officials tried (but failed) to implement in Chachapoyas, Leguía's attempts to bring the progressive forces of the North to his native land were carefully dressed in the guise of rationality and progress.

Even a cursory examination of what Leguía sought to do, however, shows that his government was obsessed by a delusion of a very specific sort. The aforementioned assumption regarding the existence of vast fields of unrealized natural and human wealth, which were just waiting to be liberated from the shackles of Peru's backward social structure, figured prominently in this delusion. For it was on the basis of such vast fields of imagined wealth—wealth that did not yet (?) exist and had to be projected into the future—that Leguía managed to bring equally vast sums of North American investment capital to Peru.

It was this capital that his regime sought to use in order to "break the great chain of forces that has enslaved [Peru] to the past" (see section epigraph). The fact that Leguía was able to leverage imagined wealth from the future to attract quite real wealth in the present speaks to an important point, not only about his efforts in particular but about such efforts in general: modernization is usefully understood as an illusory technique of spatial and temporal displacement.

The delusional nature of Leguía's vision of the future, and his faith in the power of North Atlantic capital to realize that future, is reflected in the following: based on his assumption that Peru possessed vast fields of untapped wealth waiting to be realized, his regime planned to spend a total of $250,000,000 (the equivalent of approximately $3.44 billion in 2016 dollars) on modernization projects (Galarza 1931, 110).[4] Although the president was deposed before he could reach this goal, by 1929 he had nonetheless managed to spend approximately $100,000,000 (equal to about $1.375 billion in 2016 dollars) on projects of precisely this kind.

These varied widely in form and function, from expensive, large-scale irrigation schemes to modest, small-scale hydroelectric plants; from sanitation systems for Peru's urban centers to the modernization and beautification of Lima, the national capital; from the modernization of the armed forces to the creation of a new national police force. The scale of these investments dwarfed those made in programs of this kind by virtually any previous regime.

While the Leguía government invested very large sums of money in a range of different projects, all of which were intended to modernize Peru, it was Leguía's highway-building program that absorbed much of these funds. Considering Leguía's commitment to the modernization of Peru, it is not difficult to understand why the president would have placed such a high priority on this specific program. By means of a greatly expanded highway network, Leguía sought to generalize market relations throughout Peru. He sought to vastly increase the circulation of commodities; to create new, market-based material dependencies among Peru's population; and to link individuals to a growing national and international economy. In this way, he hoped to do away with what he regarded as the backward social structures that dominated the highlands. He also sought to establish the conditions in which new, entrepreneurial forms of subjectivity could flourish.

With these goals in mind, the Leguía regime made massive investments in highway construction and in the development of the means of transport more generally. During the *oncenio* Peru's road network nearly doubled in total length, from slightly over 10,000 kilometers in the mid-1920s to just under 20,000 kilometers in 1930. The funds to underwrite the highway program came from loans from North American banks. The labor, however, had to be coerced out of the peasant population.

Drawing upon the universalizing language of citizenship (but applying it selectively to the rural cultivating population alone), a 1920 law (the Conscripción Vial) decreed that all [*sic!*] able-bodied adult men would be compelled to work on highway construction for six to twelve days per year (Basadre 1968–69, XIII, 254–57).[5] By the end of the *oncenio* the central government had distributed large sums of money all around the country to oversee the process of labor conscription and road construction. In addition, literally hundreds of thousands of Peru's most disadvantaged citizens had been forced from their homes to work in difficult and dangerous of conditions in order to advance the cause of modernizing a backward nation.

As one might imagine, Leguía's massive highway construction program provoked multiple forms of conflict and contestation, within classes and between them. It generated enormous resentment on the part of rural cultivators, who provided the labor upon which this project of forced modernization depended (Mallon 1983; Manrique 1987; Meza Bazán 1999; Wilson 2013). But the Conscripción Vial also produced significant tensions within the upper class of the Peruvian highlands, where much of the road construction took place. Elite groups with competing interests and intentions struggled with one another to control as much as possible of the funds provided by the central government to subsidize the project. They also fought among themselves—and with government planners—to steer the labor power of the Indian peasantry in directions that suited the elite.[6]

In general, however, the Conscripción Vial strengthened the position of elite factions that had allied with the Leguía government. These elites were able to use the ample resources of the highway construction program to further marginalize, hound, and harass elite enemies within their respective regions. The latter, finding themselves in increasingly desperate straits, not uncommonly resorted to displays of violence in a futile effort to shore up their deteriorating positions. The response by the authorities was almost invariably more repression. As a result, by the end of the *oncenio*, organized opposition on the part of out-of-favor elite coalitions was largely a thing of the past.[7]

Modernizing the Region: Chachapoyas during the *Oncenio*

The Department of Amazonas has always been the personal fief of my family.
It always has been and it always will be.
—Mariano Rubio Pizarro, August 10, 1990

The New Nation regime of Augusto Leguía attempted to modernize the Peruvian highlands by doing away with the feudal-like social structures and values systems that were believed to dominate that section of the national space. By eliminating these throwbacks to an earlier age, progressive elites believed, it would be possible to integrate the sierra with the coast and to make of Peru a truly integrated nation-state. Only by initiating a broad process of modernization would it be possible to overcome the forces that condemned the country to being a "beggar sitting on a bench of gold" (Drinot 2000). Only by accelerating a historical process that had become arrested in highland areas would Peru be able to realize its enormous potential for prosperity.

The modernizing reforms of the New Nation regime were broad and diverse. Although many of these reforms were implemented in the Chachapoyas region, they did not have the desired effect of eliminating feudal-like social structures and value systems. Rather, as suggested by the section epigraph—a quote taken from a member of the Pizarro-Rubio *casta*, who grew up during the 1920s—the "reforms" of the New Nation regime reinforced rather than challenged the traditional organization of power. It was only the collapse of the *oncenio* that brought about the demise of the elite political structures of Chachapoyas.

In Chachapoyas, the *oncenio* allowed one *casta* (the Pizarro-Rubio) to rise above all the others and establish itself as the unquestioned, dominant force in the region. This was in large part because of the unprecedented level of support—economic, political, and military—the Pizarro-Rubio received from the central government. This support allowed the ruling *casta* to remain in power for far longer than had ever been the case in the past.

The department-wide constellation of social forces over which the Pizarros and the Rubios presided ruled the Chachapoyas region from 1909 to 1930—a total of twenty-one years. Something of the transformed state of affairs represented by this prolonged period of control is indicated by the following: the contradictions of *casta* rule were such that, previously, few coalitions had been able to remain in power for more than five years, and none for more than ten, before being deposed by an adversary. The twenty-one-year reign of the Pizarro-Rubio thus lasted approximately four times as long as the normal period of *casta* rule, and twice as long as the longest period of coalition control.

To understand the strength of *casta*-based contradictions prior to the *oncenio*, and the ways in which the *oncenio* undermined them, we may consider the following. At the beginning of the twenty-one-year reign of the Pizarro-Rubio, the region's main opposing coalition (the Burga-Hurtado) had mounted major challenges to the Pizarro-Rubio according to the normal rhythms of *casta* politics. That is, they had done so at regular, five-year intervals, to coincide with presidential elections.[8]

The first of these challenges had been mounted during the electoral campaign of 1913, and had been led by Eloy Burga, head of the Burga-Hurtado. Something of the stature Burga enjoyed at the time is indicated by the following news item, taken from a local newspaper.

At 4:00 P.M. today Sr. Eloy Burga, prestigious political caudillo of the department, arrived in this city [Chachapoyas], accompanied by more than 200 of the most distinguished members of our society, who went to his hacienda El Molino, with the object of bringing him here [to Chachapoyas] (*La Ortiga* [*The Nettle*], January 35, 1913).

The challenge to the position of the ruling *casta* mounted by the Burga-Hurtado in 1913 was an elaborate and intricate affair that required months of secret planning and preparation. It involved the carefully coordinated efforts of hundreds of armed men, who descended on Chachapoyas from different directions, in separate columns. It also relied on the use of dynamite, which was used to set off explosions immediately prior to the arrival of the armed columns, but away from the town center, where key government buildings were located. The explosions were intended as a diversionary tactic, to draw the gendarmes and other armed retainers of the Pizarro-Rubio away from the prefecture, so that the Burga-Hurtado forces could occupy it, fortify themselves within it, and hold off attacks from their enemies.[9]

Unfortunately for the Burga-Hurtado, however, the attack did not go entirely as planned. While the explosions did succeed in drawing off some of the Pizarro-Rubio forces, *casta* leaders suspected a trap, and had most of their supporters stay put. As a result, when the Burga-Hurtado's armed columns converged on the center of Chachapoyas, the forces of the Pizarro-Rubio were well entrenched in and around the prefecture. After a pitched battle involving much violence and bloodshed, and a number of deaths, the Burga-Hurtado were forced to withdraw (see Nugent 1997, 128–39).

The second challenge to the Pizarro-Rubio was also planned by the Burga-Hurtado and was nearly executed. It also followed the normal rhythms of *casta* politics, in that it coincided with the next election cycle—the presidential elections of 1919. In the months leading up to the elections, which were held at the end of April, the Burga-Hurtado engaged in all the activities of a *casta* that was on the verge of challenging the position of the ruling group. They organized a growing number of public challenges to Pizarro-Rubio clients, using violence to humiliate and shame them wherever possible.

The Burga-Hurtado also performed in this manner in spaces that were increasingly proximate to the central, public spaces of Chachapoyas, thus demonstrating to society at large their ability to act with impunity (see Nugent 1997). The fact that the Pizarro-Rubio did not answer these challenges with counterperformances, which would have demonstrated their superior power and potency—indicated that the ruling *casta* did not feel strong enough to do so. Instead, fearing the worst, as the elections approached the Pizarro-Rubio were in a state of high alert and readied themselves for an outright assault.

Had all gone as it had in the past, the reign of the Pizarro-Rubio would likely have come to an end after ten years (the ruling *casta* having nearly been deposed in 1913). This was at the long end, but was still within the limits of the period of time a *casta* would ordinarily remain in power. Before the Burga-Hurtado could mount an assault on the Pizarro-Rubio, however, and before they could begin to take retribution on the Pizarro-Rubio for the humiliation and abuse they had endured during the previous ten years, something occurred that permanently changed the normal process of *casta* succession.

The interruption of "politics as normal" in Chachapoyas stemmed from a parallel interruption in the national capital, as reflected in the rise of Augusto Leguía, and his New Nation regime. In the three previous decades Peru's social structure had undergone profound transformations. The rapid expansion of export enclaves producing for the international market—predominantly in primary agricultural and mineral goods—had resulted in the emergence of a powerful coastal oligarchy that articulated its interests by means of their own political party—the Partido Civil. These same processes of economic expansion, however, had also resulted in the equally rapid expansion of laboring populations that had been uprooted from the countryside. These displaced laboring groups were outside the systems of social and electoral control that had long allowed the Civilistas to control the electoral process and elect their own to positions of power.

The presidential elections of 1919 thus occurred in a social context that had been radically transformed, and to a degree that the Peru's ruling elites had failed to grasp. As the voting results came in, it became clear that the candidate of the old elite—Antero Aspíllaga—would lose to outsider Augusto Leguía. Aspíllaga had promised a continuation of existing policies. Leguía, on the other hand, had promised a "new nation"—a radical break with the corrupt, elitist practices of Peru's ruling groups. Leguía's nationalizing call for a new, more egalitarian society—one that brought an end to the inherited, aristocratic privileges of the past, and that offered a more prosperous future—had a powerful appeal to Peru's laboring groups.

The Burga-Hurtado planned to seize power in May 1919, just after the presidential elections of that year. Indeed, they had planned their uprising to coincide with the elections because they were certain that when the dust had settled Aspíllaga would be the new president. Because the Burga-Hurtado were closely allied with Aspíllaga, his victory would mean that they would have the backing of the new regime in Lima. The support of the ruling regime would give the Burga-Hurtado the decisive edge they needed to move against the Pizarro-Rubio.

By early May, however, it had become clear that Leguía would emerge as the victor in the presidential elections. This came as a great surprise to the coastal oligarchy in Lima, and to the Partido Civil. It was equally surprising to the Burga-Hurtado (and the Pizarro-Rubio) in Chachapoyas. Leguía was able to hold on to the presidency despite the opposition of the country's established elite powers. He was able to do so because of the support he received from the unconventional, emergent constituencies associated with the expansion of Peru's export economy. Having won the election, Leguía went to great lengths to build up an alliance structure that could protect him from retribution by the old elite.[10]

In the Chachapoyas region, the Burga-Hurtado figured prominently among that group. As a result, just as the Burga-Hurtado were anticipating a return to regional dominance and were making preparations for an armed attack on their enemies, the expected support from their national patrons failed to materialize. Rather than being able to offer support, the members of the Civilista oligarchy found themselves under direct attack by the Leguía regime and had to fend for themselves. In these circumstances, the armed assault from the Burga-Hurtado that everyone was expecting did not take place. Instead, seeing the writing on the wall, the Burga-Hurtado retreated. Many of its leading members went into hiding.[11]

As the position of the Civilistas deteriorated nationally, so too did that of the Burga-Hurtado, and the other enemies of the Pizarro-Rubio, regionally. As Leguía consolidated his regime in Lima and persecuted and fragmented the opposition, so too did his clients, the Pizarro-Rubio, in Chachapoyas. Enjoying the direct backing of the president and the new constellation of working- and middle-class forces he was gathering around him in the national capitol, the Pizarro-Rubio in Chachapoyas were free to visit the most vicious forms of persecution imaginable upon their enemies—who had the misfortune of being associated with the discredited Civilistas.

The Pizarro-Rubio took full advantage of this freedom. Indeed, the ruling coalition visited a campaign of persecution upon their adversaries that was so broad and so systematic that many of those families chose exile and fled the region entirely.[12] But the Pizarro-Rubio did not limit their campaign of repression to their enemies among the elite. The members of the ruling coalition were equally systematic, and even more brutal, in their treatment of the numerous clients of the adversarial *casta*. These clients were scattered about the regional space, in virtually every district. Unlike their elite patrons, they did not have the luxury of abandoning their homes and their lands as political circumstances changed. This made them easy prey for the Pizarro-Rubio.

In the years following the elections of 1919 the clients of the region's out-of-favor elite families (especially the Burga-Hurtado) found their property seized and their homes destroyed (and at times burned to the ground). Individuals of both genders, all generations, and all social classes suffered attacks on their property and their person. The clients of the defeated families did their best to defend themselves, but they suffered homicides and near homicides, rapes, and castrations. Those responsible for these attacks, however, were neither prosecuted nor even arrested. This was because the police and the judiciary were in the hands of the Pizarro-Rubio. These violent attacks on the opposing *castas* were in addition to the systematic removal of all its members from positions of government power or authority. An article from *Amazonas*, a progressive newspaper published in the latter half of the 1920s, captures the situation effectively:

The Department of Amazonas Has Been Converted into a True Fief.
Twenty Years of Prostration and Servilism.

In the *oriente* of Peru there is a department that, despite the amazing fertility of its soil, the variety of its products, the spiritual richness of its children, and its infinite yearning for progress, writhes in backwardness and abandonment due to the negligence of its political representatives.

We refer to the department of Amazonas, that since its creation in 1832 up to the present is nothing but a fief, a hacienda of useless and hateful *castas*, who believe that they have the right to rule and to exploit [people] iniquitously and scandalously.

A wretched population ours . . . we have never had the good fortune of having acceptable [political] representatives before the Parliament . . . [but rather] men without ideas and lacking in sentiment . . . [who] have struggled ceaselessly over the right to exercise power, to lord over their spoils . . . to benefit themselves alone, increasing their substantial fortunes.

1909 [was] a sad hour for the department [because] one of its sons, Doctor Miguel A. Rojas, taking advantage of a high political position that he . . . occupied [he was Minister of Government during Leguía's first term in office], believed it to be in the interests of his family to cast out the ill-fated Burga-Hurtado *casta*, and . . . sent to [Chachapoyas] a . . . political authority [Prefect Pázara] who permitted women to be jailed, men to be flagellated, and the most intimate sanctuary of human dignity to be sullied, all with the goal of enthroning the Pizarro-Rubio . . . family.

Thus was born, and thus ascended this *casta*, which [since then] has monopolized everything in its favor, that allows no act of rebellion, nor even of independence, that divides what are virtually life-long public positions that are loaded with "extras" among those of its circle . . . that has taught servilism as if in a school and has introduced abjection and what amounts to a thinly masked form of slavery among the men, who in order to gain a livelihood, [to gain] bread for their children . . . must necessarily beg for a job after having had to submerge their dignity in humiliation.

Taking into account this moral corruption, one distinguished professional from Amazonas has said with reason that "Amazonas is not a department, but rather a poorly administered hacienda." And in effect, thus it is, for a region where all are abandoned to their own fate, where not even a single stone is moved in the interest of progress, where the very air that is breathed is poisoned by traditional hatreds, by morbid passions, and by bastard ambitions . . . where a free man cannot live because he feels oppressed, because he will not resign himself to sacrificing his dignity, offering homage to this *casta* that weighs like a curse on the collectivity, cannot, should not, ever call itself . . . a department of Peru. (*Amazonas* 4, no. 19 [May 1929])

As this article from *Amazonas* suggests, the violence that was visited upon the members of opposing *castas* was not limited to the interpersonal, face-to-face, physical variety—although open, public attacks of this kind were important in making public statements to society at large about the power and potency of the Pizarro-Rubio. Equally important was what we might call "structural violence." The members of the Pizarro-Rubio were now in full control of the machinery of government, including the judiciary and the police force. They used that position to manufacture evidence that implicated elite members of the Burga-Hurtado *casta* in an entire series of crimes.

In particular, the members of the Pizarro-Rubio accused members of the opposing *casta* of having abused their positions of public trust when they had controlled the apparatus of state (i.e., when the Burga-Hurtado had been the ruling *casta*). Graft and embezzlement figured prominently among the offenses of which the Burga-Hurtado were accused (although several leading members of the opposing *casta* were also accused of capital crimes like murder). These offenses were said to have occurred on an extensive scale. Having made the accusations, the Pizarro-Rubio went on to prosecute the elite members of the Burga-Hurtado for their supposed crimes. The latter, unable to defend themselves, were forced to quit the region entirely.[13]

The next presidential elections came five years later, in 1924. Had the normal dynamics of *casta* competition been at work, one would have expected a major challenge to the Pizarro-Rubio. The Burga-Hurtado would have mounted such a challenge, led by *casta* leader Eloy Burga. They would have been joined by the many other families that had suffered at the hands of the Pizarro-Rubio. By 1924, however, the cumulative effect of fifteen years of violent repression by the Pizarro-Rubio had taken its toll.

By the time of the presidential elections of that year, the Burga-Hurtado were only a pale imitation of their former selves. Indeed, the previous fifteen years of relentless persecution had taken a heavy toll on the opposing *casta*. By 1924, the parallel state structure that the Burga-Hurtado had previously employed to promote and defend the interests of their *casta* (see above, this chapter) had fallen into disuse, and was a thing of the past. That this parallel state structure was no longer being used was a poignant expression of the enfeebled state of the Burga-Hurtado. The breakdown of the Burga-Hurtado *casta* was particularly hard on those who were at the bottom of the regional class structure. The hundreds of rural cultivators who had formerly looked to the Burga-Hurtado for protection and patronage, and who had provided protection to their patrons, had also been left to fend for themselves. They had been abandoned by the Burga-Hurtado leadership, who were first driven into hiding by the Pizarro-Rubio, later into exile, and eventually into insignificance.

Just how far the Burga-Hurtado had fallen by 1924 is demonstrated by the following: Eloy Burga, the leader of his *casta*, had by this time managed to return to Chachapoyas, after having been driven into exile in 1919. His return to Chachapoyas, however, was not heralded by a procession of several hundred influential supporters, as had been the case in 1913. Rather,

Burga's return merited no response whatsoever from local notables. Indeed, instead of mobilizing armed columns of men numbering in the hundreds and using them to march against his enemies (the Pizarro-Rubio), as Burga had done in 1913 and as he had prepared to do in 1919, by 1924 he was for the most part isolated and alone, without supporters. By this latter time Burga had become almost powerless—in large part because he had lost the vast majority of his once extensive constituency.

Rather than being able to rely on his own, armed retainers to advance his position, he was reduced to what can only be described as pathetic circumstances. He was compelled to make an official request for protection to the very authorities (the Pizarro-Rubio) he regarded as his sworn enemies—the same officials he had once tried to overthrow. On April 21, 1924, Burga asked that the authorities ensure that his constitutional rights and his personal safety be protected. Several individuals, he explained in his petition, had been following him, and he was certain that they intended to kill him.[14] There is little doubt that he was being shadowed by clients of the Pizarro-Rubio.

In such an isolated state, the best that Burga could manage that year was a weak and ineffectual attempt to depose the Pizarro-Rubio. Instead of a carefully planned armed attack involving hundreds of armed men and the use of dynamite as a diversionary tactic, all that Burga could do was to assemble perhaps a dozen followers to threaten the clients of the Pizarro-Rubio as they went to the polls. The Pizarro-Rubio had little trouble dealing these "irregularities" in the electoral process.[15]

The Pizarro-Rubio were not content, however, with having eliminated Eloy Burga, the leader of the Burga-Hurtado, as a potential threat to their position. During the election cycle of 1924—a time when opposing *castas* would ordinarily have mounted an attack on the ruling coalition—the Pizarro-Rubio also felt compelled to stage public demonstrations of their potency. They did so in rural districts that were especially populous, or where their adversaries had formerly had important bases of support. Among such populous districts was La Jalca, in the province of Chachapoyas, where the Pizarro-Rubio engaged in a large-scale display of their supremacy:

Señor Prefect of the Department,

I, Francisco Culqui, Governor of the District of La Jalca . . . write to your esteemed office to inform you that I denounce the homicides committed by Don Pablo

M. Pizarro, perpetrated [in this district] on the persons of Catalino Gorp, Ciriaco Puscán, and Tomas Culqui. The facts of this crime are the following: on the 24th of June of this year the entire community at my command was gathered in the town celebrating the Festival of San Juan. The celebrations were proceeding in the most tranquil of manners until two in the afternoon of the 25th, when suddenly Don Pablo Pizarro appeared on the outskirts of our village at the head of fifty men, well-armed with "Mauser" rifles of the State, causing great alarm among the people due to the obviously subversive intentions of [Pizarro]. Immediately all the members of the community gathered in the main square, in a completely peaceful manner, to await [Pizarro's] arrival. But within moments there was complete chaos. As soon as Pizarro's men arrived they began firing their weapons at us and making terrible threats to everyone who lives here. As the authority in charge I approached Jefe Pizarro and said that there was no reason for his hostilities as the people were not at all hostile to him. Sr. Pizarro paid no attention whatsoever to what I said, but having accomplished his goals, commanded his troops to leave the town (ASC53, Decreto No. 9, 12 de Julio, 1924).

Another populous and potentially dangerous district was Santo Tomás, in the neighboring province of Luya. Here the ruling coalition engaged in behaviors that, while not of such a grand scale, were intended to make a public statement about the power and potency of the Pizarro-Rubio:

Sr. Prefect of the Department. Isaías Barrera, resident of the town of Santo Tomas . . . with the greatest respect informs you that: For some time Don Pablo Pizarro, in his murderous endeavors, pursues me tenaciously here [in Santo Tomas], where I have my house, family, and economic affairs, by means of his appointees and armed killers that he has at his disposal, because of which I . . . appeal to you to provide me with the individual rights and protections which all citizens are granted by the Constitution. Pizarro's son-in-law, Nemesio Ramos, is the person entrusted [by Pizarro] to carry out this criminal labor, because of which Ramos, in the company of the governor Dolores Yoplac, the justice of the peace Maximiliano Zabaleta, and the tax collector Tomas Cáseres assemble daily in this pueblo, armed with revolvers. Not having found me here they have fired their weapons at my wife, who escaped miraculously. . . . I have had to hide myself and my family in [the town of] Cocabamba, because of these savages [indíjenas], who are armed with a great many Mauser rifles, who shamelessly announce that they have been ordered to deliver my head to the aforementioned Ramos, in exchange for rewards or money. . . . I was not there [in Santo Tomas] when Don Pablo Pizarro arrived and Ramos, together with the aforementioned authorities went to the house of my sister-in-law, Josefina LaTorre, robbed her of everything she had in her house, and beat her, Ramos grabbing her by the hair and cowardly dragging her to . . . Colonel Pizarro. . . . [I cannot imagine] the ill fate that the poor woman would have suffered had Captain Moran [of the gendarmes] not defended her . . . refusing to consent to more outrages . . . immediately [thereafter] they went in search of her husband Isaac LaTorre. They captured him, incarcerated him, tortured him miserably, and made him sign statements swearing that no robbery or other outrages had been committed against his family. . . . The present Governor, at the order of Ramos, who [the governor] obeys blindly, jails people [without cause], and under the pretext of [levying] fines, extorts 10, 15 or 20 soles from peaceful citizens, dividing the money among the aforementioned group [of authorities]. He [the governor] commits outrages that were unknown even in the time of the . . . Inquisition. In Santo Tomas there are honorable people who suffer such a fate simply because they do not obey Ramos . . . for no other reason than they are not servile to him . . . I firmly believe, Sr. Prefect, that your impartial authority will find a remedy for the situation of many honorable citizens, and will apply the [legal] sanction that such unspeakable and monstrous crimes deserve. . . . In light of what I have explained, I ask that you provide me with the Constitutional guarantees to which I refer in this petition.

—Cocabamba, Junio 17 de 1924 (signed) Isaías Barrera
(ASC10, Decreto # 138, 21 de Junio de 1924).

By means of violent, public performances such as these, the ruling *casta* did indeed drive members of the opposition into hiding, or out of the region entirely—thus leaving their numerous peasant clients without protectors or benefactors. This applied to the leaders of opposing *castas*, who lived in Chachapoyas. It applied as well to the estate-owning clients that opposing *casta* leaders maintained in the rural districts—people such as Sr. Isaías Barrera, whose petition to the prefect is quoted immediately above. But the Pizarro-Rubio did more than simply rid themselves of elite members of the opposition and leave rural cultivators without benefactors—important though both of these were. By means of its public displays of violent domination, the ruling *casta* also sent public messages out to the regional population as a whole about the dangers of opposing them.

Nor did the Pizarro-Rubio limit their violent performances to the two instances mentioned above. The 1920s were witness to an ongoing series of public demonstrations of the same kind (although they became less common as the ruling coalition consolidated its position). These acts included crimes against property, such as petty theft, burglary, and arson, and seizure of land and livestock. They included as well crimes against person, such as assault, rape, castration, torture, and murder.

As important as the acts themselves, however, were the consequences for those who committed them—or rather, the lack of consequences. Members of the ruling *casta* who engaged in these acts of violence did so with complete and utter impunity—largely because the Pizarro-Rubio controlled the police force and the courts. In this way, the regional population was put on notice that they should be very careful indeed in all of their dealings with the Pizarro-Rubio. They were also put on notice that opposition to the ruling coalition was largely futile.

The elimination of elite opposition—in town and country alike—combined with impunity for acts of violence perpetrated by members of the ruling coalition transformed the dynamics of the *casta* order in additional ways. After 1919 there was less and less need for the Pizarro-Rubio to appoint influential, estate-owning ("strong") clients in the countryside who could help *casta* leaders control recalcitrant members of the opposition. This was because as time passed there were fewer and fewer powerful members of the opposition left to challenge the Pizarro-Rubio. And because it was no longer necessary to install such strong clients in moments of crisis (because there were fewer and fewer of these as well), *casta* leaders were not faced with the dilemmas of having to replace strong clients with weaker ones once times of danger had passed.

The problem of easing strong clients out of positions of authority once their usefulness had passed was a major source of ruling *casta* weakness. For once these strong clients had served their purpose of stabilizing affairs in the countryside, they were reluctant to relinquish their posts. This was in no small part because, having been appointed rural governor, mayor, or justice of the peace, such clients controlled officially sanctioned mechanisms of extraction. These mechanisms allowed strong clients to extort wealth legally from the region's primary (peasant) producers, thus making it easier for these clients to accumulate the wealth necessary to approach an elite lifestyle.

This was especially important because commercial pursuits offered such limited possibilities for enrichment, and because the state positions to which these strong clients were appointed came with no salary. Although the ruling *casta* usually succeeded in displacing such individuals, doing so came with a cost. For strong clients who were forced out of state positions not uncommonly resented this fact bitterly and would often seek out an alliance with an opposing *casta*. The fact that strong clients were less and less necessary to help control the countryside after 1919 thus eliminated an important source of ruling *casta* weakness.

The 1920s introduced a final change that further transformed the dynamics of *casta* rule—by eliminating another source of ruling coalition weakness. A large number of families came together in a single alliance structure to form a *casta*. All did so with the expectation that they would be provided with positions of authority and influence that would allow them to live according to the elite station in life to which all felt entitled by right of birth. There were many fewer of these positions, however, than there were aspirants to fill them. And there were no formal rules about how these positions would be distributed among those who had come to-gether to form a single alliance. As a result, it was inevitable that some *casta* members got less than they felt they deserved, and that others got little if anything. In these circumstances, it was not at all unusual for disgruntled families to participate in *casta* activities in a half-hearted manner. Nor was it unusual for these families to abandon their *casta* and look for a better ar-rangement with one of the opposing coalitions—especially during periods of political transition, when out-of-power *castas* mounted armed attacks on the ruling coalition.

As the foregoing suggests, these contradictions of *casta* rule were a function of the conditions of overall scarcity that prevailed at the time—of scarce opportunities for extracting wealth from primary producers in the countryside, and of a scarcity of lucrative positions of authority in Chachapoyas. It was these conditions of scarcity that the 1920s trans-formed, and in fundamental ways. One of the defining features of the *oncenio* was the vast sums of money the Leguía regime made available to its clients to underwrite modernization. This meant that regions like Chachapoyas found themselves flooded with wealth provided by the cen-tral government (these funds having been borrowed from foreign [for the most part US] banks).

As we will see presently, the sums of money in question were truly unprecedented. In introducing these funds into cash-poor regions like Chachapoyas, the central government (unintentionally) overcame both kinds of scarcity that had generated weakness in the organization of the *castas*. On the one hand, these circumstances did away with rural scar-city. Government functionaries in the countryside found that they no longer had to contend with powerful, local adversaries—because the

Pizarro-Rubio had driven these individuals from local jurisdictions. These functionaries also found that they did not have to rely exclusively on the extortion of wealth from primary producers (always a difficult and dangerous task) in order to enrich themselves. Rather, they could rely on the very large sums of money that were pouring into the region to subsidize modernization—and on the fact that these functionaries played a key role in making modernization possible.

Modernization funds from Lima also made it possible to overcome the scarcity of lucrative positions in urban areas—and thus to address the other main source of *casta* weakness and instability. Once the central government initiated its modernization projects, there were a range of new positions of authority and prominence that the ruling coalition could distribute among its client families. There was also a great deal more in the way of wealth that *casta* leaders could make available to their clients— which in turn made it possible for these client families to live the lives of an aristocratic elite. As a result, the kinds of "defections" that had previously characterized the behavior of such families did not occur during the 1920s. This meant that there were few processes at work to undermine the ruling coalition from within.

Conclusion

While these conditions in Amazonas were extreme, in no way were they exceptional. A similar process of consolidation by the ruling regime took place in Lima, the national capital. By systematically persecuting the opposition and by spending lavishly to build up new constituencies, Leguía's New Nation regime managed to remain in power for an extended period of time (from 1919 until 1930). For much of this period Leguía was largely unopposed. Indeed, as early as 1924, so dominant was the national constituency that Leguía built up around him, and so divided and scattered was the opposition, that in the presidential elections of that year that Leguía received 287,969 votes. His opponent, on the other hand, received 155 (Basadre 1968–69, XIII, 372–74; Herbold 1973, 100).

This same trend continued after 1924, as the *oncenio* wore on, nationally and regionally, producing a truly unprecedented state of affairs. In Chachapoyas, the families of the opposition were all greatly weakened by the Pizarro-Rubio's prolonged period of rule. So much so was this the case that after 1924 there was not a single organized elite attempt to drive them from power. By the late 1920s the elite families that were not associated with the Pizarro-Rubio had either been silenced or tamed or had been forced to flee. Indeed, by the end of their twenty-one-year reign (1930) the Pizarro-Rubio had succeeded in eliminating organized opposition from other coalitions altogether.

But the Pizarro-Rubio had done something more. They had also succeeded in defying the contradictions of *casta* rule—which had previously prevented any one *casta* from remaining in power for more than ten years at a time, or from doing permanent damage to opposing coalitions. But the Pizarro-Rubio had gone beyond simply weakening and dividing the opposition. As the foregoing suggests, the ruling coalition had managed to eliminate the other *castas* and had overcome several of the weaknesses inherent in the organization of elite coalitions. In effect, the Pizarro-Rubio had succeeded in doing away with the *casta* order altogether. In the process, they had converted themselves into a political formation the likes of which the region had never seen.

It was in the context of these transformed political conditions that the Pizarro-Rubio sought to implement the central government's modernization projects. The most important of these was the "Grand Chachapoyas Pimentel Highway," which was intended to connect the Chachapoyas region with more developed sections of the national territory, lying to the west and the south. It is to the details of this process that we turn in the next chapter.

4

Being (and Seeing) Like a State

Sr. Prefect

In reply to the orders imparted in your Oficio no. 346, of Nov. 26th . . . concerning the bridge project in this district, I came to the site, bringing with me the conscripts from the towns of: Paclas, San Jerónimo, Chosgón and nearby haciendas, on the 16th of the present month . . . and I have the great satisfaction of communicating to you that the work on the bridge . . . has now been completed.

— Governor, District of San Jerónimo

Introduction

It was in this context of a weak, scattered, and divided opposition that the Pizarro-Rubio began to implement the central government's modernization schemes.[1] The most important of these was the Grand Chachapoyas-Pimentel Highway. National planners and progressive elites had high hopes for this roadway. In their estimation, it would link the Chachapoyas region with the more forward-looking, developed parts of the country, to the west and south. Projects like this one were sacropolitical in nature. They were viewed as having powerful redemptive qualities—as being able to help do away with the traditional social orders and archaic value systems that had long dominated the highlands.

After 1930, the highway project would be plagued by intense competition between different families of the elite and different branches of government. The project would also be characterized by extreme dysfunction.

Progress on the highway would take place at a veritable snail's pace, or would often come to a complete standstill, as project managers found themselves unable to recruit a workforce. Thus, after 1930 it was not at all uncommon for project plans to call for 500–1,000 men to be laboring at the project's work sites, but for conscription officials to be able to deliver only a small fraction of that number.

After 1930, dysfunction and paralysis paralyzed this project, and many other government projects. It was this dysfunction and paralysis that made it increasingly difficult to embed the remarkable (a massive program of forced labor) in the routine (normal, everyday administration). It was the inability to embed the remarkable in the routine that ultimately led to the outbreak of a plague of dark fantasies, in which government officials were subject to deeply paranoid fears about dangerous others who were invisible to the naked eye.

The dysfunction and delusion associated with the project after 1930 is especially interesting when one considers what transpired before 1930, when the Pizarro-Rubio dominated the region. What was remarkable about work on the highway project prior to 1930 was how utterly unremarkable it was. Although the project relied upon a great many of the same mechanisms, and although it faced many of the same challenges, conscription was an orderly and unproblematic affair. The literally hundreds upon hundreds of workers required for highway construction would gather at the project's work sites, put in their time, collect their (very modest) pay, and return to their villages.

As the order and regularity that characterized this process suggests, during the 1920s government officials had no difficulty conscripting a workforce. As a result—unlike what would transpire after 1930—they did not have to explain away their inability to find laborers. This was true despite the fact that, prior to 1930, "the state" controlled even less in the way of armed force than it would come to control later. During the 1920s the gendarmerie in Chachapoyas was miniscule in size and was dwarfed by the enormous Indian-peasant population that made up the workforce.[2]

Despite this fact, however, work on the highway project progressed steadily, in the complete absence of labor shortages, and without delusion or displacement. Government officials had no need to invoke interference from quasi-phantom forces, as they would be compelled to do later. Indeed, one would never have anticipated that highway construction would subsequently become so difficult or problematic.

The developments surrounding conscription during the 1920s are interesting because they focus attention on the conditions of possibility of "state-ness." What are the circumstances that make it possible to be (and see) like a state (Scott 1998)? The implementation of Leguía's modernization projects during the *oncenio* was accompanied by the kind of order, regularity, transparency, and effectiveness that are often associated with "real" states. The latter are widely regarded as institutional structures that exercise a monopoly on the legitimate use of force, and that have eliminated violence-wielding competitors (Centeno 2002; Lopez Alva 2000; Tilly 1985).

The material presented here, however, points in the opposite direction. The ability of the central government to impose its will in Chachapoyas was contingent not upon the elimination of violence-wielding actors like the Pizarro-Rubio coalition but on their preservation. Indeed, when the last of these nonstate actors (the Pizarro-Rubio) was finally eliminated from the scene (in 1930)—when conditions resembled what would conventionally be understood as a state monopoly on the use of force—government officials found themselves incapable of governing the region. As we will see, in the absence of coercion-wielding *castas* (from 1930 onward), conditions became increasingly chaotic and ultimately culminated in a crisis of rule.

In the pages that follow I examine the dynamics of conscription surrounding the Grand Chachapoyas-Pimentel Highway. Work on the highway project began in September 1926 and continued until August 1930—when Leguía was overthrown, and the *oncenio* came to a crashing halt.

The Grand Chachapoyas-Pimentel Highway

The highway project was part of Leguía's national program of highway construction, the main provisions of which were set out in the 1920 Ley de Conscripción Vial (also called the Ley de Caminos). According to this law, funds for the highway would come from the central government (the Ministerio de Fomento). They would be given to provincial highway committees (*juntas provinciales de conscripción vial*), which were established by the same law. These juntas were composed of the provincial mayor, judge, and army officer (who was in charge of military conscription).

One of the reasons that the Pizarro-Rubio were so enthusiastic about the highway project was that it provided huge sums of money to cover construction costs. The scale of these subsidies was wholly unprecedented. Because the Leguía government had engaged in massive foreign borrowing, it was able to flood highland regions like Chachapoyas with sums of money the likes of which had never before been seen.

Some figures will provide a more concrete sense for the scale and significance of these government subsidies. Beginning in September 1926, the Ministry of Development provided each of the provincial highway committees of Chachapoyas, Luya and Bongará with S/. 3,000 every month, to cover the expenses involved in highway construction. This represented an *enormous* amount of money by local standards; highway labor conscripts were paid only 20 centavos [a fifth of a sol] per day). It also represented a huge increase in the funds available to the ruling coalition.

Prior to September 1926 the central government had provided regional officeholders with *very* little in the way of funds. There were virtually no monies for public works. Of the limited funds available, virtually all were used to pay the salaries of public employees, who often went without pay for months at a time. Furthermore, the vast majority of government functionaries—district governors, mayors, and justices of the peace—received no salary whatsoever.

The injection of thousands upon thousands of soles every month into a cash-scarce regional economy had a profound effect on regional political relations. This sudden windfall allowed the ruling coalition to greatly strengthen its position and also to increase the size of its following. These funds also made it possible for the ruling coalition to engage in public performances of power and potency that underscored the predominance of aristocratic sovereignty—and to do so by forcing the clients of defeated *castas* to labor on the Grand Chachapoyas-Pimentel Highway.

Some of the funds for the highway project paid the salary of the highway engineer. Other monies were used to pay foremen, and to purchase supplies (in particular, explosives). The vast majority of the funds, however, were used to pay laborers. Conscripts were compensated at a rate of 20 centavos a day.[3] As this suggests, the monthly highway subvention provided the Pizarro-Rubio with resources that could be used to conscript on an extensive scale.

These "ordinary" expenditures, however, were only the beginning. The Leguía regime also provided additional "extraordinary" funds to cover the costs associated with unusual or unanticipated construction problems. These subsidies ranged in size from S/. 10,000 to S/. 17,000.[4]

The *juntas provinciales de conscripción vial,* however, were not directly responsible for mobilizing the workforce for the projects they oversaw. Rather, this task fell to the juntas of the many districts of which each province was composed. These committees were made up of the district governor, mayor, and justice of the peace—the unpaid appointees who had long managed everyday political life in the countryside. Prior to conscripting laborers, each district junta would first compile a detailed list of all individuals in the district who were obliged to provide labor services. The junta would then take the measures required to mobilize a workforce.

In comparison to the enormous difficulties surrounding corvée during the 1930s-40s, what was remarkable about forced labor during the 1920s was how completely mundane and ordinary it was. Indeed, it was as if the dynamics of conscription during the *oncenio* were an inversion of those of the post-*oncenio* period. Several features of forced labor activities during the reign of Leguía highlight these differences.

First, a seemingly unique form of organization facilitated corvée during the 1920s—one that revolved around the *juntas de conscripción.* Although the juntas were created by the Ley de Caminos, it would be a mistake to regard them as acting in the name of or as seeking to promote the goals of the central government. Rather, the juntas enjoyed virtually no independence from the ruling *casta.* Indeed, they were controlled by the Pizarro-Rubio coalition. *Pace* Weberian understandings of strong and weak states, however, it was the juntas' "weakness"—their inability to establish any autonomy from the ruling coalition—that made them effective at conscription.

The fact that institutions established by the central government had been subsumed by a powerful, nonstate political organization—and that this was a source of strength rather than weakness—is reflected in several features of the juntas. First, in theory, the members of each junta represented not only a range of interests but also a "separation of powers"—which was assumed to be inherent in government itself. Indeed, the committees were designed to include representatives of the key constituencies that had vital, and potentially opposed, interests in the conscription process. Thus, the municipal government was to represent the interests of the citizenry, who were obliged by law to provide labor services but who also had inalienable rights. The military was included in the juntas to ensure that its interests in conscription were not neglected in the rush to build highways. The judiciary was included to ensure that in meeting their corvée needs both the civil and the military branches of government abided by the rules and also respected the rights of the citizenry.

While the juntas were to operate within a legal framework based on the principle of a separation of powers, these committees violated those precepts at every turn. In Chachapoyas, the autonomy of the civilian, military, and judicial branches of government assumed by the Ley de Conscripción Vial was not a thing of fact but of fiction. There was nothing even remotely resembling an internally differentiated bureaucracy that operated within a legal framework to balance opposing interests.[5] Even so, the absence of such a bureaucracy did not act as an obstacle to conscription. To the contrary; what made the *juntas de conscripción* effective instruments of corvée was not a separation of powers among different branches of government but rather the unity of interests among all committee members.

Because the Pizarro-Rubio had become such a dominant force in the Chachapoyas region, they were able to appoint their clients to all positions in the bureaucracy, in every branch of government. Rather than represent separate and opposed interests—as was assumed by the architects of the Ley de Conscripción Vial—these individuals represented a single set of concerns. This was true of the members of each district *junta de conscripción*. As members of the same *casta*, they were able to work together toward the same goal (conscription). It was also true of the members of each provincial junta. As members of the same *casta*, they could likewise work together in a coordinated fashion toward the same end.

But it was not just the fact that each individual junta could work together in a cooperative manner. Because a single, overarching *casta* coordinated the activities of all conscription committees, all could work toward promoting labor conscription. Thus, all of the district juntas were able to support the activities of all other district committees. Similarly, all provincial committees were able to assist other provincial juntas. Furthermore, higher order (i.e., provincial) committees could support the efforts of lower-order (i.e., district) juntas, and vice versa. This made for a degree of coordination and integration that was unprecedented for the region as a whole. It also helped establish a region-wide structure of surveillance that people who were subject to conscription found very difficult to evade.

In the Chachapoyas region, subprefects—as high-ranking members of the ruling coalition—played a crucial role in coordinating the process of labor conscription.[6] So too, however, did the departmental prefect—another ruling coalition member—who was the president of the Central Council of Roads (the Junta Central de Caminos). This body was responsible for the maintenance and construction of all roadways in the department of Amazonas. The subprefects and the prefect were thus the individuals who made sure that the coalition members who occupied key government posts in the provincial and district government worked together to conscript a work force. This is reflected in the following *oficio*, sent by the mayor of the province of Chachapoyas (the head of the Provincial Conscription Committee) to the subprefect of the province:

> [Seal of the Provincial Highway Committee of Chachapoyas]
>
> 26 of July of 1928
>
> Sr. Subprefect of the Province of Chachapoyas [el Cercado]
>
> Today, the Conscription Committee over which I preside has resolved that the highway conscripts from the districts I will mention presently are to present themselves in [Chachapoyas] in order to lend their services to the work on the [Grand Chachapoyas-Pimentel] highway, which is currently under construction. [These districts are]: Quinjalca . . . San Nicolás . . . San Miguel . . . Santa Rosa, Totora . . . Omia . . . San Pedro, Chuquibamba, and Balzas.
>
> With the goal of ensuring that these orders are strictly complied with, I ask that you dictate the measures necessary to ensure that the Sr. Municipal Mayor [of each of the districts of the province of Chachapoyas] in cooperation with the Sr. Governor of each district work together to mobilize the respective labor contingents [of their districts].
>
> Dios guarde a Ud.
>
> Benjamin Reina
>
> [seal of the Provincial Council of Chachapoyas]
>
> (ASC38, 26 de Julio de 1928)

A second distinctive feature of labor conscription during the *oncenio* was that it was characterized by what today would be called a high degree of regularity and transparency.[7] Regarding the regularity of corvée, the district *juntas de conscripción* would first compile detailed lists of everyone who was called upon to provide labor services. The district committees would then issue three successive calls for labor. The first call was for workers between the ages of 18 and 21, the second for men between 21 and 50, and the third for laborers between 50 and 60.[8] The precise timing of these calls was determined by the junta of the province to which the district belonged. In consultation with the prefect, the provincial conscription committee was responsible for devising a staggered work schedule for all the districts in its jurisdiction. This schedule ensured that work crews would replace one another on a regular basis, and thus that there would be no delays or interruptions to impede highway construction.

During the second half of the 1920s provincial mayors, as the heads of their respective provincial highway committees, regularly drew up plans that detailed the order in which the districts of their province were to provide highway conscripts, the number of men each district would provide, the dates when these labor "contingents" would be expected to work, and the locations where they were to present themselves. Indeed, the provincial mayors were expected to draw up these plans without fail, every year:

[Seal of the Provincial Highway Committee of Chachapoyas]

Chachapoyas, 19 March 1930

Sr. Prefect of the Department, and President of the Central Council of Roads. Chachapoyas

Oficio No. 8.

This *oficio* acknowledges receipt of your esteemed note no. 17, of yesterday, in which you inform me that the Council over which you preside, in its session on the 18th of this month, has decreed that work on the [Grand Chachapoyas-Pimentel] Highway is to be resumed, and that the Council . . . has asked that the appropriate measures be adopted.

In reply, I am pleased to report that the Conscription Committee over which I preside, in a session that also took place on the 18th of this month, has decided to publish the lists for the First Call of conscripts from the District of [Chachapoyas], and also to formulate the guide for the general call for conscripts from this province [as a whole], detailing in it the dates when the workers of each district are to appear for this project [and] the number of conscripts who will be provided to the Sr. Engineer.

Dios guarde a Ud.

[seal of the Provincial Council of Chachapoyas]

(ASC38, 19 de Marzo de 1930)

In addition to the regularity of conscription, another feature of corvée during the *oncenio* that distinguished it from would come later was its transparency. In this regard, two facts stand out as noteworthy. First, the lists of conscripts compiled by the juntas were placed in highly visible, public locations. Furthermore, the lists were posted well in advance of the time the individuals were to provide labor service. These lists declared not only when but also where men in each age category would be required to labor.

The fact that this information was made public prior to the time the men were expected to appear at their respective work sites had clear advantages from an organizational perspective. Indeed, the success of the labor rotation schedule for the various districts depended in no small degree on everyone knowing far in advance what was expected of them, and when and where it was expected. Unlike what transpired after 1930, however, this knowledge did not become the basis of widespread evasion on the part of would-be conscripts. After 1930 evasion becomes such a generalized problem that the authorities go to elaborate lengths to conceal from the general public the details of who was to be conscripted, and when they would be expected to labor (see Chapter 6 and 7). Prior to 1930, however, it was just the opposite. There were few surprises concerning what was supposed to happen, and what did happen:

[Seal of the Highway Conscription Committee of the Province of Chachapoyas]

Sr. Prefect, President of the Central Council of Roads of the Department.

Oficio No. 11.

I am honored to remit to your esteemed office, together with the present *oficio*, two printed copies of the decree issued today, by myself, President of the Highway Conscription Committee of the Province of Chachapoyas, calling up the respective labor contingents, so that they come together to contribute their labors to the construction of the highways from this city [Chachapoyas] to Bagua-Chica and Leimebamba [i.e., the Grand Chachapoyas-Pimentel Highway], the work in question to be resumed on the 5th of May, in accordance with the resolution passed by the Council over which I preside.

I also remit to you five copies of the lists of the first calling of 360 highway conscripts from the District of Chachapoyas, who are to appear on the date indicated to continue with the work on the highways.

With the goal of having the abovementioned decree displayed by edict as of the sixth of the present month at 3 pm, I ask that the Council over which you preside instruct the members of the Guardia Civil [*la fuerza pública*] to carry out this task.

Dios guarde a Ud.

(ASC38, 4 de Abril de 1930)

As the documents quoted above show, the order and regularity of the conscription process was not based only on the formulation of province-wide plans, which detailed how many workers from each district would be expected to labor, and when and where they would expected to do so. Nor was this order and regularity based solely on the fact that all political officials—from the prefect down to the governors, mayors, and justices of the districts—worked in concert, as members of a single coalition, to mobilize the work force (although this was crucial).

The success of labor recruitment during the 1920s was also based on the existence of long lists from each district detailing who was obliged to provide labor service. These lists included the full names and ages of all males between the ages of eighteen and sixty. Months prior to the period when the contingent of laborers were to be called, all district officials were apprised of the schedule. Several weeks prior to the time the men of the district were to be called to service, the lists would be posted in prominent public places. Figure 4.1 shows a typical list, from 1928, for the district of Chachapoyas.

The existence of these lists, of course, required that detailed information be collected in each district about the men who were to serve as highway conscripts. It was the job of the district mayor, working in concert with the governor and the justice of the peace, to compile these lists. Because these three individuals were all members of the ruling coalition, they were able to work together toward the same end.

Because the ruling coalition had fragmented and dispersed the opposing *castas*, individuals who would otherwise have resisted conscription had no patron or protector to whom they could turn for assistance. As a result, compiling detailed information about potential conscripts was a relatively straightforward affair. This was in stark contrast to what would transpire after 1930, when these district officials answered to different patrons, had conflicting interests, and worked at cross-purposes.

The fact that there were few surprises about what was supposed to happen, and about what did happen, had important implications regarding the relationship between knowledge, publicity, and power during the *oncenio*. The ruling *casta* was sufficiently confident in its own coercive capacities, and in its ability to monitor and control people's movements through space, that it did not hesitate to adopt procedures that would become an anathema to modernization efforts after 1930. Indeed, the Pizarro-Rubio were willing to go so far as to warn people publicly, and in advance, about official plans to force them to work against their will.

In other words, the Pizarro-Rubio were utterly unconcerned about a possibility that would become a virtual certainty after 1930—that anyone who was advised about government conscription plans would do everything in their power to evade this enormously disruptive intrusion into their lives. During the 1920s, conscripting elites regarded the population as powerless to resist. The Pizarro-Rubio were certain that there was no possibility of escape from their system of surveillance—that indigenous

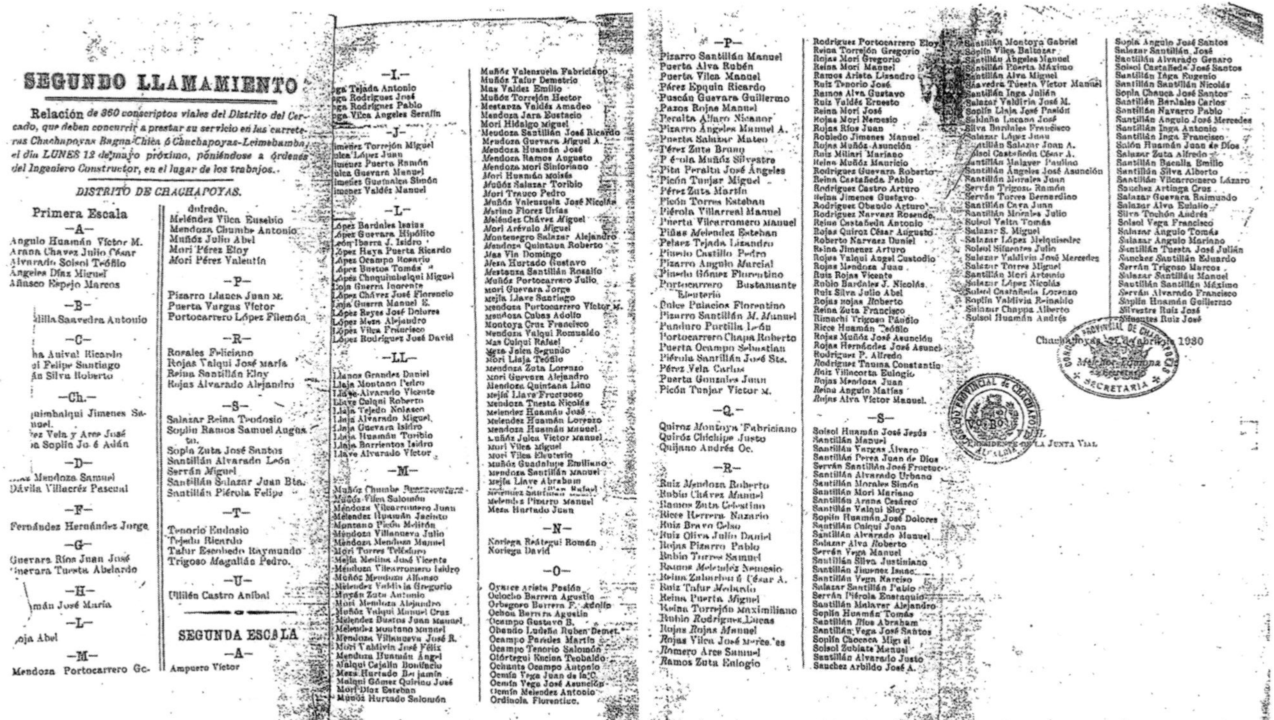

FIGURE 4.1. Conscription list for public works. *Source:* ASC38.

cultivators would either remain in place and submit, as they were supposed to, or that those seeking flight would be easy to locate and discipline.

Nor were these elites mistaken. A third distinctive feature of labor conscription during the *oncenio* was that it was very effective. The officials who were responsible for organizing corvée succeeded in assembling the unusually large number of workers required for the highway project week after week, month after month, with little resistance or evasion on the part of the conscripted population. Indeed, there were very few individuals who even attempted to evade their responsibilities under the law, and even fewer who succeeded. Furthermore, there were regular, routine procedures in place to deal with those who did choose evasion.

Indeed, the unity of the ruling coalition prior to 1930 meant that the conditions of power that shaped the generation of knowledge about subaltern groups were far different than they would come to be:

Presidency of the Conscription Committee of Luya
9 April 1930.

Sr. Prefect, President of the Central Council of Roads.

Oficio #8. In compliance with your *oficio* #20, of the 3rd of the current month, I write to inform your office of the following: that in accordance with the decisions of your Conscription Committee, I have requested that all the [district] Mayors of the Province send their respective conscript lists [the *padrón vial*], with the respective ages, names and details concerning those who have fled, in an effort to evade their obligations [*omisos*] . . . for the Highway project. . . .

Dios guarde a Ud.

Manuel Malaver (ASC38, 9 de Abril de 1930)

These procedures worked in part because the ruling *casta* had such detailed information about the conscript labor pool. Equally important was the fact that district officials took great care in monitoring who did and did not work and were able to name the specific individuals who had absented themselves. Also important, however, was the fact that the members of district committees could rely upon the assistance of junta members in other districts and provinces to track these men down and compel them to comply with their obligations.[9] In other words, what made labor conscription so effective during the 1920s was the existence of a region-wide structure of surveillance, imposed by the ruling *casta*, which made it possible to monitor the movement of people through space.

Confirming Conscription

In the 1930s and 1940s, the state functionaries who were responsible for conscripting the workforce for modernization were confronted with an ongoing scarcity of laborers. As we have seen, the labor pool projected into being by central planners was not a thing of fact but rather of fiction—which meant that labor-conscripting government functionaries were forever in search of a workforce that was not entirely there. Being unable to produce what did not exist, these functionaries were compelled to write to their superiors on an ongoing basis offering excuses for why they were unable to comply with what they have been ordered to do. Indeed, the archives are literally overflowing with correspondence of this very kind.

During the *oncenio*, however, conditions were the opposite of what they would be in the period that was to follow. Rather than write to their superiors with excuses about why they were unable to do as they were instructed, the various functionaries and juntas that were responsible for corvée would do just the opposite. They would write to explain that all was going according to plan. Those that would do so included the provincial conscription committees, which would regularly provide the prefect with progress reports about work on the highway project:

[Seal of the Provincial Council of Luya]
Presidency of the Conscription Committee [of Luya]
21 June 1930.
Sr. Prefect, President of the [Central] Council . . . of Roads
Chachapoyas
Oficio No. 36.
The aforementioned districts [Conila, Lopecancha y Tingo], and also Santo Tomas, having completed their highway labors, with their contingents at [the work sites of] Utcubamba and Caclic, the Council over which I preside, in our last session, has decreed; that the districts of Luya and Luya Viejo are to send the conscripts at their disposal [to those sites] in the following form: the first 50 men to [the] Utcubamba [work site] every 12 days and the second 50 to [the] Caclic [work site], until the conclusion of the work, and without the omission of a single conscript. . . .
Manuel Malaver (ASC38, 21 de Junio de 1930)

But it was not just the provincial conscription committees that wrote to the prefect on a regular basis to reassure him that progress was being made. District conscription committees were also in constant communication with the prefect, and with other authorities, to apprise them of how their work was proceeding. In stark contrast to what was to transpire after 1930, however, they did not write with excuses about why they were unable to comply with orders to produce laborers. Rather, they wrote to inform their superiors that work was proceeding as it should have:

[Seal of the Office of the Governor, District of San Jerónimo]
The Yomblón Bridge
Sr. Prefect

    In reply to the orders imparted in your Oficio no. 346, of Nov. 26th . . . concerning the bridge project in this district, I came to the site, bringing with me the conscripts from the towns of: Paclas, San Jerónimo, Chosgón and nearby haciendas, on the 16th of the present month . . . and I have the great satisfaction of communicating to you that the work on the bridge . . . has now been completed.

        Dios que a Ud.

        [signature] (ASC40, 19 de Diciembre de 1929)

    Or, they wrote from their work sites to ask for the equipment or supplies they needed to do their work more effectively:[10]

[Seal of the office of the governor of the district of Levanto]
10 May 1930.
Sr. Prefect of the Department. Chachapoyas. Oficio # __ [blank]

    The community at my command has begun the construction of the bridge at "Purud," but our work has faltered because we have encountered [an area of] hard rocks, which makes it impossible for us to continue. As a result, we ask that you provide us with two drills, each one of one meter in length, and two sledgehammers and with these materials we are certain that we can overcome all difficulties and can complete the bridge in as little time as possible.

        Dios que a Usted.

        [signature] (ASC40, 10 de Mayo de 1930)

    Alternatively, the district conscription committees would write to reassure the prefect, as head of the Central Council of Roads, that they would cooperate fully with all highway construction:

[Seal of the office of the governor of the district of Bagua Chica]
Sr. Prefect of the Department of Amazonas.

    I have the pleasure of informing your office that the [departmental highway] Engineer, Sr. Benjamin Carrillo . . . arrived in this district on Sunday the 24th . . . without incident.

The following day he called us together to explain the important mission with which he has been entrusted, that of directing the work on the highway from this locale to the city [of Chachapoyas]; as directed by our Illustrious leader, Sr. Augusto B. Leguía and the Ministry of Development; a project of singular importance, being carried out by your Prefecture . . . for such grand benefits. Please accept my humble note of gratitude, and also that of the people I represent . . . we commit ourselves to you and to the highway project, everyone in this entire region, and will cooperate in every way we can with the Highway Project.

On the 26th of this month the work on the Highway began, with the number of people that the Engineer regarded as necessary; on Monday, Dec. 2nd, there will be 134 citizens at work on the Highway from this district.

> Dios que á Ud.
>
> [signature, governor of Bagua Chica]
>
> (ASC40, 30 de Noviembre de 1929)

It was not just district and provincial political appointees, however, who, as key members of the ruling coalition, worked together with one another to advance coalition ends. As implied above in the *oficio* about the Yomblón bridge, the same applied to important landowners, who also cooperated with the Pizarro-Rubio—at times in ways that seemed counterintuitive. Indeed, after 1930, when government functionaries sought to conscript the resident workforce of haciendas, they were threatened with violence, and were compelled to desist in their efforts (see Chapter 6 and 7). In stark contrast, during the 1920s the relations between many hacienda owners and the ruling coalition were close and collaborative. So much so was this the case that hacendados made their resident workforce available to coalition leaders for highway construction despite the fact that estate owners relied on that same workforce for their own well-being:

[Seal of the office of the subprefecture of Chachapoyas]

Sr. Prefect of the Department

Oficio No. 469

I have received an official communication from the governor of the district of Levanto, in which he explains that the peons and sharecroppers of Sr. Julio Eguren, who belong to the hacienda Quipachacha, all have their respective highway conscription certificates/vouchers, and are prepared to [go to] work when they are called.

I explain this in response to your Oficio No. 150, of the 26th of the present month.

> Dios guarde a Ud.
>
> [signature] (ASC40, 30 de Noviembre de 1929)

In comparison with what was to come after 1930, several aspects of these processes are noteworthy. The first is the level of detailed information that the ruling coalition was able to generate about the population to be conscripted. The provincial conscription committees drew upon lists made of up specific names, from each district in their respective provinces. As can be seen from the list for the urban district of Chachapoyas (see Figure 4.1), these could be quite detailed and long. But the lists for the rural districts, which were less populous, while not as long, were just as detailed.[11] This meant that the authorities always knew the specific individuals who were obliged to serve as labor conscripts. It also meant that government officials based their activities on efforts to conscript those specific individuals.

Second, the provincial and district conscription committees kept careful records about who had labored on the highway project, and how many days they had labored. Once any specific individual had served their time, they were not called up again—something that would change dramatically after 1930.

Third, the authorities kept equally careful records of who had not served as required by law. In stark contrast to the post-1930 period, there were very few of these latter individuals. Like those who had served, those who had not were known and listed by name.[12] Government officials invested much time and energy in tracking down these "*omisos*" and making sure that they did not evade their obligations. Officials made no effort to recruit above and beyond the individuals on their respective lists.

The records that the provincial conscription committees maintained regarding the specific individuals who were obliged to contribute to the highway project were thus detailed and systematic. Indeed, these records were sufficiently detailed that the provincial conscription committees were able to enforce an additional provision of the Ley de Conscripción Vial. This provision gave people the option of meeting their obligation to the highway project by providing a cash payment rather a contribution of labor (see Meza Bazán 2011, 308). Because the provincial highway committees had detailed information about the specific individuals that made up the conscription pool, they were able to ensure that everyone who was supposed to make a contribution did so—whether in labor or cash.[13]

In this way the provincial highway committees were able to collect considerable sums of money. The committees then used the funds provided by these individuals (the *redenciones viales*) to further the cause of highway construction:

[Seal of the Caja de Depósitos y Consignaciones]
Sr. Prefect of the Department, President of the Central Council of Roads.
Oficio No. 257.
Sr. Prefect,

In reply to your esteemed *oficio* No. 143 of the 25th of the present month . . . I have imparted the instructions necessary to our branch in Lámud [capital of the province of Luya] asking them to inform the Sr. President of the Highway Committee of the province of Luya to dispose of the funds he has at his disposal from the *redenciones viales* of his province.

Dios guarde á Ud.

[Signature] (ASC40, 26 de Noviembre de 1929)

Most surprising of all, however, was the following: in a complete reversal of what was to come after 1930, in the 1920s there were no complaints whatsoever of labor shortages. This is not to say that the members of the ruling coalition did not struggle with one another. They did indeed, especially about who was to receive and control how much of the funds provided by the central government for public works:

[Seal of the Court of the 1st Instance, Province of Chachapoyas]
Sr. Prefect of the Department, President of the Central Council of Roads.
Oficio no. 563.
Sr. Prefect,

In reply to your esteemed *oficio* No. 134, dated the 11th of the current month, I must explain the following:

With regard to the incomplete accounts that you have provided, there is no precise figure regarding the location of the funds for the "Chachapoyas-Bagua Chica" Highway [a portion of the Grand Chachapoyas-Pimentel Highway], which were deposited in the Caja de Depósitos y Consignaciones. There is no debit [entry] for the Lp. 300.0.00 [3,000 soles], the subvention that corresponds to the month of September, nor is it clear what has happened to the Lp. 100.0.00 [1,000 soles] that was to be used for the Leimebamba [portion of the] Highway. You have also made inappropriate charges to [the] Treasury [of the Provincial Highway Committee of Chachapoyas]. You have . . . charged to this Treasury the Lp. 50.0.00 [500 soles] due to pay for the delivery of funds from Cajamarca, which we have no obligation to pay, a sum that has been added to the Lp. 74.8.00 [748 soles] due for the delivery of funds from Moyobamba, which constitute an unjust charge regarding our funds.

These are the observations that I have made thus far with respect to said accounts.

Dios Que á Ud.

[signature] (ASC40, 12 de Noviembre de 1929)

The members of the Pizarro-Rubio also fought with the central government and sought to rid themselves of the limitations that central officials sought to impose on them regarding how the highway funds were to be used. Initially, coalition leaders found themselves unable to free themselves of these limitations:

[Seal of the Caja de Depósitos y Consignaciones]
Sr. Prefect of the Department and President of the Committee for the Construction of the Chachapoyas-Bagua Chica Highway:

We have the pleasure of bringing to your attention that the Committee over which you . . . preside . . . has received, on the 14th of this month, the following telegram from our Central Office:

"[The] Lp. 1,000 Peruvian pounds [10,000 soles] [placed at the] disposition [of the Provincial Highway Committee [for the] Highway to the Coast [may be] used for that project alone and said funds may not be transferred to other projects without supreme authorization [from the Ministry of] Fomento."

Dios que a Ud.
[signature] (ASC40, 19 de Setiembre de 1929)

Toward the end of their reign, however, the Pizarro-Rubio finally succeeded in ridding themselves of these limitations:

[Seal of the Council of Highway Conscription, Province of Chachapoyas]
Oficio No. 20
Sr. Prefect:

I am honored to acknowledge receipt of your *oficio* No. 41, dated today, in which you explain that the Central Council of Roads, over which you preside, has decreed that the conscription contingents for the [Grand Chachapoyas-Pimentel] highway are to be used to repair other roadways in the Department, as authorized by telegram by the Dirección de Vías de Comunicación.

Dios guard á Ud.
[signature] (ASC38, 28 de Abril de 1930)

But what the members of the ruling coalition virtually *never* did prior to 1930 was what they always did after 1930: struggle in vain to conscript a workforce and compete with each other to control it. To the contrary: rather than having been faced with consistent, systematic shortages of labor, as was the case after 1930, the Pizarro-Rubio were able to mobilize large quantities of conscripted labor, year after year. Furthermore, they were able to do so even from remote, rural districts, at a great distance from the work sites of the highway project—a task that would prove to be impossible after 1930:

[Seal of the Office of the Governor of the district of Ocallí]

Sr. Prefect of the Department

The [District] Conscription Committee over which I Preside, in compliance with the orders of Sr. Vasquez de Velazco, former Prefect and President of the Departmental Highway Construction Council has today delivered . . . the receipts for the highway conscripts from this district of Ocallí, of which there are 200, who are prepared to [go to] work on the highway whey they are called.

Dios que á Ud.

[Signature] (ASC40, 30 de Octubre de 1929)

Making the conscription capabilities of the Pizarro-Rubio all the more remarkable was the fact that the ruling coalition was able to mobilize such a large workforce in the 1920s without having recourse to armed force. It was not the gendarmes but rather the governors, mayors, and justices of the peace—unpaid government functionaries, who administered everyday life in the rural districts—who conscripted labor for the highway project. In what amounted to a complete inversion of what transpired after 1930—when the Guardia Civil (the National Police) were essential to virtually all aspects of conscription—in the 1920s it was *very* rare for the gendarmes to be involved in virtually any aspect in this process.

Engineering Aristocratic Privilege

During the 1920s the Pizarro-Rubio were thus able to eliminate virtually all opposition from the region's other elite families. The latter were confronted with such relentless persecution that many fled the region entirely. Those that remained kept such a low profile that for all intents and purposes their continued presence in Chachapoyas was irrelevant to the region's political dynamics. The fact that these families were compelled to absent themselves from political life meant that the very large number of clients that these families had formerly maintained among the rural cultivating classes were left without benefactors or protectors. This in turn meant that extensive sectors of the rural peasantry were vulnerable to the predations of the Pizarro-Rubio.

It was in this context that the ruling coalition began to implement the central government's modernization schemes. As we have seen, the most important of these was the Grand Chachapoyas-Pimentel Highway, a project that was a part of President Leguía's nationwide highway construction program, the provisions of which were set out in the *Ley de Conscripción Vial* (the Law of Highways). Drawing upon the unprecedented sums of money made available for this project—and also on their own expanded network of clients in the Chachapoyas region, and the absence of competing elite coalitions—the Pizarro-Rubio were able to conscript large quantities of labor. Furthermore, they were able to do so a regular, consistent basis.

The period beginning on August 1 and ending on August 13, 1927, provides a good example of the ability of the ruling coalition to conscript labor, as expressed in the activities of the Provincial Highway Committee of Chachapoyas (which was filled with Pizarro-Rubio members). Between its three active work sites, during this two-week period the committee mobilized the labor of 783 highway conscripts, who labored for a total of 6,652 days. There were no *omisos*. In the two-week periods that followed, the number of conscripts ranged from a low of 742 (who labored for a total of 6,294 days) to a high of 876 (who labored for a total of 7,458 days). There were very few *omisos*. Furthermore, the committee identified each one by name, kept careful records of the details of their transgressions, and pursued them with great zeal.[14]

The story was much the same during the same period of the following year. In the first half of the month of August 1928, the Provincial Highway Committee of the Province of Chachapoyas compelled 813 highway conscripts to work on the highway project. These individuals labored for a total of 7,332 days. Thereafter, the number of conscripts ranged from a low of 746 (who labored for a total of 6,720 days) to a high of 890 (who labored for a total of 8,035 days).[15] As had been true the year before, there were very few *omisos*. When one remembers that these figures represent the contributions of only one of the three provinces that were responsible for contributing conscripts for the highway project, it is clear that the Pizarro-Rubio were succeeding in coercing a great deal in the way of forced labor (see Figure 4.2 for a sample page from one of the payroll account books).

In sum, during the 1920s the families that made up the Pizarro-Rubio did not struggle in vain to conscript a workforce of the size required for the Grand Chachapoyas-Pimentel Highway, as elite families would be compelled to do continuously after 1930. Nor did they struggle among themselves to conscript the laborers they needed to maintain the region's traditional aristocratic order—which called upon the Indian peasant population to provide labor services for church, state, and private interests.

Nor did the elite families of the region fight with one another to control the regional labor supply—a problem that became endemic to the region in the 1930s. As long as the ruling coalition was intact, there were no labor shortages. Nor did anyone complain of not having access to the labor force they required.

Nor could it be said that there was no progress made on the highway project in the 1920s, as would be true for most of the period after 1930—when work was accompanied by endless delays and setbacks, and often came to a complete standstill. There was in fact extensive progress made on the Grand Chachapoyas-Pimentel Highway during the 1920s.

This is especially interesting when one considers that the terrain through which part of the roadway was constructed at this time—which ran from Chachapoyas toward the canyon floor of the Utcubamba River—was among the most difficult and rugged of any of the terrain it would have to negotiate (the only section more difficult being the canyon of the Marañon).[16]

The problem with the highway project during the 1920s was not that there was no progress, but rather that the extensive progress was of the wrong sort. It quickly became apparent that the Pizarro-Rubio did not view the Grand Chachapoyas-Pimentel Highway in sacropolitical terms. The importance of the project was not that it would connect the region to the nation and unlock all the potential progress and uplift that interconnection promised. Rather, the importance of the highway project was that it had the potential to express and reinforce the power and prestige of the region's ruling elite coalition.

Indeed, the elite families that that made up the ruling coalition used this major public works project to serve as a testament to their regional preeminence. They did so in several ways. One of these was simple graft. As later investigations would show, *huge* amounts of money that had been made available for this project, and for public works in general, simply disappeared into the pockets of the families that made up the ruling coalition. According to some accounts, literally hundreds of thousands of soles—and perhaps as many as a half a million—went missing (see Nugent 1997, 271–77). What was significant about this massive diversion of public funds, however, was not just its scale. Equally important was the fact that it was common knowledge that it was taking place, but that there was no public mention of this fact during the entire reign of the Pizarro-Rubio. The ruling coalition exercised such extensive control over the mechanisms

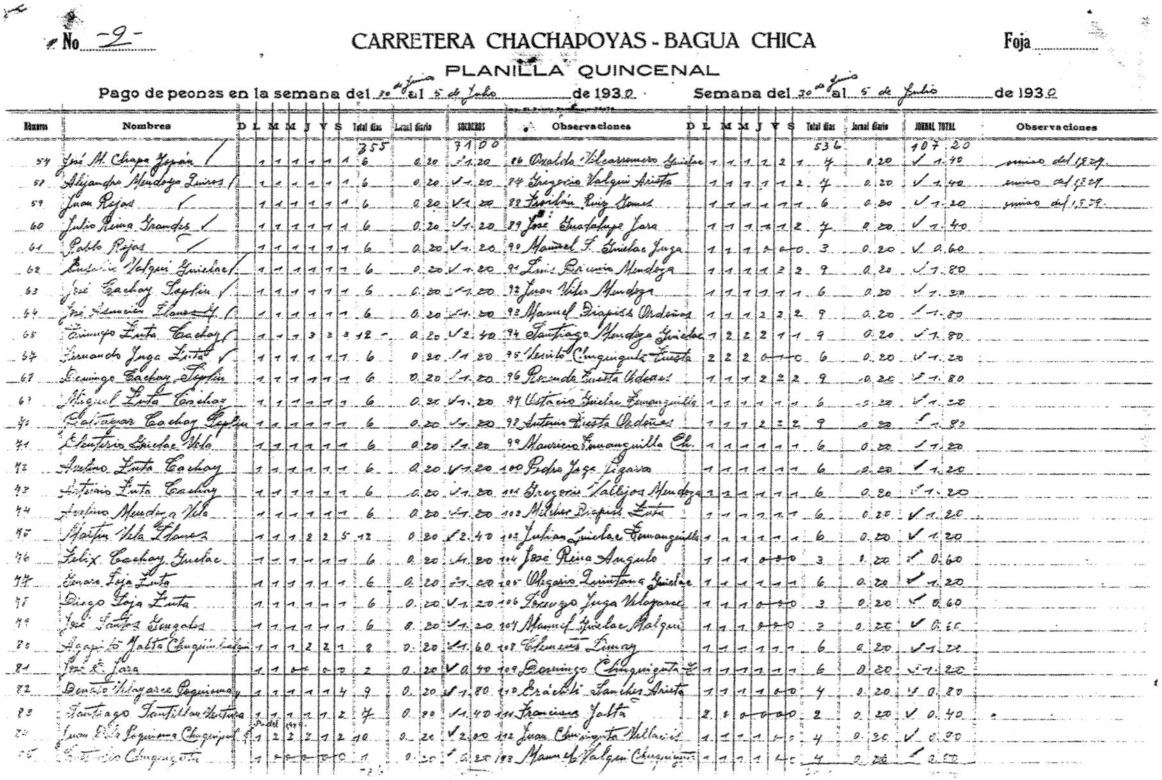

FIGURE 4.2. Public works payroll sheet.
Source: ASC38.

of public discussion and debate in the Chachapoyas region, and over the institutions of justice, that no challenge to their position was possible.[17] This meant that the ruling coalition was able to directly contradict what the "state stated" (Corrigan and Sayer 1985) regarding the use of state funds to construct a new future for the nation. Furthermore, they were able to ridicule state goals and intentions with complete impunity.

The ruling coalition took additional steps, however, to ensure that the Grand Chachapoyas-Pimentel Highway would act as a vehicle for the aggrandizement of the Pizarro-Rubio, and the form of sovereignty (aristocratic) that was the basis of their position. They did so by demonstrating their ability to further contradict what the state stated—in this case, regarding the importance of highway construction as a means of breaking with Peru's feudal past, and establishing an integrated, modern nation-state. Rather than using the highway project as a way of doing away with the premodern social structures and value systems that the central government considered the source of the country's problems, the Pizarro-Rubio did just the opposite. They drew upon this large-scale public works project to show the continued dominance of just such a premodern social structure and value system.

The Pizarro-Rubio did so by pursuing a seemingly unlikely strategy; they did everything in their power to shift the logic that informed decisions about the route the roadway would follow. As the ruling coalition organized the construction of the highway, considerations of nation building became secondary to those of aristocratic privilege and the inherited right to rule. In the process, those in the ruling coalition flaunted their ability to use conscripted labor toward ends considered "inappropriate" according to the criteria of nation building, and to use that labor force toward the aggrandizement of the Pizarro-Rubio.

The ruling coalition did indeed manage to conscript large quantities of labor, on a regular basis, during the 1920s. They used that labor, however, in ways that government planners did not intend. In the process, the Pizarro-Rubio transformed the Grand Chachapoyas-Pimentel Highway from an artery of interconnection into a public statement about the priority of aristocratic privilege—one that was built directly into the physical environment. They did so by "reengineering" the highway project.

The Pizarro-Rubio took systematic steps to ensure that the highway was built so that considerations of efficiency, ease of use, transitability, even the all-important goal of using the roadway to connect the region to the rest of the nation, mattered little. Instead, the ruling coalition used the project as ruling *castas* had long used the initiatives of the central government (see Chapter 3). They used it toward two, interrelated ends. The first of these was to demonstrate the ability of the ruling coalition to contradict the principles of nation building and popular sovereignty that had long dominated official discourse. The second way that the Pizarro-Rubio used the Grand Chachapoyas-Pimentel Highway project was as yet another opportunity to make public statements about the preeminence of their own coalition vis-à-vis opposing coalitions.

In the hands of the Pizarro-Rubio, what was intended as a great artery of interconnection that would be to the equal benefit of all was transformed into an expression/reflection of privilege and difference. From the perspective of the Pizarro-Rubio, the purpose of the highway was to bring ever-greater visibility to the families that mattered, and to relegate the families that did not matter to increasing obscurity and invisibility. In other words, only certain families were deemed worthy of seeing and being associated with the important activities, personages, and processes implied by the construction of this highway. And only certain families were deemed worthy of being seen by those would travel the highway.

With this as their guiding logic, the members of the ruling coalition did indeed reengineer the highway. They ensured that it would end up taking a path that would appear bizarre, nonsensical, and absurd from the perspective of those concerned with nation building. For those who were motivated by the logic of aristocratic sovereignty and intercoalition competition, however, the path taken by the roadway made perfect sense.

From the perspective of anyone concerned with promoting national interconnection, the most logical place to begin highway construction in the Chachapoyas region would have been at the town of Balzas. This town was located far from Chachapoyas, in the south of the region, in the Marañon River canyon, on the east side of the river (see Map 1). Beginning here would have made the most sense because a highway was already being built immediately across the river, in the department of Cajamarca, up the opposite side of the Marañon canyon and further to the west, where transportation networks linking the north of Peru to the rest of the national space were already well developed. Balzas was thus the nearest point of connection to the existing road network in the department of Amazonas. Starting highway construction at this point, and continuing north toward Chachapoyas, would have allowed the artery of interconnection to extend from the existing network into new territory in an interconnected fashion.

Although it made literally no sense from the perspective of expanding the existing highway network, or promoting national interconnection, work on the Grand Chachapoyas-Pimentel Highway began in a section leading into the city of Chachapoyas. Because Chachapoyas was located at a considerable distance from Peru's existing transportation network, beginning construction here meant that the highway would remain literally a road to nowhere, and for decades. Even so, it was no accident that the project began near Chachapoyas, for the estate homes of virtually all of the region's elite families were located in the immediate environs of the city.

It was not simply, however, that construction began at a place that made no sense in terms of either engineering or interconnection. In addition, in the section adjacent to Chachapoyas, where much of the early work was concentrated, the roadway went through a series of what appeared to be the most tortured of twists and turns and illogical pathways. Constructing the thoroughfare in this manner had two interrelated purposes. On the one hand, the highway was reengineered so that it would pass by the estates of all the important families associated with the Pizarro-Rubio. On the other hand, the pathway chosen by the ruling coalition was equally informed by the need to ensure that the highway systematically avoided all the estates associated with the defeated Burga-Hurtado coalition (in particular, El Molino, the fortified hacienda home of the Burga family).

In some circumstances, the families that made up the ruling coalition collaborated with one another to determine the route the roadway would follow—as revealed by an article from the progressive newspaper *Amazonas*, which made extensive commentary on the project:

When the construction of the [Grand] Chachapoyas-Pimentel highway was announced our spirits soared. . . . Never did we think, [however], that the directors of . . . a work of [such] transcendental importance for Amazonas would defraud our hopes and destroy the enthusiasm of our hardworking people. . . . Up to today more than 8,000 highway conscripts have worked and in spite of this they have scarcely managed to do more than a few meters on the outskirts of the city. . . . This has been due to the fact that the Sr. Engineer in charge of the project has changed the project over and over again . . . because of [pressure from] the established interests of local tyrants [*gamonales*], who are not content to wickedly exploit the poor Indians, but who also take advantage of the . . . Engineer to ensure that [he] change the plans he presented to the

Minister of Development [Fomento]. . . . [I]nstead of following the shortest route the roadway runs through a series of curves by the haciendas of said tyrants, to the detriment of . . . the State and, what is more painful, with the sacrifice of the people and the consent of the political authorities (*Amazonas*, Año 1, Número 4, 1 de Febrero de 1927).

In other circumstances, however, the families that made up the ruling coalition competed with one another to determine the path that the highway would take—as in the example below, in which feuding clients of the Pizarro-Rubio in the town of Bagua Chica each back their own expert in an effort to steer the roadway in the desired direction (see Basadre 1968–69, XIII, 255):

In the town of Bagua Chica, capital of the district . . . on the 31st of December of 1929, at 2 pm, the members of the District Highway Committee met in the Municipality, with the object of . . . conveying to you, Sr. Director of Public Works and President of the Departmental Highway Council, our concerns about the route officially approved for the highway "Pimentel-Chachapoyas"; it having become known recently in this Region that the Sr. Engineer Carrillo has selected a route completely at odds with that selected by the town of Bagua Chica, [the new route] running along the right margin of the "Utcubamba" river, across very rugged terrain, having to cross deep ravines and swift streams at every step, which will present serious obstacles to the rapid prolongation of the highway, [problems] which will not face the route studied previously and in great detail by Sr. Garcia Chepote, a very intelligent Engineer, who recommended that the highway be built along the left margin of the river already mentioned, in this way passing directly through the town of "Bagua Grande," through a section that is completely flat, from the [M]arañon [river] all the way to the town of "Chosgón," in the district of "San Jerónimo," this being an extension of 100 kilometers, more or less; we therefore ask, Sr. Director of "Public Works" and President of the Highway Council of the Department, in the name of all the highway conscripts of the district that we represent, that you decree officially, and in the strictest of manners, that the conscripts only be used as originally planned, and in this way realize in the shortest time possible the aspirations of our National Leader [*Mandatorio*] and the [congressional] Representatives of Amazonas, and in this way ensure that the highway from Chachapoyas to the coast be a perfect one.

[Seal of the District Council of Bagua Chica]
[signature] (ASC38, 31 de Diciembre de 1929)

Whether the elite families of the Pizarro-Rubio cooperated or competed to determine the path that the Grand Chachapoyas-Pimentel

Highway would take, however, the message was the same. It was the ruling coalition rather than the central government that would determine the logic that guided the construction of the highway. As a result, it was the ruling coalition that would determine the significance of the highway project for the Chachapoyas region. The Pizarro-Rubio made it abundantly clear that they had little interest in the central government's sacropolitical efforts to connect the region to the nation. Rather, from the perspective of the ruling coalition, the purpose of this major public works project was similar to that of all public works projects—and all forms of central government involvement in the region. The function of all these forms of central involvement was to reflect and reinforce the aristocratic order that was overseen by the region's ruling coalition of forces.

Conclusion

In sum, during the *oncenio* a series of important transformations in political life occurred in the Chachapoyas region. First, during this period the Pizarro-Rubio were able to rise up above the other *castas* to become the undisputed, dominant force in the region. Second, the Pizarro-Rubio succeeded in converting themselves into more than a *casta*. Rather, they were able to consolidate a coalition the likes of which the region had never seen. Third, as a result of the prolonged period of rule that they enjoyed, and the unprecedented levels of support they received from the central government, Chachapoyas's new political configuration managed to dismantle the other *castas*, and in the process succeeded in eliminating the *casta* order as a whole.

Fourth, having done away with the region's other elite-led coalitions, the Pizarro-Rubio were able to prey upon their former adversaries' clients, who found themselves without benefactors or protectors. In this context, the ruling coalition was able to conscript large quantities of labor, on a regular basis. Furthermore, they were able to do so without having to enlist the support of the forces of order. The ruling coalition was also able to generate detailed, accurate information about the regional workforce. This information proved invaluable to the Pizarro-Rubio as they went about the task of recruiting labor.

Fifth, although the ruling coalition was indeed able to conscript labor on an unprecedented scale, the leaders of Pizarro-Rubio were scrupulous about ensuring that the workforce was used toward "inappropriate" ends. Rather than utilize their army of conscripts to promote the cause of national interconnection, which was the government's explicit purpose in building the great artery of interconnection, the ruling coalition went out of its way to demonstrate its ability to contradict what the state stated. Instead of using the workforce at their command to promote the sacro-political cause of nation building, the Pizarro-Rubio used their army to further the aggrandizement of the ruling coalition—and to underscore the priority of the principles of aristocratic sovereignty, upon which their rule was based.

When and why it is possible to be (and see) like a state (Scott 1998)? Views of the state that find inspiration in the writings of Max Weber (1980) regard it as an institution that exercises a monopoly on the use of legitimate force within a given territory. According to these views, state formation depends in no small part on the ability of central powers to eliminate violence-wielding competitors, who interfere with the monopoly on force the state seeks to establish. Developments in Chachapoyas, however, suggest a very different interpretation. The ability of the central government to impose its will in this remote section of the national space was contingent not upon the elimination of violence-wielding actors but on their preservation. Indeed, as we will see in Part Three, when these nonstate actors were no longer present—when conditions resembled what would conventionally be understood as a state monopoly on the use of force—government officials found themselves incapable of governing the region. The absence of coercion-wielding *castas* after 1930 meant that conditions became increasingly chaotic, ultimately culminating in a crisis of rule.

5

Divided Elite and Disordered State

Sr. Prefect.

    Yesterday the Governor of this district . . . dishonored the Mayor, and completely without cause dragged him by force to jail, where he remains, his clothing ripped, and only because the Mayor objected to the efforts of the Governor to force all the citizens of this [district] to provide him with personal labor on his own lands, and to fine those who refuse the sum of one sol per day, [while] claiming that his demands are for the good of the District. . . . We ask that you free us from this situation, which is completely lacking in justice.

    —Francisco Salazar, Alderman

Introduction

The end of the *oncenio* represented a major watershed for the nobility of the Chachapoyas region. From this point onward, they suffered a rapid and calamitous fall from grace, as their powers and privileges were greatly reduced. The cause of their difficulties was the collapse of the old *casta* structure. The extended networks of closely linked families that had once worked collaboratively to extort, coerce, and compel splintered into separate pieces after 1930, leaving individual elite families alone and isolated, competing with other families to make do.

Control of political office remained the only way that the region's noble families could have any hope of maintaining their aristocratic station. With the breakdown of the *castas*, however, there were no longer any reliable strategies that elite families could follow that would guarantee them access to these positions. Compounding the difficulties faced by these families was an additional fact: the positions that had been so effective in supporting them during the *casta* period changed in character. They were much less lucrative and prestigious than they had been in the past, and thus were far more limited in their ability to sustain an elite lifestyle.

Finally, even if an aristocratic family succeeded in securing an appointment to a political position, the competition of the post-*casta* era was such that there was no certainty that they would be able to hang onto that post. This combination of factors meant that elite families felt deeply insecure about their ability to maintain themselves as elites. The fact that they were confronted with the prospect of a calamitous decline in position, and that there were no reliable means to guard against that prospect, made elite families truly desperate about their situation.

Contributing further to the distinctive political dynamics of the era was an additional factor—one that pitted aristocratic families against one another. With the splintering of the *castas*, something occurred that would have been unheard of in the past. Families that had formerly belonged to warring elite coalitions found themselves occupying influential positions within the government apparatus at the same time. These families had longstanding and bitter enmities with one another. As they fought out old battles in new terrain (i.e., within the government apparatus) they undermined the coordination and unity of purpose that had obtained among government officials prior to 1930. And they replaced that coordination with a highly destructive, competitive, and disordering dynamic.

Things Fall Apart: On the Structural Disintegration of the Administrative Sphere

Several factors contributed to the disorder and dysfunction of political affairs during the post-*casta* era. The first of these involved changes in the politics of elections. During the *casta* era, elections for the region's key political positions (senator and deputy) were violent affairs, fought out between opposing *castas*. The *casta* that prevailed represented a powerful coalition whose desires the central regime could not ignore. For the central government needed a strong regional ally that would support it against competing national coalitions, which had supporters among the *castas* in Chachapoyas.

As a result, the executive branch of government, which in theory made appointments to the key positions that controlled the administrative apparatus—departmental prefect, provincial subprefects, judges, and chiefs of police—in practice ceded that right to ruling *casta* leaders (who had prevailed in the region's "elections"). This meant that congressional deputies would appoint subprefects and judges, while senators would select the prefect and the chiefs of police. These appointees were themselves prominent members of the ruling *casta*. They would use their own powers of appointment to fill the remaining positions in the bureaucracy with clients of the ruling *casta*. In this way they ensured that their *casta* controlled the entire state apparatus.

After 1930, these conditions changed in important ways. With the collapse of the *castas* the central government was no longer forced to rely on a powerful *casta* ally in Chachapoyas to control threats from opposing *castas*. This meant that the government in Lima was no longer compelled to relinquish rights of bureaucratic appointment to *casta* leaders, who would use that right to reward *casta* followers and reproduce the position of the *casta* as a whole. Rather, the various offices of the central government were much freer to name individuals of their own choosing to positions throughout regional government.

With the collapse of the *castas* the central government succeeded in eliminating one of the key powers that ruling *castas* had enjoyed—a power that had prevented the government from acting in its own name. This change helped the central government establish what would conventionally be understood as a monopoly on the use of armed force in the region. Despite this fact, however, as time passed state officials found themselves less and less able to govern the region. In the absence of a *casta* to lend order and consistency to the behavior of government officials, a range of conflicting and contradictory interests came to inform state activity.

Indeed, in the highly competitive, zero-sum conditions of the post-*casta* era something of a war of all against all broke out between individual elite families, as each did everything in their power to retain their elite status. Unlike the highly visible, armed struggles of the *casta* era, however, this was a cold war. The violence of the post-*casta* era went underground, so to speak. It became masked behind new discursive and behavioral weapons, as elite families waged war on their enemies surreptitiously. With the dawn of the post-*casta* era aristocratic families were compelled to conceal their struggles for advantage behind a mask of concern for the common good. This produced conditions of bureaucratic involution and in-fighting that were unprecedented in scope and scale. It also produced dysfunctional conditions that were rarely acknowledged as such.

The Central Government's Modernization Projects

It was in this context of growing elite competition and fragmentation that successive central regimes pursued policies that were "sacropolitical" in nature. These regimes sought to implement modernization projects that were intended to free the country from the weight of its unfortunate past, and in the process bring to life a stagnant social formation. The resources the government made available for these projects were unprecedented in scale and represented an important new form of wealth above and beyond what could be coerced out of the rural cultivating population by tributary means (Wolf 1982). The additional wealth associated with these new projects thus represented a crucial resource upon which aristocratic families could potentially draw in attempting to limit the rapid deterioration of their elite status. The dilemma that elite families faced was how to gain access to these resources.

The central government's modernization projects varied widely in form, but the most important of these projects were: (1) an extensive network of roads, highways, bridges, and airfields, which would (in theory) help bring into being a national market by establishing direct interconnections between sections of the national space that had long operated in isolation of one another; (2) an equally extensive network of schools, where an army of teachers would steep highland children in national cultural values; (3) new water, sewage, and sanitation facilities, improved marketplaces, and a series of small hydroelectric plants—to introduce the highlands to improved living conditions; (4) improved bureaucratic infrastructures to enumerate, monitor, and improve the well-being of the population; and finally (5) uniform procedures for recruiting the rural population into the armed forces.

In addition to injecting large sums of new wealth into the regional economy, the post-*casta* state of redemption also introduced new positions into the government bureaucracy. The posts in question—for example, the highway engineer and his support staff, the construction contractors and their support staffs—were entirely separate from the political positions in the old bureaucracy, which ruling *casta* leaders had once distributed to ruling *casta* followers as a form of patronage.[1] Establishing ties with the individuals who were appointed to these new posts was crucial for any elite family that hoped to maintain its elite status. But the dilemmas involved in forming such ties introduced additional competition and dysfunction into regional political life.

During the *casta* era, the ruling coalition was of such strategic importance to the central government that appointments to positions of this kind would always have been made or approved by the ruling *casta*. During the post-*casta* era, however, this was no longer the case. As a result, the individuals who were selected to oversee modernization projects were not beholden to any regional political coalition. Indeed, these individuals represented the very kind of potentially threatening force that the *castas* had been at great pains to control and domesticate prior to 1930.

With the fall of the *castas*, however, it was no longer possible to eliminate the potential threat represented by positions such as these by absorbing them into the ruling *casta*. Instead of being able to absorb them into one ruling coalition, a large number of competing aristocratic families— each desperate to maintain their deteriorating elite status—would converge upon and court these individuals, doing whatever they could to make a connection with them. Each elite family tried equally hard to ensure that other elite families were unable to make such a connection.

The appearance of appointees from Lima was thus one source of the unprecedented instability that characterized the post-*casta* era. Other factors, however, further contributed to this instability. Whether the Chachapoyas region was the site of any given modernization project was determined by decision makers in the national capital. These included the members of Congress and the various government ministries. There was no telling if or when the region would be the recipient of government largesse. When this did occur, however, it often happened with little advance warning.

Once a new project began, it would introduce abrupt changes into regional affairs. This was due in part to the forces already mentioned; with the fall of the *castas* the appointees from Lima who were named to oversee these projects were no longer beholden to local political coalitions. Considering that these project managers had resources of which all aristocratic families were in desperate need, and that the managers needed the assistance of some elite families to carry out their projects, these individuals found themselves at the center of intense rivalries between competing elite families.[2]

In other instances, however, it was not appointees from Lima but individuals from local families who found themselves appointed to oversee or implement modernization projects. These circumstances introduced a related form of disorder into regional political life. For the individuals who were so appointed unexpectedly found themselves in a position to wield resources, and to forge connections, that would have been unthinkable just a short time before. Furthermore, in most cases no one had expected them to be selected for these positions of responsibility.[3]

Because of their unexpected good fortune, however, their "stock" went up appreciably, and in short order—making them interesting and important in ways that had not previously been the case. Furthermore, what was true of appointees from Lima was also true of these local project managers. Because of the resources they had at their disposal, and their need to ally with some other elite families, they suddenly found them-selves at the center of intense rivalries, in which their peers went to elabo-rate lengths to make connections and to be sure that competing families did not.[4]

Exacerbating the unpredictability and instability of the post-*casta* period were the irregular and unpredictable patterns of funding for mod-ernization projects. The following scenario was not at all uncommon. The central government would grant permission for a particular project to be carried out and would appoint a manager or managers (whether local or Lima-based) to oversee its implementation. The government would also make monies available to begin work on the project. Completely without warning, however, funding would suddenly disappear. And because money was no longer available, work would have to be stopped, and the project suspended. As funds disappeared, managers and implementers—and the elite families they had enlisted to support them—would find themselves with nothing to do.[5]

Complicating matters further was the fact that it was unclear when, or even if, the funds to continue the project would be forthcoming. In the (perpetual?) meantime, the alliance that had come together around the project would be put on pause, as it were. And because it was so difficult to know if the project would be resumed, for how long, with what regularity, etc., the managers—whose stock had recently gone up—would find that their stock had gone down.

Erstwhile project managers experienced a rapid fall in status in part because they were unable to deliver on promises (regarding the project) they had already made to local families they had enlisted to help them with the implementation process. Equally important, however, was a second consideration. With the suspension of funding for a project, local elite families would be compelled to reassess the strategic importance of these individuals into the future. And it was impossible to do so in any kind of reliable manner. Indeed, it was unclear to what extent these individuals would turn out to be valuable allies. The "popularity" of these figures therefore waxed and waned rapidly and unpredictably. For the most part, they were the center of attention and rivalry only for as long as, and for the periods during which, they had resources at their disposal.

The instability and unpredictability of post-*casta* political affairs was accentuated by the fact that the individuals who were appointed to manage and oversee modernization projects changed frequently, with little advance notice. Several factors contributed to these frequent changes in personnel. First, the Chachapoyas region was what would now be regarded as a "hardship post." It was located at a great distance from the national capital, and could only be reached after a long, arduous, and often dangerous journey.[6]

Furthermore, there was very little in the way of amenities to make it worthwhile for those who completed the journey to stay in the departmental capital. And there were even fewer amenities available in the capitals of the different provinces. As a result, individuals who were appointed to oversee modernization projects were constantly petitioning their superiors in Lima to be transferred elsewhere.[7]

A second factor that produced frequent changes in the personnel who were in charge of modernization projects was the unreliability of funding. It was not at all uncommon for projects to be suspended or discontinued. In the latter case, those who had been appointed to manage or oversee a project would find that they had made the long journey to Chachapoyas for no reason and would be forced to return to the national capital. Or, they would discover that they had been transferred to a different region of the country altogether.[8]

Their departure, however, was very disruptive to local political alliances. It meant that the intense rivalries fought out between local elite families to decide who would benefit from the resources associated with that project had been fought for nothing—that enemies had been made for no reason, and also that friendships had been formed that were not to last. Indeed, the frequent departure of project managers meant that the individual families, and the ephemeral alliances of families that had temporarily come together around each discontinued project, were undermined.

Each of these networks formed as a result of intense competition between local elite families. These families did everything in their power to establish ties with project managers, in order to counteract what would otherwise be a rapid deterioration in their social status. The fact that the group of families that had prevailed in this contest suddenly found that their efforts had been for naught was deeply disruptive to the continuity of political alliances. It was equally damaging to the efforts of these families to maintain their elite status—and to their ability to feel secure that they would be able to do so into the future. For a project manager or an elite family that had been an important ally one day could become a liability just a short time later.

Adding further to the unpredictability of the post-*casta* era was the following; it was often not clear whether a project had been discontinued or suspended. If there was no official decision or announcement from Lima stating that a given project had been terminated—and it was rare for such an announcement to be made—both the project and the personnel associated with it could languish for months, with no clue about what the future might hold. At times the manager of a project that had gone into a state of de facto suspension (because additional funding was not forthcoming) would discover, after months of receiving no support, that new monies had been authorized.

Even so, it was often the case that the funds were less than had been expected, that they had been designated for new purposes, or that they arrived during times of year when it was difficult to use them (if the project involved the use of local labor—and virtually all did—planting season, harvest season, and the rainy season were difficult periods). Changes of this kind would mean that some existing relationships with elite families could be reactivated. It also meant, however, that others would have to be modified or broken, while new relationships would have to be formed.[9]

Regardless, the fact that it was unclear whether a project had been discontinued meant that there were risks involved for elite families who decided to abandon the project manager and seek out new relationships. For if the project was resumed, these families would have lost access to an important source of wealth and connections. The lack of clarity surrounding the future of modernization projects also meant, however, that there were risks involved in not abandoning the manager of a suspended project.

A family that remained loyal to the manager of a suspended project, and to the other families that had come together around that project, risked forgoing opportunities to forge connections with new projects and new project managers.

A final variation on the abovementioned pattern involved projects that were discontinued but were subsequently restarted. In these cases, it was necessary to appoint a new project manager (local or Lima-based). If this individual was an appointee from Lima, he would have to make the long trip to Chachapoyas, which would result in further delays. In anticipation of his arrival, however, local elite families would begin to politic among themselves, and would attempt to use whatever contacts they had in Lima to reach out to this individual. Whether local or not, however, the new project manager would become the focus of a new round of rivalries between the region's elite families. The appointment of a new manager would also undermine whatever relations had been formed with elite families by the old manager and would make it possible for new families to curry favor.[10]

There were, of course, periods when funding for the central government's modernization projects was available, and the relevant managerial personnel was in place. During such times, however, efforts to implement these projects introduced additional dimensions of disorder into regional political affairs. This was because the ability to carry out these projects was dependent on the ability of government officials to establish a new political geography, and to superimpose it on the region's longstanding political geography (based on the territorial/administrative divisions of district, province, and department). This new geography not only was independent of the old one but also represented a direct threat to its viability. This was because the new geography relied upon the labor of primary producers, who lived within, and were subject to, the demands of the old territorial units. As a result, whenever the interests that represented these two geographies collided—which they inevitably did during the course of modernization—conflict was sure to ensue.[11]

The longstanding political geography of the Chachapoyas region was established at the founding of the Peruvian nation-state and might be thought of as a geography of stasis. It was based on the abovementioned nested hierarchy of territorial/administrative units upon which national administration depended. The geography associated with these units was one of fixity and boundedness. For the most part, each unit was expected to be self-contained and self-functioning.

There were ways in which districts were answerable to the province to which they belonged, and provinces to the department of which they were a part. Even so, for the most part, the minimal unit of administration—the district—was expected to look after its own affairs. This was especially true of matters related to corvée labor. While not unheard of, during the era of the *castas* it was rare indeed for the population of a district to be called upon to provide forced labor beyond the confines of that district.

There were three (unpaid) government functionaries who were responsible for overseeing everyday political life in the districts. They were the governor, mayor, and justice of the peace. Under the *casta* structure, these three were rarely called upon by their superiors to "export" the labor of their district elsewhere. Instead, their primary administrative obligations consisted of mobilizing the workforce of their district to maintain "public works." That is, the main activities for which the district population was responsible was the upkeep of roads, trails, and bridges within the confines of their district. Equally important tasks included the maintenance of government buildings (including schools) and religious structures (churches and chapels). In addition, members of the elite who owned haciendas located within the district could often prevail upon district functionaries to provide them with labor—but only if the hacendado was a member of the ruling *casta*.

The central government's modernization projects introduced a new political geography that threatened to disrupt this geography of stasis—one that might be thought of as a "geography of movement" that was a direct by-product of the state of redemption that had been declared for the country as a whole. The geography of movement threatened to disrupt the geography of stasis in part because the modernization projects associated with the government's state of redemption failed to respect the inward-looking nature of district governance, and the fact that each district was responsible for the maintenance of its own public works.

Some of the new projects introduced by the central government drew only on the labor force of a single district. Many others, however, required laborers from multiple districts, who were compelled to collaborate on projects that extended through a number of different districts (new highways were a good example). While every effort was made to ensure that the workforce of any given district was not compelled to work outside of district boundaries, it was not at all uncommon for them to have to do so. This meant that district functionaries were called upon to mobilize the population of their jurisdiction so that the workforce could absent itself from that jurisdiction.

Whether the central government's modernization projects relied upon the labor supply of a single district or several, the district functionaries who were responsible for mobilizing the workforce for these projects were faced with the same problem. To the extent that they cooperated with these new calls for labor, they would be undermining their ability to fulfill their longstanding obligations to the state, the church, and the elite. For the new labor demands associated with the state of redemption were not accompanied by any reduction in the demands associated with the region's longstanding structure of administration—with the demands associated with its geography of stasis. Rather, district functionaries were expected to mobilize the workforce of their respect districts to serve the needs of two conflicting projects of rule at the same time.[12]

The conditions of the post-*casta* era were such that *continuities* in relationship were a thing of the past. During the *casta* era, one always knew with whom one had to ally in order to gain access to positions of wealth and power. The positions were those of the old government administrative hierarchy. Membership in a *casta*, generally arranged by means of marriage alliance, was the stable and predictable means by which such positions could be accessed. During the new, post-*casta* period, however, all this changed. After 1930, elite families never knew with whom they should ally in order to maintain their elite status. Nor did they know what strategies they should pursue in order to do so.

While access to positions in the old government administrative hierarchy certainly helped elite families maintain some semblance of their former positions, these posts were neither as lucrative nor as reliable as they had once been. The new cold-war-like conditions of the post-*casta* era, and that fact that there was no longer a ruling *casta* on hand to coordinate the activities of those who occupied posts in the government bureaucracy, meant that the positions were fraught with problems and difficulties. Furthermore, while occupying these posts might help the occupant make connections with project managers—and thus gain access to the wealth associated with modernization projects—this was anything but guaranteed. Finally, because the managers of these projects came and went, and because the funding for these projects was so erratic, an individual who was a valuable ally at one point in time could prove to be a liability just a short time later. Perhaps most damaging to the continuity of political relationships, however, was the fact that there was no way to tell whether or not such people would be an asset or a liability.

In sum, with the collapse of the *casta* structure the aristocratic families of Chachapoyas went into a period of steep and rapid decline. The disintegration of the elite coalitions that had dominated political life prior to 1930 meant that the broad networks of kin-allied families that had formerly worked together to dominate regional affairs fell apart. In their place, individual elite families were left alone and isolated, desperately seeking some way of maintaining a social status that was increasingly difficult to maintain. As a result, these families fought viciously among themselves to preserve whatever they could of that status.

Power, Knowledge, and Publicity

As the foregoing suggests, after 1930 it was no longer the case that broad, stable coalitions of closely allied families and their extensive networks of followers fought for control of the state apparatus as a whole. Rather, during the post-*casta* era individual elite families (and their narrow circle of temporary allies) fought over *fragments* of the state. And because these competing families occupied official posts within the state apparatus at the same time, they also fought over the inner workings of government.

In order to wage war on their adversaries—who were scattered across the new bureaucratic field of battle—elite families employed two main strategies. First, every family went to great lengths to show that it was entirely dependable, reliable, etc.—that it was an ideal ally—whether to fill positions in the government bureaucracy or to assist a project manager with a modernization project. The best way to do so was for a family to show that it could fulfill all the obligations associated with the position(s) it did control. Second, every family went to equally great lengths to show that adversarial families were entirely unsuitable as potential allies—that they were unreliable, untrustworthy, dishonest, etc. The best way to do so was to prevent other families from fulfilling the obligations associated with the positions they occupied. Because the successful completion of most official tasks required cooperation among several government functionaries, it was a simple matter for any one functionary to interfere with the effectiveness of others, even as he pretended to do the opposite.

But elite families went beyond obstruction—beyond employing "weapons of the moderately strong" (Scott 1985)—in their efforts to undermine the credibility of opposing families. In order to discredit their adversaries, they also employed discursive means of attack. All families having created conditions in which it was virtually impossible for any family to carry out its duties, each elite family would then use denunciation (Fitzpatrick and Gellately 1997) to accuse their enemies of corruption, negligence, indifference, etc. The power of these accusations came from more than the fact that the practices were illegal. At least as important was the fact that they interfered with the state of redemption that had been declared for the country as a whole. Ironically, they were also offenses for which the accuser was in no small part responsible.

Charges of this kind began to circulate through government offices in increasingly large numbers. Indeed, in their desperation to retain whatever they could of their former powers and privileges, and to eliminate potential competitors for those powers and privileges, all elite families took to employing this strategy of generalized denunciation on a systematic basis. As they did so, a wholly new dynamic took shape among the various offices and branches of the government bureaucracy. Functionaries who had formerly cooperated with one another to carry out official extortion during the *casta* era went to great lengths to interfere with one another during the post-*casta* era—to disrupt the official activities of their foes. The effect was to produce extensive disorder in the operation of the state.

The fragmentation of *casta* coalitions, and the involution and competition that came to characterize intrabureaucratic relations, did much to undermine "public administration" during the post-*casta* era. For the present purposes, however, what is significant about these changes is that they undermined the region-wide structure of surveillance that had been so important in enabling labor conscription during the *oncenio*. As this structure of surveillance collapsed, so too did the coordination, regularity, and transparency that characterized forced labor during the 1920s. This in turn made it increasingly difficult to embed the remarkable in the routine.

It is especially interesting that conscription became increasingly disordered during the post-*casta* era because many of the same branches of government and positions in the state bureaucracy were involved in implementing corvée. As had been the case during the 1920s, district functionaries—the governor, mayor, and justice of the peace—continued to have the primary responsibility for mobilizing labor for modernization projects.[13] In an inversion of the state of affairs that obtained during the *casta* era, it was common for each of these functionaries to regard his peers as adversaries rather than collaborators during the post-*casta* era. As a result, each sought to interfere as extensively as possible with the activities of the others (see chapter epigraph).

The fact that state activities were so extensively disordered, however, was not only because district functionaries were at odds with each other. Equally important was the fact that their superiors in the provincial capital—the subprefect, mayor, and judge—often had this same antagonistic relationship with one another. As these officials pursued their competing agendas, they also came into direct conflict with one another, as each sought to show that he could fulfill all the obligations of office and that his adversaries could not. As we will see presently, because of the central place of forced labor in promoting modernization, many of these obligations revolved around conscription.[14]

This meant that it was not at all unusual for provincial officials to be actively involved in attempting to prevent their counterparts from being effective agents of corvée. It also meant, however, that provincial officials were unlikely to assist district functionaries with conscription problems in their district. It also meant that provincial officials could not be counted upon to reach out to functionaries in other districts in their province when the functionaries in any one district found that they could not locate missing conscripts. It also meant, however, that provincial officials were unlikely to cooperate with their counterparts in other provinces.

In sum, the collapse of the *casta* structure meant that government functionaries distributed throughout the entire state apparatus were much less likely to cooperate with one another to achieve collective goals. Instead, those who worked in the various offices of the government bureaucracy found themselves in direct competition with one another. For they had come to belong to small, unstable, ephemeral factions, with opposed interests and aspirations. The success of one could come only at the expense of the others. As these ever-shifting groups made war on one another, the effect was to disorder the operation of state—and to do so behind a façade of concern for the common good.

As noted above, one consequence of this new state of affairs was that it undermined the integrated structure of surveillance that had been crucial in enabling conscription during the *oncenio*. During the *oncenio* the laboring population had found it very difficult to disappear from the conscription rolls or to remain undetected by *casta* surveillance. So much so had this been the case that the vast majority of those who were subject to forced labor had chosen to comply with government demands despite their highly onerous character. Indeed, evasion was largely futile during the 1920s. Few people even attempted it, and fewer still succeeded.

During the 1930s and 1940s these conditions changed dramatically, as competition between feuding members of the government apparatus rendered the *oncenio*-era structure of surveillance ineffective. As this structure broke down, the laboring population found that evasion was much easier than it had been. They were quick to take advantage of the transformed state of affairs. Faced with ever-increasing demands for their labor, and state officials who were unable to track their movements, many would simply go into hiding whenever they learned that government conscription agents were approaching. They would return to their homes when these functionaries had left.

There are indications, however, that as the post-*casta* period wore on, some rural cultivators chose what they anticipated would be a more long-term solution to the threat of corvée. The evidence is fragmentary, but it suggests that a number of peasant households responded to the increasing burden of conscription as their ancestors had in the early colonial period. They chose permanent dislocation rather than temporary flight:[15]

Sr. Prefect of the Department

I have the honor of informing your . . . office that . . . in recent years numerous individuals from . . . Colcamar, Tingo, Luya, and Lámud . . . from the neighboring province of Luya . . . have taken up residence in the district under my command. . . . Despite their obligations . . . these individuals refuse to join with the rest of population in participating in . . . public works . . . that . . . contribute to the well-being of the District and the Nation. . . . These individuals are able to evade their duties . . . because they are protected by the Mayor and the [members of the] Municipal Council . . . who compel the[se individuals] to provide labor for their own private purposes. . . .

This . . . has resulted in serious irregularities in public administration. . . . I bring these [facts] to your attention so that your . . . esteemed office may take the measures you deem appropriate (ASC42, 11 de Octubre de 1941).

Rural cultivators appear to have been aware that their inability to avoid conscription during the 1920s had been based on the ability of district functionaries to compile detailed, comprehensive conscription lists. These lists included information regarding the names and ages of all the adult males who lived in each district. After 1930, however, many rural cultivators sought to prevent the authorities from compiling accurate lists, and in this way to become invisible to government officials. Some sought to do so by offering bribes to the district functionaries who compiled these lists (in particular, district mayors). Others, however, decided that the best strategy was to leave their homes entirely, and to take up residence in another district. This, they hoped, would help them remain beyond the gaze of the conscription authorities, and therefore safe from corvée demands.

These strategies proved to be very effective. It became increasingly difficult for the authorities to compile detailed lists naming the specific individuals who lived in each district—lists of the kind that had enabled conscription during the *oncenio*. This alone made it increasingly difficult for the authorities to "see like a state" (Scott 1998). But names were of less and less use to government officials during the post-*casta* period for additional reasons. During the 1930s and 1940s it was often the case that the district functionaries who were responsible for conscription had competing and opposed interests. Each was determined to show that he could meet his obligations to conscript labor while his counterparts could not. As rural cultivators sought to disappear from official conscription rolls, they needed a benefactor who could help them maintain their invisibility.

As indicated in the block quote immediately above, because district functionaries were increasingly at odds with one another, they were more than happy to provide this "service" to those who were in need of a political patron. For in so doing, each functionary could better thwart the conscription efforts of his adversaries. He could also establish ties with new constituencies that could help him meet his own obligations to conscript. As we will see in the next two chapters, after 1930 this led district functionaries to accuse one another "corruption." In this context, *corruption* references an especially egregious crime. It refers to more than simply using political position for personal gain; rather, in the case at hand it means that state functionaries have interfered with the sacropolitical goal of bringing Peru's moribund social formation to life. They have done so by diverting laborers away from modernization projects that were intended to redeem the nation and toward pursuits that that were said to reflect the "unbridled personal greed" of unprincipled government personnel. These accusations became increasingly common as the post-1930 period progressed. They had been unheard of prior to 1930.

Because it was so much easier after 1930 to disappear from official conscription rolls, due to the willingness of district functionaries to act as unofficial patrons for rural cultivators who were seeking to do so, government officials discovered that it was increasingly difficult to know with any certainty who lived where. While there were population estimates for the region as a whole, and although they were broadly accurate, district officials found that compiling the kinds of detailed, district-by-district lists of conscripts that had acted as the basis of corvée during the *oncenio* was very much a fool's errand. Indeed, most officials abandoned any attempt to do so, for these lists were of little use. Without a region-wide structure of surveillance to locate specific missing workers, names were of limited utility to those responsible for conscripting laborers.

As a result of this transformed state of affairs, government officials were compelled to take a new approach to conscription. They abandoned their earlier efforts to compile lists that named the specific individuals in each district who were expected to provide labor for modernization. Instead, they attempted to locate the total number of workers from each district or province that were required for any given task. In the process, the "unit of conscription" shifted from the individual conscript to the administrative unit (district or province)—to population in the aggregate.

As officials took this new approach to conscription, the regularity, transparency, and effectiveness that had formerly characterized corvée disappeared. Now that evasion was possible, and now that it was no longer feasible to search for a large number of specific individuals, the relation between power, knowledge, and publicity underwent an important transformation. During the 1930s and 1940s it no longer made sense for the government to be so public or transparent about conscription activities— to post lists of conscripts in public places, for example, or to do so well in advance of the time these individuals were expected to work. Instead, knowing that the population would flee the moment they were forewarned, officials did everything they could to *conceal* that information—to ensure that information about corvée remained secret.[16]

Laboring populations were not denied all information about what they would be called upon to do. They were informed of the total number of days they were expected to work, especially on large-scale projects like the Grand Chachapoyas-Pimentel Highway. In the process, they learned that these obligations were considerably more onerous than those of the *oncenio*.[17] And in the case of large-scale projects, provincial officials continued to devise schedules that detailed how many men the various districts would be expected to provide and during which periods. But the authorities were careful to keep these schedules to themselves. When and where rural cultivators were to offer their labor services was not made public, for fear that people would go into hiding.

Even so, details regarding the when and the where of work obligations would often leak out. In these circumstances, the men from rural cultivating families that had chosen not to move to a new district would seek to conceal themselves—although they could not be sure that they would learn of the government's plans far enough in advance to evade the authorities. Families that had relocated to a new district were in a different position. For it was the very functionaries who had informally agreed to become their benefactors and protectors (the governor, the mayor, and the justice)—who had agreed to shield them from corvée—who were responsible for organizing corvée. As it was these government functionaries who were responsible for implementing forced labor policies, they were the first to learn of official conscription plans. These unofficial patrons were therefore in an ideal position to protect their clients, or not, as they saw fit.

These developments made conscription a much more fraught and problematic process than it had been during the *oncenio*. Not even a visit to the district from the police—which became commonplace during the 1930s and 1940s but had *never* been necessary during the 1920s—could produce the desired number of conscripts. Indeed, because evasion became so much easier after 1930, and because functionaries like the district governor, mayor, and justice were often working at cross-purposes, it proved impossible to locate anything but a small percentage of the workers being sought for modernization. This in turn meant that government planners had to deviate from their own (secret) schedules and were compelled to go back to the same districts over and over again, way ahead of schedule. The fact that they did so further disordered conscription. It also generated more and more resentment on the part of rural cultivators and gave them more and more reason to flee when faced with the threat of corvée.

Imaginary Fields of Labor

As important as were the abovementioned forces in making it difficult to conscript a workforce, the ultimate cause of the scarcity of labor encountered by government officials during the post-*casta* era was to be found elsewhere. If there had been not a single case of evasion or concealment, if not one family had moved to a different district to disappear from the conscription rolls, there still would have been labor shortages of the most severe kind. This was because scarcity was being generated by other, more fundamental forces. Particularly important in this regard was the fact that the elite were deeply fragmented and divided after the *oncenio*—that the apparatus of state came to be a terrain of conflict that was fought over by individual elite families and by shifting, ephemeral elite alliances.

With the collapse of the *casta* structure it was no longer the case that officials in all branches of government were members of the same coalition. Nor was it the case that they all worked together to pursue the common interests of their *casta*. To the contrary; everyone was at pains to show that they could fulfill the obligations of their own position. They were equally at pains to show that their elite adversaries, whether in the same or in other branches of government, could not. The competitive logic that obtained between these different branches of government, and between different positions in the same branch of government, combined with the modernization plans of the central government to introduce a dysfunctional and delusional dynamic into the conscription process. This meant that every functionary was determined to produce every conscript expected by his superiors—down to the last man.

Because of the sacropolitical nature of government efforts to modernize the region, however, it was inevitable that these functionaries would fail to produce the labor force in question. According to the logic of sacropolitics, the entire population was to be mobilized to accomplish great things. The populace was to liberated from the oppressive, archaic social structures and value systems that had weighed so heavily upon them (and upon the nation as a whole) so that they could participate in generalized processes of redemption. Only in this way could Peru be freed from the dead weight of the past. Only in this way could Peru's moribund social formation be brought to life.

The state of redemption declared by successive central regimes involved highly ambitious plans to modernize the highlands by implementing a wide range of forward-looking modernization projects. Most of these projects relied on the conscripted labor of the peasantry. As the number and scale of these projects suggests, implicit in the central government's plans to redeem the country through mass sacrifice was the assumption that the government would be able to draw upon a vast field of untapped peasant labor. As we will see, this field did not exist in fact but rather in the imaginations of central planners. Once planners had imagined this field of labor into being, however, government officials in Chachapoyas went on to insist that it was there—despite overwhelming evidence to the contrary.

They did so for a simple reason. With the dawn of the post-*casta* era the aristocratic elite of Chachapoyas was faced with a rapid and calamitous decline in social position. In an effort to counteract that process, elite families sought to gain access to the new quantities of wealth associated with the modernization process. In order to prove themselves worthy clients, each elite government official was under great pressure to show that he could carry out all of his duties, and that his adversaries could not. Since these duties increasingly revolved around providing laborers for modernization projects, all officials were determined to produce every worker they had been called upon to provide.

Complicating their efforts to do so, however, was the following: the cumulative demands of all the various government offices assumed a laboring population that was two to three times the actual population size. The fact that much of the workforce demanded by government planners did not exist, however, did not dissuade each government functionary from seeking to produce every worker he was expected to produce. As a result, the war of all against all that broke out within the terrain of government was of a particular kind. It was fought over the control of an (only partially existing) rural labor supply.

The extensive disorder and dysfunction that accompanied official efforts to modernize Chachapoyas was deeply unsettling to the government officials who were responsible for the process. As we will see in the chapters to come, it was the fact that officials proved to be so ineffectual at bringing their modernization projects to fruition that they found so distressing. Virtually all projects and plans were accompanied by endless delays and continual setbacks, and for reasons that seemed to make little sense. Some projects stagnated and were abandoned completely. Others were begun but then were left unattended, in a state of partial completion for years at a time—making it unclear whether or not work on these projects continued or had been suspended.

Still other projects managed to crawl along, but at a proverbial snail's pace. Occasionally a project appeared to have been completed. But as often as not, government officials discovered subsequently that the work they thought had been finished had been poorly done and had to be redone or undone. Due to labor shortages, however, it was difficult to do so, because of which it proved impossible to bring the project to completion.

Still other projects were in fact completed but subsequently broke down, were never repaired or rebuilt, and were left to rust, collapse, or decay. A few projects were actually finished and remained potentially operational. But in a great many cases the roads and the highways, the bridges and the airfields, the schoolhouses and the vocational training centers, the sanitation systems and the electrical grids turned out to be a huge disappointment. They ended up not being used, being used only minimally, or being used in ways project designers had not intended.[18]

As a result of this state of affairs, the landscape of modernization as a whole took on the appearance of something unfinished. It came to consist of projects that were variously abandoned, obsolete, or broken down, that were partially done, poorly done, or in need of being undone. There was little evidence, however, of anything moving *forward*. The fact that there was no visible progress toward progress suggested a temporality very different from the one imagined in the logic of sacropolitics and its associated state of redemption. Despite the commitment of central planners to bring to life a moribund social formation, and their determination to do away with the premodern attitudes and social structures that were standing in the way of progress, it proved far more difficult than they had anticipated to seize control of and direct the historical process.

Indeed, the visible evidence of government officials' own work on modernizing projects and plans conveyed a message that had little if anything in common with a narrative of advance. Implicit in their inability to move forward on modernization was a temporality in which time seemed suspended, unchanging. Rather than each project steadily advancing, and all projects combining to create the impression that they were part of something bigger, something grander, the perpetually unfinished nature of the government's many projects and plans undermined the impression that these projects were part of a larger, sacropolitical nation-building effort. Because these projects did not advance, they created the impression that they were a part of nothing, that they were leading nowhere. Indeed, the fact that a great many of these projects served no useful purpose suggested that modernization was a farce, a chimera, a dead end.

Ironically, the unfinished (and unfinishable) nature of state activity applied with special force and clarity to the government's two most important modernization initiatives—military conscription and highway construction. It is difficult to imagine projects that could have absorbed more in the way of time, energy, and resources, and that could have been more of a constant and inexplicable source of frustration to government officials. It is equally difficult to imagine projects that could illustrate with greater clarity the inability of government officials to move ahead with modernization.

But it was not just that the landscape of modernization—the end result of work on government projects—took on the appearance of something incomplete, something suspended in time. A similar temporality characterized official efforts to carry out the work on these projects. No matter what officials did, these projects never seemed to go anywhere. Furthermore, nothing that government officials did to rectify the situation seemed to make any difference. No matter what new strategy they employed, no matter what reform they undertook, the same, underlying problem remained. It was the inability to assemble an adequate workforce that undermined the success of official plans to improve the region. Indeed, the government's projects of improvement languished in what amounted to a state of perpetual liminality.

As one after another of their efforts foundered and failed, government officials became increasingly frustrated by the situation they faced. As they became more and more bewildered by their inability to move forward with modernization, they became less and less able to accept the idea that their problems were the result of ordinary causes—that they were the result of causes that made any sense. In these circumstances, it was not long before officials sought to account for their difficulties by invoking extraordinary causes—by invoking interference from "actors" whose behavior was said to be as irrational and inexplicable as their own inability to realize official projects and plans. The most important of these dangerous and irrational actors were political subversives (in particular, members of APRA), corrupt state functionaries, and naïve, childlike Indians.

But it was not only that officials attributed their inability to modernize the Chachapoyas region to interference from forces that were irrational, unethical, and intractable—forces that functionaries regarded as the very antithesis of the state and its sacropolitical schemes of improvement. As time passed, and their modernization schemes continued to founder, government officials attributed to these forces ever greater degrees of potency, irrationality, and intractability. In other words, the authorities attributed to these forces a kind of magical, or diabolical, agency. Only in this way, it seems, could government officials account for their failure to make any significant headway with the modernization process.

Conclusion

After 1930, the inability of government officials to mobilize the work-force they sought had two effects that have important implications for academic debates regarding what the state is, where it is located, what gives it power and potency, and on what basis one may know whether it is present or absent. First, officials' inability to conscript labor after 1930 made them question whether their regime was truly a state. Officials in Chachapoyas were especially preoccupied with this question because they found themselves unable to compel the population to provide labor services despite the presence of a police force, a judiciary, and a state bureaucracy, and despite the ongoing performance of political rituals and the generalized use of state symbolism.

The fact that the conventional trappings of rule were all present, while the ability to coercive or compel was absent, made the familiar organs of state seem like little more than an empty shell. It also convinced government officials that what they were accustomed to regarding as un-problematic signs of "state-ness" could not be taken at face value—that the existence of a police force, a judiciary, and so on, could not be assumed to indicate the presence of a real state. Indeed, government officials were bewildered by the inability of their regime to "be like a state" despite the presence of all the conventional trappings of rule. So puzzled were they that they produced an elaborate explanation to account for this apparent anomaly—one that attributed the dissipation of power and potency of their state to the concentration of power and potency in a competing (but imaginary) polity.

Although there was very little evidence to support such a view, government officials ultimately came to the conclusion that the integrity of their regime's state institutions had been deeply compromised by the activities of political subversives. The latter, it was believed, had surreptitiously filled the ranks of the police, the judiciary, the state bureaucracy, and so forth—a vantage point from which they had been able to undermine normal state activities. Although these subversives were posing as public servants, they were only feigning loyalty to the central government and were biding their time, waiting for the appropriate moment to strike. As a result, while the governing regime took on the appearance of a real state, officials concluded, appearances were not to be trusted. The state was indeed an empty shell, with little if anything of substance within.

The second effect that was produced by officials' ongoing struggles with conscription is related to the first. The steady deterioration of the state's capacity to mobilize a corvée labor force convinced government officials that something had to be interfering with their efforts. Only the most malevolent of forces, they believed, would seek to do so. Only the most potent and powerful of forces could have succeeded. That powerful and malevolent force, officials concluded, would have to be comparable in scale and complexity to the state whose activities were being thwarted. In other words, only something state-like would have been capable of interfering with the power of a state. Ultimately, government officials' inability to coerce or compel despite the presence of all the trappings of rule convinced them that the activities of their regime were being undermined by a subterranean counterstate.

The malevolence of this underground polity, government officials concluded, stemmed from the fact that it had been organized by the members of a radical political sect (APRA) that had committed itself to the violent overthrow of the existing order. The power and potency of the Aprista counterstate was harder to understand but appeared to stem from the deep fanaticism of party members—from the fact that they would stop at nothing to achieve their subversive ends. The Aprista counterstate, government officials surmised, was buried somewhere deeply underground and therefore could not be seen with the naked eye. The fact that this underground polity was malevolent, potent, and largely invisible meant that it represented a grave threat to the ruling regime.

Government officials had only the most limited and circumstantial of evidence to support their view that this underground state existed. They had even less evidence that this underground polity had the trappings of rule associated with conventional states. Even so, officials assumed that the only kind of polity that would be capable of thwarting their own designs would be a fully formed and complex affair—one that partook of all the signs of state-ness associated with conventional regimes. Indeed, officials ultimately came to believe that they saw glimpses of underground state-ness everywhere.

Furthermore, unlike the visible trappings of rule associated with their own state, government officials believed that the (imagined) signs of state-ness of which they caught glimpses pointed to the existence of a polity that was anything but an empty shell. To the contrary; officials regarded these as conclusive proof that the subversives had elaborated a subterranean polity that was filled with power and potency. They attributed to that polity all the capacities that their own state so obviously lacked. And they went to great lengths in what proved to be a futile attempt to eliminate their underground enemy.

These developments in Chachapoyas do indeed raise questions about what the state is, where it is located, who is in charge of it, what gives it power and potency, and what may be taken as evidence of its presence. During the 1930s and 1940s, what would conventionally be understood as a "real" state—one that confronted not a single violence-wielding competitor, and that had all the trappings of rule visible to everyone—was regarded as artificial and empty. What would conventionally be regarded as an imaginary state—which could not be seen and was not able to display any conventional state trappings—was regarded as malevolent, potent, and real.

In the next two chapters, I explore the dynamics of state failure with respect to modernization initiatives in the Chachapoyas region. I do so by focusing on the projects of the post-*oncenio* era that called for the largest number of conscripts: military conscription and highway construction. As we will see, these two initiatives alone called upon government officials to produce a pool of conscripts that was approximately *twice* the size of the actual population. The fact that this workforce was more imagined than real did not prevent government functionaries, however, from seeking to convince their superiors that they were doing everything they could to produce it. Nor did it prevent these functionaries from generating elaborate explanations concerning why they were unable to do so.

As I show, the central government's distorted vision of rural labor abundance combined with the realities of competition between government functionaries to disorder the state. In the process, what had formerly been "ordinary acts of administration" became the most tortuous, drawn out, and unsuccessful of affairs. As we will see, this applied in particular to the government's modernization schemes. The authorities found it impossible to carry out tasks that they associated with the normal operation of the state (in particular, processes related to conscription). They also found that it is impossible to identify the problems that prevented them from moving forward with the modernization process.

Because of the inevitable shortages of (imaginary) labor generated by the modernizing state apparatus, delusion and displacement became central to these projects. Even so, both delusion and displacement were

carefully concealed beneath a veneer of the norms of bureaucratic procedure and the language of the everyday. As I show in Chapter 8, however,
delusion and displacement were never far from the surface. As the authorities became increasingly perplexed by their inability to move ahead
with modernization, even minor disruptions of official projects and plans
could throw government officials into a panic—even when no effort was
being made to do so. In other words, it took little to pierce the armor of
the ordinary with which the state sought to protect itself, and to send the
authorities running to find some extraordinary explanation for why their
efforts to modernize were failing.

In these circumstances, the authorities found it increasingly difficult to carry out even the most mundane of administrative activities. They
found it less and less possible to embed the remarkable in the routine, as
the (anti-)rites of purification that absorbed so much of government activity failed to purge the state of what it was not allowed to be. Indeed, state
officials found it increasingly difficult to transform what were in reality the
violent, irrational, and delusional practices associated with modernization
into mundane, rational acts of administration. Keeping up the appearance
of the ordinary and the unremarkable became more and more challenging
in a context in which efforts at establishing routine routinely and systematically failed.

Part III

The Antiepistemology of the Everyday

6

The Sacropolitics of Military Conscription

Sr. Lieutenant, Chief Conscription Officer for the Province.

In response to the contents of your *oficio* No. 122, . . . I have sent
the most strict of orders to the Subprefects of the Provinces of Luya,
Bongará, Chachapoyas, and Rodriguez de Mendoza, and also to the
Chief of Police, that they are to capture all citizens who are obliged
to offer obligatory military service. As the Lieutenant knows, however,
the simple inhabitants of this department do not comprehend their
obligation to serve the Nation, and once the political authorities
[i.e., the district governors] advise the individuals [in question] that
they are to present themselves [for military service] they flee to the
montaña, where they hide themselves, because of which the political
and military authorities are unable to catch them, despite having made
every effort to do so, [circumstances that are] aggravated by the small
size of the police force and the enormous size of the Department.

   —Prefect, Department of Amazonas

Introduction

As noted throughout this volume, government efforts to modernize the Chachapoyas region involved efforts to represent the most violent,
delusional, and coercive of practices as ordinary, unremarkable acts of administration. The process by which the government sought to transform
the extraordinary into the ordinary—to systematically misapprehend and
misrepresent the social world—was an unusually subtle one. On the one

hand, officials had to purge the state of what it was not allowed to be. On the other, they sought to mobilize the population to make the nation what it should have been. I have suggested that a particular kind of overstatement was integral to this process—one based on what Yurchak (2003, 2006) has called a "hegemony of form." Particularly important was officials' obsessive adoption of a hypernormalized form of expression that made extensive use of a language of the normal, the routine, and the everyday. This discursive form created a disjuncture between the internal, self-referential world of government representation and the social realities that government communiques were intended to describe and engage.

In the process, official discourse represented the social world not "'as it was' but, rather, 'as it ought to [have been]'" (Boyer and Yurchak 2010, 205). Unlike the late socialist contexts explored by Yurchak, however, there was no acknowledgement of this disjuncture. Indeed, the process of purging upon which state formation depended relied crucially on the denial of any such disjuncture. Instead, government officials insisted on carrying on endlessly about the state and its social worlds in precisely the terms imagined in official discourse. In the process, the authorities did much to ensure that affect, imagination, and delusion were effaced from the entire domain of state activity. So broad and systematic was this self-representation, I have argued, that it is exceptionally difficult to see through it—to not mistake the veil of the ordinary and the everyday in which official activities shrouded themselves with the state itself.

Those who spoke in the name of the state thus employed a particular kind of overstatement as they went about the daily, mundane task of transforming the extraordinary into the ordinary, the remarkable into the routine. What is truly remarkable about the power of overstatement—about the state in its unremarkable guise—is how completely opaque it is. Based on what is contained in the documentary record, one would have almost no awareness of virtually any of the contradictions that so plagued government practice. One can see virtually *nothing* through the state's endless performance of the ordinary—other than a set of activities that are so routine, so regular, and so mundane that they are worthy of little more than being ignored.

The material presented in this chapter and the next is intended to illustrate the ways in which documentary practices act as (anti-)rites, which seek to purify the state of what it is not allowed to be. The chapters are also intended to illustrate the ways in which these (anti-)rites invert the ordinary and the extraordinary, and attribute to the forces of order an indispensable role in protecting the former from the latter. Something of the power of state documentary practices to effect this transformation, and to perform this inversion, is indicated by the following: during the middle decades of the twentieth century (1920–1956) successive governing regimes in Peru sought to force literally hundreds of thousands of subalterns out of their homes, and away from their fields, to work in difficult and dangerous conditions with little pay, to advance the sacropolitical cause of modernization. Throughout this entire violent and coercive episode, one would never know from the documentary record that there was anything even remotely unusual about what the authorities were seeking to accomplish. What is represented in official discourse as extraordinary—and therefore in need of explanation—is the fact that there are forces at work that seek to interfere with the state's conscription efforts. What is presented as ordinary is the projects and plans themselves.

The Sacropolitics of Military Conscription

It was in the context of the disordering, intrabureaucratic competition described in the previous chapter—in which shifting factions of the elite used state office to compete with one another for control of the (largely fictive) labor supply—that the central government sought to implement its new modernization projects. The government's sacropolitical efforts to modernize the Chachapoyas region in the decades after 1920 were truly mammoth in scale and included a great many different programs and projects. Despite their diversity, however, the vast majority of the government's numerous modernization initiatives had something important in common. Most relied for their successful completion on the ability to conscript the labor of the rural peasantry. As the number and range of these projects suggests, implicit in central plans to modernize the highlands was the assumption that there was a vast field of untapped peasant labor on hand—a "population," waiting to be mobilized, animated, brought to life for the good of the nation.

The degree to which this assumption was based on sacropolitical considerations—on a fantasy of abundance rather than on a sober, informed assessment of the characteristics of the regional population—is revealed by the following; not only did state officials never even enquire about how many people might be available to support their modernization schemes, they studiously ignored the information that existed about this topic.[1] The "population" that government officials and regional elites were so anxious to put to work, for the mutual benefit of all, was not a thing of fact but of fiction. It was conjured into being, bit by bit, from the imaginations of individual bureaucratic planners, each estimating the labor supply needed to realize the plans of his particular office. These individuals went so far as to quantify their fantasies about the labor supply—to express their desires in the form of that most neutral of media—numbers: "so many laborers were required for task A, so many additional laborers were needed for task B," etc. While no one office (with the exception of the military) made labor demands that were in excess of the population size, the cumulative effect of all demands exceeded the population many times over. Government officials were thus confronted with a major problem. They conjured and insisted on recruiting a labor supply that did not exist.

Having imagined into being a vast field of peasant labor, planners in each government office went on to insist that the fictive labor force they required was there—despite overwhelming evidence to the contrary. Indeed, the number of workers sought by government agencies was rarely if *ever* forthcoming. It seems never to have occurred to state officials, however, that the problem was with their own plans and projections. Instead, finding themselves perpetually unable to locate the (nonexistent) labor force they were so certain was there, government planners and project managers went on to demonize, pathologize, or to render otherwise problematic, specific elements of the population. These planners and managers also turned to the regulatory and coercive branches of government for assistance in dealing with these dangerous social elements. When even they were unable to procure this (fictive) labor supply, a crisis ensued.

I next show how this distorted vision of rural labor abundance combined with the intensive competition that obtained among elite families, and with the involuted nature of bureaucratic infighting, to disorder the state. I also analyze the ways that state functionaries represented and responded to this disorder. The obligation to employ the categories of liberal rule to characterize profoundly illiberal activities, I suggest, led government functionaries to produce official narratives filled with elisions, silences, and fabrications that masked key problems. The obligation to misrepresent both the problems officials faced as well as the solutions to those problems, I argue, shaped the official response to these problems in distinctive ways. It focused government efforts at surveillance and control on concerns that were as misdirected and illusory as was the state's fictive supply of labor.

To repeat, one of most striking features of the documentary record is the following: based on what is contained within it, one would never know that the forces of order were in pursuit of a largely fictive population. To the contrary; one would conclude that the problems that the government faced did indeed consist of the ordinary, mundane, practical problems of rounding up rural cultivators. One would never know, in other words, just how delusional official projects and plans were. Instead of seeming remarkable—of seeming violent, delusional, and coercive—these projects and plans appear to be entirely unremarkable. So much so is this the case that there is no reason to give them a second thought. It is in this sense that documentary practices acted as (anti-)rites, which sought to purify the state of what it was not allowed to be. It is in this same sense that these (anti-)rites inverted the ordinary and the extraordinary and attributed to the forces of order an indispensable role in protecting the former from the latter.

The Role of Military Conscription in Disordering the State Apparatus

As we saw in Chapter 4, during the regime of Augusto Leguía (1919–1930) the central government committed itself to the formation of a "New Nation" that would bring Peru directly into the modern age. On the one hand, establishing a New Nation meant breaking definitively with the antiquated, aristocratic practices of the past. On the other hand, it meant launching programs to reform the administrative apparatus, strengthen the armed forces, develop the country's infrastructure, and expand the market economy. In the process, the central government sought to make present what was absent—a truly national economy and society and a modern nation-state. Toward that end, Leguía's government introduced a whole series of sacropolitically inspired innovations in economic, social, and political life. A number of Leguía's programs were continued by subsequent regimes, if in modified form.

In terms of their impact on subaltern groups in highland regions like Chachapoyas, the most important of these reforms were those that sought to strengthen the armed forces and develop the infrastructure.[2] The success of these programs depended upon the ability of district-level functionaries (governors, mayors, and justices of the peace) to impose additional surveillance, to conscript additional labor, and confiscate additional wealth from a rural cultivating population already pushed to its limits. As a result, these programs brought out a number of the disordering contradictions in government administration that characterized the post-*casta* era. It is to the details of the government's attempts to reform military conscription, and to the conflicts engendered by these efforts, that we now turn.

The regime of Augusto Leguía, and those of subsequent national leaders, invested much in the way of resources and expertise in an effort to strengthen and modernize the armed forces. One essential component of government efforts to form a more modern military revolved around official attempts to create and enforce new procedures for conscripting men into the army. Although the Ministry of War had sought to implement these procedures in the Chachapoyas region during the *oncenio*, the ruling Pizarro-Rubio coalition had confounded all efforts on the part of the military to conscript from the large number of clients that the ruling *casta* maintained among the peasantry. As a result, it wasn't until after the fall of Leguía, and of the Pizarro-Rubio, that it became possible to implement the new procedures.[3]

Once the Pizarro-Rubio bloc had been driven from power (in August 1930), and the *casta* structure had unraveled, changes in conscription procedures were swift in coming. Within a year the Estado Mayor—the army General Staff—had made it clear that henceforth, the Department of Amazonas would be expected to actually fill the conscription quotas that already existed on paper. In theory, men of any social class were eligible to be inducted into the army, for a period of no less than two years. In practice, however, it was overwhelmingly the sons of rural cultivating families who were forced to suffer this fate.

These plans of the Peruvian military provide a useful point of departure for understanding the way that fantasy and sacropolitics informed the most mundane of everyday government activities in the Chachapoyas region—and how this in turn disordered the operation of the state. Nowhere were state fantasies about rural labor abundance more in evidence than within the armed forces. Nowhere was this more clearly reflected than in the military's use of that seemingly most neutral of media—numbers.

The official correspondence of the military was clear and unequivocal about the number of men who would be required to join the armed forces. Each year the army insisted on its right to conscript 425 men from each of the department's four provinces (see below). The military discovered, however, that it was extremely difficult to realize that goal. This was due in part to the large number of men being sought. Indeed, 425 men per province per year represented a significant strain on the labor supply, the degree of that strain depending on the population of the province. To focus on the figure of 425 men, however, is to vastly underestimate the impact of the military draft on rural society. At any given point in time the number of individuals the armed forces sought to induct into its ranks was far higher.

According to the law of military conscription, all able-bodied men were required to spend a minimum of two years as soldiers. In fact, however, absences were considerably longer. Informants report that it was rare for men to be gone for less than five years. Many men never returned at all. In other words, during any five-year period, the armed sources sought to draft approximately 2,125 men from each of the region's four provinces. Comparing the number of individuals the army assumed to be available with the number actually available, however, is nothing short of bewildering. For it reveals just how delusional the plans of the armed forces were. There were in fact fewer than 2,125 adult men in all but one of these four provinces, and barely that number in the remaining province (see below for details). In other words, as suggested by a standardized figure for all provinces regardless of population size, the military made its conscription calculations in complete ignorance of and disregard for the characteristics of the actual society in which it sought to intervene.

These seemingly cold, indifferent calculations on the part of the armed forces were actually informed by what might be thought of as the "heat of military passion"—a passion that was born of deep anxieties within the armed forces about what they regarded as the truly shameful state of the country's affairs. Since the late nineteenth century, the armed forces had regarded themselves as the only truly national force in a society that was profoundly corrupt and deeply divided by partisan interest. The military saw itself as the country's salvation because it and it alone could rise above the petty, self-interested political struggles that characterized civilian life to articulate and defend the common good and the national interest.[4] The armed forces could take on their unique nationalizing role, however, only if they were able to shape and mold a large number of raw recruits (especially the indigenous population) into highly disciplined soldiers who would understand and honor their obligation to serve the national interest. Recruitment was the first crucial stage in this process.[5]

The military thus made its calculations about conscription needs based on a fervent belief in its own unique ability to save the nation—and to do so by making present what was at the time so painfully absent—an impartial, apolitical state apparatus, and a truly national citizenry. The army had not the slightest regard for or even interest in the actual society from which it sought to conscript the disciplined, nationalized soldiers of the future. As a result, its calculations were completely out of touch with the realities of what the regional population could endure.

Indeed, were the plans of the armed forces to have been implemented, this one branch of government alone would have stripped the countryside of virtually its entire adult male population! The thousands upon thousands of fields that dotted the landscape, and that were the basis of peasant livelihoods, would have been empty, deserted. Agrarian production would have come to a standstill. The regional food supply would have disappeared. Despite the impossibility of conscripting the entire agrarian workforce, however, from this point onward the army's chief conscription officer in Chachapoyas put relentless pressure on the regulatory and coercive branches of government to do just that—to scour the countryside in search of all the would-be conscripts the army required. As a result, the government functionaries who were responsible for finding real people to fill the ranks of the military's "contingent of blood" (as the army referred to the unit in question) were faced with a perpetual and unavoidable deficit of future soldier/citizens.

During the period of *casta* control, peasant clients of the ruling elite faction often managed to avoid the draft by appealing to their political patrons, who would intercede on behalf of their clients by declaring them ineligible (or by leaving their names off of the draft registers; see Nugent 1997). With the end of the *oncenio* this was no longer possible. By the 1930s the *casta* structure had disintegrated, and had been replaced by shifting, short-term alliances of individuals that fought out a war of all against all within the state apparatus. In these new circumstances, there was no single, broad, unified coalition that could use its control over the government apparatus as a whole to shield its clients from conscription. Instead, each short-term, shifting elite alliance used the limited state offices available to it in an effort to meet its own conscription obligations. They used these same offices in an effort to ensure that other alliances were unable to meet theirs.

From this time onward, there were no *castas* on hand to interfere with the conscription process. As a result, conscription could proceed (among the peasantry!) on a more uniform basis. In the early 1930s, the army General Staff began to issue stern warnings about the new state of affairs. The General Staff advised departmental prefects to inform the district functionaries within their jurisdictions that they would no longer be allowed to exercise favoritism in selecting conscripts, as they had in the past. Furthermore, the authorities warned, functionaries who refused to abide by the new regulations would face dismissal as well as the possibility of trial by military tribunal:

Sr. Mayor of the Province of Chachapoyas.

The Sr. Director of Government, in circular No. 92, of the 6th of September, advises this office of the following:

"The office of the Sr. Minister of War has received continual complaints from the Territorial Service [from the army conscription officers stationed in each provincial and departmental capital, who were responsible for overseeing the military draft] concerning certain [district] functionaries who refuse to comply with the Law of Obligatory Military Service, and who behave in the most unscrupulous manner with respect to it. At the request of the Sr. Minister of War, the Ministry of Government issues the following decrees: (1) That every year, in the second half of December, the Prefectures will issue instructions to the Subprefects, and they to the Governors and Lieutenant Governors, to actively propagandize among the populations under their command, encouraging them to register for conscription; (2) That mayors [who were in charge of maintaining the registers of vital statistics] who are denounced for interfering with the registration process, or who extort funds from the inhabitants [in exchange for leaving their names off of the registration lists] will be removed from their posts, and will be ineligible ever to return; (3) That once the contingents [of conscripts] have been assembled, in whole or in part, in the provincial capitals, no political official may release any of the conscripts without the permission of the Chief Conscription Officer for the Province [the *Jefe de la Circunscripción Provincial*]; (4) That the Guardia Civil will participate in an active manner to ensure that everyone complies with all the provisions of the law. (ASC6, 3 de Octubre de 1933)

By means of communiqués such as these, the General Staff singled out "corruption" as a major cause of the army's inability to recruit the number of individuals the military required. The Ministry of Government also sought to ensure that district functionaries like the mayor would no longer be able to use the conscription process to enrich themselves. In order to prevent them from doing so, the Ministry of Government built in new safeguards that called for the direct involvement of government personnel like the Guardia Civil, who were not beholden to the region's elite families or to their clients in the countryside (like the mayor). The *guardias* were to impose surveillance over the entire conscription process. It was up to them to ensure that corrupt public servants like the mayor did not undermine the success of military recruitment. The decrees issued by the Ministry of Government were also designed to ensure that such corrupt functionaries would be purged from the ranks of the state.

From this point onward, in addition to monitoring the activities of the regional population, different branches of government also began to impose surveillance upon, and to represent a threat to, one another. Should the police conclude that functionaries like the mayor were not doing their utmost to make conscription a success, or that they were interfering with conscription efforts in any way, the consequences could be serious. For the *guardias* could denounce any of these functionaries to the military authorities, as a result of which a mayor, governor, or justice could find himself out of the job and unable ever to return. This was no idle threat. A number of government personnel who were denounced by the Guardia Civil were removed from their posts. Some were fined and a few were even jailed.[6]

But it was not just the police who were empowered to report upon the misdeeds of district functionaries like the mayor, who occupied the lowest rungs of the state bureaucracy. The language of the decrees issued by the Director of Government created the possibility for a more general structure of surveillance—one that extended well beyond the Guardia Civil. *Anyone*—including other district functionaries—could denounce his or her mayor for extortion or for tampering with the draft registration lists.[7] Furthermore, anyone (including mayors) could report that political officials—even those of high rank—were seeking to follow the time-honored practice of freeing conscripts after they had been assembled in a provincial capital. In other words, the decrees made it possible for government personnel in general to watch and to report upon one another's behavior. As we will see, because these personnel found themselves having to produce quantities of labor that did not exist, and because they were involved in a war of all against all, governors, mayors, *guardias*, justices, and other officials all had strong reasons to denounce one another to higher-ranking authorities.

The military's efforts to find corrupt functionaries who could be held accountable for the difficulties involved in military recruitment, however, were seriously misguided. Implicit in this culture of blame was the assumption that conscription had met with such limited success because of the greed of "unscrupulous" individuals—whose behavior had to be policed and whose misdeeds had to be punished. It is true that government functionaries were deeply implicated in the very behaviors that the Ministry of Government sought to prohibit. But the ministry's decrees ignored the reasons that governors, mayors, and justices found it impossible *not* to engage in these practices on an extensive scale. By focusing on self-interested individuals, the decrees ignored the existence of a complex set of regional interest groups who all depended on the labor of rural cultivators to maintain their well-being—and who struggled among themselves to control that labor. It was not unprincipled individuals but rather the dynamics of an entire social order that compromised the success of military conscription. Because of the role of governors, mayors, and justices in meeting elite demands for labor, it was inevitable that these personnel would seek to interfere with the draft.

Such a perspective on regional society, however, could not be broached in political discourse, for it suggested a more radical critique of the power structure than government officials were willing to entertain. Instead, it was necessary to displace the problem onto some alternative source—in this case, district mayors and other "unprincipled" government personnel. Displacing blame for the problems of the social order writ large onto the shoulders of corrupt individuals helped maintain the illusion that regional society as a whole was consensual and egalitarian—a vision that was wholly divorced from everyday social realities, but one that was in harmony with Peru's self-conception as a modern nation-state. But it was also to separate these individuals from the broader social networks of which they were a part—and whose interests they did little more than represent. It was also to render those networks invisible. District functionaries like the mayor were in the awkward position of having to mediate the efforts of the multiple groups who all sought to maintain access to peasant labor in the post *casta* period. It is to the needs of these groups, to the role of district functionaries in seeking to serve those needs, and to the role of displacement in misconstruing both problems and solutions that we now turn.

In addition to being responsible to the military authorities for helping to implement the draft, governors, mayors, and justices were also answerable to regional, aristocratic patrons —or were themselves those patrons. The military's efforts to conscript on a more systematic and uniform basis after 1930 threatened the interests of the traditional landed elite, who relied upon access to the labor and wealth of rural cultivating families to maintain their aristocratic lifestyles. At times, landed elites did not hesitate to engage in open defiance of the central government's new conscription procedures:[8]

Sr. Frigate Captain and Prefect of the Department of Amazonas.

As you will see from the present document, in compliance with your order of yesterday, and accompanied by the gendarme Francisco Poquima, I attempted to capture the individuals [residing in the hacienda "Rojas Cucho"] who have evaded their responsibility to provide obligatory military service: it was at one o'clock in the afternoon when we arrived at Rojas Cucho, the hacienda that is owned by Sr. Pedro Quiroz, and that has as its representative an individual named Cruz Sánchez Aliaga and a son [of the owner] who said he is called Julio Abel Quiroz; in the [illegible] of the hacienda we found that the peons we encountered were in an uproar about our visit . . . there were [also] indications that many other [peons] had hidden themselves, despite our efforts to conceal the purpose of our mission. . . . I proceeded to interview everyone that I could find, accompanied by the [hacienda] representative, and by don Julio Abel Quiroz, and after two hours I showed him the *oficio* that I had in my possession, which authorized me to seize all peons who had managed to evade the [conscription] law.

Despite having employed the most efficacious means of prudence and tact, [at this point] it became difficult to proceed, because by word and gesture the [hacienda's] representative instructed the peons to conceal themselves; and in the presence of J. A. Quiroz, Manuel Mendoza Huaman, Manuel Santillan Huaman, and other workers of Rojas Cucho, [the representative] Sánchez repeated what he had said to me earlier, that he had a direct order from his *patrón*, don Pedro Quiroz, that none of his workers were to be allowed to leave the hacienda, regardless of having been called by law [to serve in the army], and that before he [Sánchez] would allow [the peons] to be taken blood would run and cadavers would be left lying on the ground. (ASC38, 4 de Marzo de 1932)

When confronted with hacienda owners who refused to release their peons to serve in the army, the prefect would respond initially by instructing the governor of the district where the hacienda was located to try to resolve the problem. To the extent that the landed elite was prepared to offer armed resistance to government efforts to expropriate their labor force, however, governors were ill prepared to deal with such cases. As a result, they would ask for the assistance of the forces of order—resulting in con-frontations of the kind described in the example above. Rarely were these resolved in favor of the armed forces.

Indeed, resistance on the part of hacienda owners to surrendering their workers to serve in the army was ubiquitous throughout the region after 1930. Government officials recognized the limited degree to which they could successfully challenge the landed class over this issue, even with the assistance of the police:

Sr. Prefect of the Department.

On the 26th of the present month, the Departmental Headquarters [of the Territorial Service] received telegram No. 150 from the General Command, which says:

"Departmental Head. Chachapoyas. No. 150. [You are to] deploy [every] effort [in order to] comply [with the] orders issued [concerning the] draft [so as to] not repeat [the] problems [of the] previous year."

I have the honor of . . . asking that you take the measures necessary to en-sure that the gendarmes at your command are more active this year in capturing the conscripts called upon to serve in the contingent of blood, forcing—if it were at all possible—the landowners to deliver the conscripts that they have hidden within the boundaries of their estates. (ASC20, 27 de febrero de 1932)

As the foregoing suggests, the labor force conjured into being by government planners was imaginary in two senses. One of these concerned the size of that labor force. As the various offices that were involved in the modernization effort calculated the number of workers needed to com-plete their particular projects, they conjured a working population of fic-tive proportions. But there was a second sense in which the labor force that government officials sought to mobilize was imagined rather than real. As the difficulties of recruiting in haciendas show, much of the rural popula-tion that the General Staff insisted was available for conscription was in fact not available. Rather, a great many people were involved in relations of dependence that either precluded or rendered deeply problematic any and all efforts by the armed forces to intervene in their lives. Characterizing them as a "population" that was waiting to be put to work elsewhere ig-nored these relationships. It also remained silent about the circumstances that made it extremely unlikely that anything but a small portion would ever be available.

Indeed, as suggested by the documents quoted above, during the post-*casta* era the army's conscription officers were never able to overcome the resistance of the region's hacendados and their peons (for the stark contrast with the period preceding, see Chapter 4). As a result, the number of individuals who were actually available to be drafted was far less than even census materials would suggest. The realities of this situation, however, had no impact whatsoever on the number of men the army insisted were available for the draft. Rather, conscription officers continued to pressure the regulatory and coercive branches of government to deliver the same number of men as before. In other words, the conscription procedures of the armed forces proceeded in complete disregard of actual conditions on the ground.

But it wasn't just the traditional landed elite who put up fierce resistance to the draft. The rural peasantry also did everything in their power to avoid losing family members to the army. It is not difficult to understand why. The prolonged absence of men who were forced into the military was extremely disruptive (emotionally, economically, socially, and politically) to the individuals themselves, and to the families and communities from which they were forced to absent themselves. During any five-year period the military sought a total of 8,500 from the department as a whole to serve as soldiers.[9]

It is instructive to compare the number of peasant men sought by the military with the number of rural households that could provide the armed forces with the conscripts they desired. According to the national census of 1940, there were 3,310 rural households in the province of Chachapoyas, 1,376 in the province of Bongará, 5,160 in the province of Luya, and 1,583 in the province of Rodriguez de Mendoza (MHC 1942, 5–6). These figures suggest that in the province of Chachapoyas, the demands of the military for conscripts meant that, on average, every household in the province was expected to sacrifice two thirds of one of its productive members. In the province of Rodriquez de Mendoza the situation was worse. Here, on average, each household was expected to give up 1.3 members. In the province of Bongará the demands of the military were heavier still; each household was expected to give up 1.5 members! Only in the largest and most densely settled province, Luya, did the demands of the military average out to less than one half of a person per household (0.41 people).[10]

But these figures significantly underrepresent the hardships imposed on rural cultivating families by the new procedures regarding military conscription. For the individuals sought by the armed forces—adult males—played a crucial role in the reproduction of agrarian households. According to the national census of 1940, there were 2,021 adult men in the province of Chachapoyas, 1,441 in the province of Bongará, 4,980 in the province of Luya, and 1,415 in the province of Rodriguez de Mendoza (MHC 1942, 9–10).[11] The fact that the military sought 2,115 men from each province meant that in three of the four provinces of Amazonas the new conscription procedures of the armed forces threatened to deprive rural society of its entire adult male workforce! Only in the province of Luya were there more adult men than the number sought by the military. Here, the armed forces' conscription quotas threatened to deprive peasant society of almost half of the adult male labor force.[12]

But even these figures significantly understate the pressures that the Office of Military Conscription placed on the rural cultivating population, and the delusions under which this branch of government labored. For those who were drafted into the armed forces were required to serve only once. This meant that, regardless of the number of men who returned from serving in the military, none could legally be expected to serve again. They were permanently lost to the military as a potential source of recruits. Thus, every five years there were 2,125 fewer men to conscript in every province than there had been previously. Furthermore, the number of adolescent boys who came of age during any five-year period was far less than the number that each province was expected to provide. As a result, not only was the military faced with a deficit of future solder/citizens. It was also faced with a deficit that grew steadily through time. But this fact did alter the expectations of the armed forces. They continued to insist on 2,125 men per province over a five-year period, without fail.

The above discussion, however, does not fully capture the degree to which the activities of the military were informed by delusional views of the rural populace—the degree to which conscription officers viewed that world as it should have been rather than as it was (Yurchak 2003, 2006). According to the law of military conscription, it was only young men (age 18–25) who were subject to the draft. In practice, the armed forces treated Indian/peasant men of any age as potential draftees. The number of individuals who were legally liable to serve in the army, however, was only a small proportion of all adult men. According to the census of 1940, in the province of Chachapoyas there were 932 young men of draftable age (as opposed to the 2,125 the military sought). The province of Bongará had 665, and Rodriguez de Mendoza had 487. Luya had the largest number (1,721), but even here there were fewer individuals than the number imagined and pursued with such zeal.[13]

The Everyday Contradictions of Military Conscription

Because the rural population regarded military service with such horror, it was exceptionally difficult to find the number of conscripts desired by the military. It was up to the governors of the rural districts, working in conjunction with the mayors, the justices, and the Guardia Civil, to do so. Faced with a recalcitrant population that was not adequate in size to sustain such a major assault on its productive labor supply, and with mayors and justices who had no reason to cooperate with them, it was inevitable that these district governors would fail in their efforts to find the number of conscripts they sought. The archives are literally overflowing with documents attesting to the difficulties governors encountered in seeking to find a sufficient number of draftees.

Some of the difficulties that governors experienced in attempting to fill the draft quotas for their respective districts stemmed from the procedures they were compelled to follow by the chief conscription officers who oversaw the recruitment process. Under the new regulations, in the second half of December of each year, prefects were to advise the subprefects, and they were to instruct the governors to encourage the inhabitants of their districts to register for the draft. The prefects and subprefects were always careful to do so. In the *oficio* with which this chapter begins, the prefect sought to explain to the chief conscription officer how existing rules and procedures contributed to the difficulties he experienced in seeking to conscript the population. Such complications, however, were of limited interest to the military authorities. According to the procedures they had established, every year district governors were under strict orders to have a designated number of conscripts ready to be picked up by the Guardia Civil at a prearranged date in the capital of the district. Every year the governors were compelled to write to the prefect asking for additional time, explaining that they had been unable to find the number of conscripts required. Cognizant of the difficulties involved, both the prefect and the army's conscription officers who were in charge of recruitment generally acceded to the governors' requests for extensions. Even then, however, governors were unable to comply with the orders of their superiors.

As time dragged on and the conscripts were not forthcoming, the conscription officers who were responsible for assembling the *contingente de sangre* for each province would complain to their commanding officers.

Drawing upon a culture of blame, they would assert that the department's political officials—not only the governors, justices, and mayors, but also the subprefects and even the prefect—were not cooperating with the conscription efforts as fully as they should. One of the high-ranking military officers who was in charge of conscription for a group of provinces (the territorial commander) would then write to the prefect:

Sr. Lieutenant, Chief of Police.

    The Sr. Lieutenant, Chief Conscription Officer of the Province, in an *oficio* from yesterday, advises me of the following:

"Today I have received the [following] radio communication from the Sr. Captain and Territorial Commander [of Conscription]: Provincial Chiefs [of] Moyobamba, Tarapoto, Saposoa, Chachapoyas, Jumbilla, Lámud. Circular No. 228. "[You are] guilty [of] failure [to] comply [with the] remission [of the army's] contingents [of blood] [by the] dates [previously] indicated. [Your failure] suggests little interest [on your part in] complying [with the] orders [of this] office. Stop. [You must] incite [greater] fervor [on the part of the] political authorities [and must also] make clear [to them that continued] negligence [on their part will] result [in them being] placed [at the] disposition [of] military justice for punishment. Stop. [This] Command [will not] tolerate excuses [of] any type and [will] insist [upon] strict compliance [with the] orders [already] imparted even [if] failure [to do so] results [in] prison [sentences] for [those] responsible." (ASC6, 25 Noviembre 1933)

    Warnings such as these had ripple effects throughout much of the state apparatus. Threatened as they were with possible jail time for their failure to produce the desired number of conscripts, governors and lieutenant governors were compelled to step up their efforts to find men who could be drafted—even if it meant ignoring the provisions of the law concerning who was obligated to serve. Governors and their lieutenants were particularly prone to ignore the age requirements of draftees—to capture men who were too old as well as boys who were too young—or to pressure men who had already served to serve again.

    But it wasn't just these functionaries who came under increasing pressure from the military authorities. Although the chief conscription officer for the Province of Chachapoyas sent the message from the territorial commander quoted above to the prefect, the prefect sent it on to the chief of police. He did so because the police were equally responsible for procuring the number of conscripts desired by the military authorities and were equally liable for punishment if they failed to do so. As we have seen, however, the Guardia Civil had also been empowered by the army General Staff to denounce district personnel like the mayor or governor if they were not lending their full support to the conscription process. The police did not hesitate to do so. Indeed, denunciations of this kind became commonplace. To take but one example:

Seniors Governor and Lieutenant Governor of Huancas.

The Commander of the Guardia Civil . . . informs this office that despite repeated requests for assistance . . . you refuse to cooperate with police efforts to capture the men who seek to evade their Obligatory Military Service. I order you to provide all assistance [possible] to the pair of *guardias* sent to [Huancas] to capture these [men]. Failure to comply will result in you being removed from your positions and placed before a military tribunal. (ASC7, de Febrero de 1935)

Functionaries who had been denounced by the police, and who still refused (or were unable) to comply with the orders of the military authorities, could find themselves dismissed:

Sr. Prefect of the Department.

TOPIC: Request for a change of Governors.

I have the honor of . . . placing before your consideration the following:

Article 112 of Law 1569 states the responsibilities of [political] authorities who fail to offer their assistance to the Chief Conscription Officer of the Province when he is seeking to carry out his duties.

The lack of culture of the inhabitants of this zone [Rodriguez de Mendoza] . . . is a very negative factor, which interferes with the regular functioning of Public Administration, which can be reduced or neutralized by drawing upon the experience and moral value of qualified individuals.

In that the Governors of the districts of Huambo and Santa Rosa refuse to assist this Office in its attempts to capture the men who are obliged to provide Obligatory Military Service, despite having been asked repeated times, and despite having been denounced [for lack of cooperation] by the Guardia Civil [*la fuerza pública*], I ask that you have the aforementioned governors replaced, and I attach a slate of [alternative] candidates. (ASC28, 4 de Mayo de 1938)

As the police took to denouncing the district authorities for their failure to assist with the government's conscription efforts, and personnel like the governor and lieutenant governor found themselves reprimanded and threatened by their superiors, relations between district functionaries and the Guardia Civil rapidly deteriorated. Governors, mayors, and justices would often respond to the new environment of danger in which they were forced to operate by employing passive resistance—as in the example cited immediately above, which culminated in threats from the prefect. But the response of district functionaries was not entirely passive. Faced with the prospect of being denounced by the police, district personnel took to making denunciations of their own. They took to protesting the heavy-handed and abusive behavior of the police who came to their districts in search of conscripts. Some of these denunciations focused on the *guardias'* mistreatment of the general populace:

Sr. Lieutenant, Head of the Guardia Civil.

The Mayor of the Province of Luya informs this office that . . . district mayors [in his jurisdiction] report that the *guardias* who are on commission in Ocumal and neighboring Districts to capture conscripts [to serve in] the *contingente de sangre* are forcing the inhabitants to surrender their chickens and ducks. . . . Please take whatever steps you consider most efficacious to ensure that these abuses come to an immediate end. (ASC34, 17 de Marzo de 1935)

Other denunciations dwelled upon the tendency of the police to usurp the official functions of the district functionaries, or to disregard their authority altogether.[14]

Sr. Lieutenant, Head of the Guardia Civil.

My office has received a telegram from the Governor of Leymebamba that says the following:

"I communicate to you abuses [committed by] Guardia Duenas [who is] on commission [with the] Territorial Service [i.e., on commission to conscript men into the army], [who has shown] contempt [for] my authority, [has] threatened to take me prisoner, [has] jailed various underaged youth [who he intends to] conscript [and has] broken into [the] homes [of the] elderly [for the same purpose]. I request [that you] provide assistance [so that these] abuses [are brought to an] end."

Please take whatever measures you consider most appropriate to ensure that these abuses do not continue. (ASC34, Oficio # 254, 29 de Junio de 1935)

For the most part, the police and district personnel limited their conflicts to the realm of official discourse, each denouncing the other to his superiors. At times, however, as shown in the *oficio* quoted above, the tensions between the police and district personnel threatened to turn violent. But it wasn't only the Guardia Civil who could become physically abusive:

Sr. Lieutenant, Sector Head.

I have received your *oficio* no. 122 . . . which describes the attacks on the police who were on commission in the Province of Rodriguez de Mendoza to capture
men . . . obliged to serve in the contingent of blood. I have ordered the police post in
Mendoza to arrest the governor of Limabamba, Benigno Torres, and Atanasio López,
who perpetrated the attacks . . . and who swore that they would not allow the *guardias*
to complete their mission. (ASC6, 17 de Agosto de 1933)

This behavior speaks to the highly conflictual nature of the relations between the police and district functionaries.

As the military authorities increased their pressure on political officials and the forces of order, the police became a real threat to district
functionaries. The latter, however, were unable to name the true source of
their difficulties. These were threefold. The first was the fact that they were
expected to provide labor to multiple elite patrons at the same time. The
second was the fact that the labor in question had to be coerced from the
peasantry, at the point of a bayonet. The third was the fact that the labor
force that district functionaries were being asked to conscript was largely a
figment of the imaginations of central planners.

In an effort to protect themselves from the accusations of other functionaries, and from the Guardia Civil, governors and mayors (and secondarily, justices) became more guarded about their actual activities. In order
to protect themselves from blame by their superiors, district functionaries
became ever more creative in producing explanations that would displace
the problem on to some alternative source—one that could be named in
political discourse. The four most common objects of displacement were
the following: (1) the region's torrential rains, which washed out trails and
roads, making it impossible to travel through the districts to round up
young men (invoking the rains was a short-term delaying tactic); (2) the
corrupt behavior of other district functionaries, who were said to be ex-
torting wealth from the rural populace, or to be providing members of the
old elite with labor (in exchange for money); (3) the inability of the Indian
peasant population to understand the importance of military service as
a key nation-building activity—a failing that caused them to flee to the
montaña when confronted with the obligation to serve; and (4) the Party
of the People, whose subversives encouraged the peasantry to ignore their
obligations as citizens to provide labor and wealth to support government
projects.

All of these explanations reflect the aforementioned process of displacement. They were intended to shift attention away from the actual sources of the difficulties district functionaries confronted with respect to conscription, and toward alternative sources, which could be broached in political discourse. Explanations such as these had a huge advantage for district functionaries, not least because they focused attention on forces that were outside their control. Some—in particular the weather—were outside the ability of anyone to control. Others—the existence of unscrupulous government personnel who were involved in extortion, or in illegal labor trafficking—played upon preexisting fears of the military authorities. Still other explanations—the inability of the Indian peasantry to comprehend the importance of nation building—reinforced racial prejudices about the rural population. None of these explanations, however, dealt with the actual reasons that there were such enormous problems with conscription. As a result, the government was left chasing phantoms.

Asserting that government functionaries were unable to procure labor because of interference from these sources did important cultural and political work, for it played a crucial role in constructing the state as bounded, autonomous, and legitimate. Attributing the problems of the modernization effort to phantom forces obscured the preponderant role of state activities in creating the very problems that government functionaries had to contend with on a daily basis. It also displaced responsibility for these problems onto external sources, which were said to threaten the completion of important state tasks.

In other words, what was represented as remarkable—as being in need of careful observation and amelioration—were the efforts of dangerous, irrational, and unethical others to interfere with state projects and plans. What was implicitly represented as unremarkable—as not being worthy of note—were the projects and plans themselves. That this construction inverted what was remarkable and what was routine is perhaps obvious. What may be less so is the fact that it also constructed the very idea of the routine operation of the state. Indeed, this inversion of the routine and the remarkable positioned those who represented the state as those who were best suited to monitor the activities of a range of dangerous others. This same inversion positioned these officials as those best able to protect the modernization process from those who threatened it. This same inversion positioned government officials as those best able to safeguard the normal, everyday operation of the state. Thus did official discourse help construct the image of an autonomous and legitimate state that was beleaguered by its enemies.

District personnel succeeded to a considerable degree in producing explanations that displaced the difficulties they faced in organizing military conscription from their actual causes to phantom sources. Even so, as the documents quoted above reveal, military officials questioned the degree to which district functionaries were truly committed to the cause of conscription and accused them of collusion in helping men of draft age avoid their obligatory service. The military was not far from wrong. It is not difficult to understand why these functionaries might have been inclined to help potential conscripts avoid military service (in exchange for a fee!). To the extent that governors, justices, and mayors cooperated with the military authorities, they were undermining their own ability to comply with other important duties and obligations that came along with their positions—all of which required access to a large labor force.

Some of these obligations were customary and extralegal. In addition to being in government service, district personnel had obligations to range of elite patrons. Even though the *castas* of old were no longer operational after 1930 and the alliances of the post-*casta* era were fleeting and ephemeral, access to district-level political office still depended on having political connections. As a result, governors, mayors, and justices were still beholden to members of the elite, who continued to look to these government personnel to provide labor that was essential to the success of elite enterprises. Indeed, because the position of the old elite families was rapidly deteriorating, and because they were desperate to retain whatever they could of their aristocratic status, they put ever-increasing pressure on district functionaries to provide them with labor.

In addition to these customary, extralegal obligations, governors, mayors, and justices also had entirely legal administrative duties to perform that further compromised their interest in capturing young men to serve in the army. Among the most important of these responsibilities was to maintain the infrastructure of the districts that had been entrusted to them. This was no small task. Because of the region's heavy rains and exceptionally rugged terrain, it took a sizeable labor force to maintain Amazonas's roads, trails, and bridges, its schoolhouses, churches, and public buildings. Governors and mayors were expected to call out the district population to see to these duties on a regular, ongoing basis.[15] Failure to do so meant that they were answerable to their superiors in the govern-ment hierarchy (in particular, the provincial mayor, the subprefect, and the prefect).

As changes in conscription procedures put such heavy strain on the rural labor supply, governors and mayors (and secondarily, justices and priests) found it necessary to compete for control of this labor force. In an effort to prevail in this competition, district functionaries began denounc-ing one another to their superiors, each arguing that his counterparts were interfering with his ability to carry out his duties. At times, mayors would denounce governors:[16]

Sr. Governor of Quinjalca.

This office has been informed by the mayor of your district that the inhabitants of [Quinjalca], at the initiative of the Municipal Council, are involved in the construc-tion of new School for boys, and that you are not offering your full support to this project, which is one of general interest to the Nation. . . . I therefore order you to exhort all citizens within your jurisdiction, without exception, to collaborate with the Municipal Council in this project, which is to the collective good of all the children [of Quinjalca]. . . . I also instruct you to provide this office with a written report every two weeks [explaining] what steps you have taken [in this regard]. Should you fail to comply with [these orders] you will be at risk of losing your position. (ASC5, 9 de Noviembre de 1934)

At other times, governors would denounce mayors:

Sr. Mayor of Soloco.

The Governor of your District has sent an *oficio* to this Prefecture explaining that you excuse many inhabitants from contributing [their labor] to the diverse Public Works projects that have been initiated [in Soloco] while other citizens collaborate fully, demon-strating their patriotism and their sincere desire to ensure the progress of [their] District.

With respect to projects of collective interest, which must be based on the vol-untary [*sic*!] effort of all the citizens of Soloco, this lack of consistency cannot be tolerated, and . . . therefore I direct you to exhort everyone, without exception, to participate in these [public works] projects, [by] persuading them that the projects are of general interest. . . . This office will not accept excuses or delays of any kind . . . and will hold you responsible [should they occur]. (ASC34, 13 de Noviembre de 1935)

What is significant about this competition between governors and mayors for control of the district labor supply is the form that it took. That form was denunciation. For competition by means of denunciation created a climate of mutual suspicion and distrust among the government functionaries who were responsible for administering the same district.[17]

Because of the necessity of describing all government activity in terms of the precepts of popular sovereignty (see, for example, the document quoted immediately above), neither district functionaries nor higher-ranking government officials could acknowledge either of the two main problems that they confronted in seeking to implement their various modernization projects. First, they could not acknowledge that their own efforts were highly coercive in nature—that they violated the most basic rights guaranteed to all citizens by the Constitution. At times, the need to deny the coercive dimension of state activity, and to frame the government's entire modernization effort in the language of popular sovereignty, produced communiqués that were nothing short of absurd. Thus, even as they struggled to impose massive programs of forced labor on Peru's most vulnerable citizens, officials like the prefect would commonly invoke the constitution in criticizing functionaries who sought to use force to compel people to do their bidding:

Sr. Governor of Chiliquin.

The citizens of your district have complained on numerous occasions to this office that you force them to perform labors against their will, for your own personal benefit, and without offering to pay them. . . .

You will remember that article 55 of the Constitution states [the following]:

ARTICLE 55.—No one may be forced to work for another without their free consent, and without being offered the suitable remuneration. (ASC5, 10 de Noviembre de 1934)

Second, district functionaries who were pressed to explain their failure to carry out the orders of their superiors could not name the other main source of their difficulties. This was the fact that they were obliged to provide labor to multiple elite patrons at the same time, who had collectively imagined into being a labor force of fictive proportions. Instead, functionaries would invoke the same phantoms (corrupt functionaries, naïve Indians, and subversive Apristas), and would employ the same strategy of displacement, in their effort to explain away their inability to do what could not be done.

In short, because of their many competing obligations regarding labor, district functionaries were very reluctant to allow the military authorities to make off with the entire adult male workforce. Men who entered the military posed especially serious problems for these government personnel because conscripts were "lost" to them for years at a time—often permanently. To the extent that governors, mayors, and justices did cooperate with the Territorial Service, they undermined their own ability to comply with other elite demands—both licit and illicit. This in turn left them vulnerable to criticism, punishment, and at times even legal action.

The only way that district personnel could manage these conflicting demands from multiple patrons was to honor none in their entirety, but to respond to all in part. At the same time, governors, mayors, and justices would engage in displacement in an effort to explain away their inability to comply fully with the commands of their superiors. Partially effective though this strategy was, the combination of partial compliance with displacement had a powerful disordering effect on the operation of the state apparatus. On the one hand, it became increasingly difficult for district personnel to work together in a unified manner toward any collective goal, as they had during the *casta* period. Instead, as each became the target of the recriminations of others, district personnel came to regard one another as sources of potential danger.

On the other hand, governors, mayors, and justices found it equally difficult to work in a collaborative manner with their superiors in government. Because district personnel were being asked to implement programs that could not be implemented, and because their superiors were responsible for holding them accountable for their failure to do so, governors, mayors, and justices were also compelled to regard their superiors as a threat. As we have seen, they sought to manage that threat by engaging in displacement. Even so, many district functionaries were relieved of their duties for failure to comply with the orders of higher-ranking government officials. Some were fined. A few were even forced to spend time in prison.[18]

There were thus limits to the degree to which partial compliance combined with displacement was an effective strategy of threat management. Indeed, there were times when the multiple pressures to which governors, mayors, and justices were subject became intolerable. Despite the threat of punishment, these district personnel would at times simply refuse, en masse, to comply with the orders of their superiors. The effect on the operation of the state could be crippling:

Sr. Lieutenant, Chief of the [Guardia Civil].

The Sr. Comandante of the Fifth Territorial Military Headquarters, in telegram No. 349 of the 8th of this month, informs me of the following: "[The] Chief [Conscription Officer for the Province of] Luya . . . requests [that you] provide him with *guardias* [in order to] assist the [political] authorities [of the] districts [of] his Province, [who are] unable [to] capture conscripts [for the army]. [The] authorities [say that they would] prefer to resign rather than [have to] capture [the] conscripts [themselves]. . . ." (ASC5, 12 de Junio de 1935)

In other words, high-ranking government officials responded to the disorder they themselves had provoked with their massive program of forced labor by displacing responsibility for that disorder onto the shoulders of an imaginary construct—"corrupt, unscrupulous functionaries"— whose behavior government officials then sought to police. In the process, government officials made distinctions that were at once arbitrary but nonetheless crucial to the reproduction of the state. The reason that there was a continual labor shortage, however, had nothing to do with the criminal inclinations of individual public servants. Although the notion that there was a clear distinction to be made between selfless and selfish government functionaries helped mark the boundaries of an imagined legitimate state and initiated a procedure for purging that state of what ailed it, this distinction was entirely fanciful. As we have seen, the shortage of labor was a direct by-product of the assumptions and actions of *all* state offices and all government workers. In their zeal to carry out modernization schemes, they had collectively imagined into being a labor force of fictive proportions. And they had then become distraught over their inability to locate the labor supply they had dreamed into existence.

While the need to police the potentially corrupt behavior of public servants appeared to reference an actual problem, it actually created a false one. It converted the problem of labor scarcity—which was a function of state fantasy—into an issue of individual morality. It also masked the circumstances that made it inevitable that all functionaries would be compelled to "betray the public trust" on an ongoing basis. Government policy nonetheless singled out corruption and unscrupulous functionaries as issues of major concern—as being one of several forces that threatened to undermine the entire sacropolitical modernization effort. As a result, the government became deeply invested in attempts to monitor and control unacceptable behavior on the part of its own public servants. Those who refused to behave honestly were said to represent a major threat to the success of government plans and projects. In reality, however, the entire problem of corrupt individuals was largely a phantom concern and had little to do with the problems the government faced.

Conclusion

In the preceding pages, we have reviewed correspondence between the government officials who were involved in conscripting labor for the armed forces. There was a kind of annual cycle to these efforts to draft rural cultivators into the armed forces. The cycle began with official requests for military conscripts, which were forward to district-level functionaries by the departmental prefect. The cycle continued through a series of episodes in which district-level functionaries asked for extensions in order to comply with the orders of their superiors, explaining that any of a series of factors were interfering with their ability to deliver conscripts in the numbers demanded. These factors included the region's torrential rains and the naïveté and ignorance of the Indian peasantry. They included as well corruption on the part of government officials. As we will see in detail in Chapter 8, these factors also included interference from political subversives.

The annual cycle of efforts to conscript the rural peasantry into the military concluded with the failure of government functionaries to produce the number of conscripts demanded by higher-ranking officials. Throughout this entire process, which repeated itself from one year to the next, the problems that the government faced seemed to consist of the ordinary, mundane, practical problems of rounding up rural cultivators. Indeed, what is so striking about the documentary record is the following: on the basis of what is contained within it, one would never know that the authorities were in pursuit of a largely imaginary pool of recruits. One would never know, in other words, just how delusional official projects and plans were. Instead of seeming remarkable—as violent, delusional, and coercive—these projects and plans seemed entirely ordinary and mundane. So much so is this the case that there is no reason to give them a second thought. It is in this sense that documentary practices acted as (anti-)rites, which sought to purify the state of what it was not allowed to be. It is in this same sense that these (anti-)rites inverted the ordinary and the extraordinary and attributed to the forces of order an indispensable role in protecting the former from the latter.

The challenges that district functionaries faced in seeking to find adequate numbers of men to serve in the army were multiple. They were not limited to the resistance they encountered from the representatives of traditional landed power, who were seeking to maintain customary, extralegal means of accessing labor. Nor did the difficulties they confronted stem only from the fact that they were representatives of the central government, and thus were obliged to maintain the means of transit (bridges, trails, etc.) of their respective districts. Nor were their problems exclusively a result of the peasantry's resistance to the draft. While these factors contributed in important ways to the dilemmas that governors, mayors, and justices faced in seeking to comply with the orders of the military authorities, additional factors further contributed to the difficulty of filling the new draft quotas. Changes in conscription practices were not the only reform introduced in the Chachapoyas region during the post-*casta* period. After 1930 successive central regimes sought to implement a range of other sacropolitical modernization projects in the highlands of Amazonas. In addition to the government's attempts to regularize military service, the most important of these were the programs that sought to develop the region's infrastructure. Government efforts to implement these programs acted to further disorder the operation of the state. It is to a consideration of these processes that we turn in the next chapter.

7

The Sacropolitics of Labor Conscription

Sr. Prefect of the Department of Amazonas.
    I have the honor of bringing to the attention of your . . .
office . . . the [fact] that the Subprefect of Chachapoyas, Nestor
Alvaro Santillan, promised to have the obreros for the Districts of his
Province appear for work on the [Grand] Chachapoyas-[Pimentel]
Highway during the first half of March. Not a single [obrero] has yet to
appear . . . because of which work on the project . . . has come . . . to
a standstill. . . . . I ask for your assistance, Sr. Prefect, in correcting this
problem. . . . .
    —Chief Engineer, Department of Amazonas

AS WE SAW IN THE PREVIOUS CHAPTER, the plans of the armed forces to conscript the regional population were in many ways delusional. These plans were informed by interests and aims that were sacropolitical in nature—by the military's unwavering faith in its unique ability to save the nation. The armed forces sought to do so by creating something that it believed did not exist—a truly national citizenry. The armed forces were intent upon mobilizing and animating a population that was largely inert, stuck as it was in premodern social structures and value systems. The military, however, was only one of many branches of state that looked to the countryside to provide the labor necessary to redeem the nation. Each additional government office that did so further inflated the imaginary labor supply, deepened the real labor deficit, and called forth phantoms to explain the failure of its projects and plans.

A case in point is the Office of Highways, which was motivated by sacropolitical concerns that had much in common with those of the military. The Office of Highways was responsible for the construction of the Chachapoyas-Cajamarca-Bagua Highway (formerly, the Grand Chachapoyas-Pimentel Highway). This highway was part of the extensive network of roads, bridges and airfields that figured so prominently in the state of redemption that the central government had declared. Indeed, the highway was an integral part of the government's plans to overcome the backward, feudal state of the Peruvian highlands—by doing away with the sierra's premodern attitudes and institutions. In the process, government officials sought to bring to life a moribund, stagnant social formation—one whose dead weight represented a serious obstacle to the progress of the nation.

As is true of a great many sacropolitical contexts, notions of excess—of going beyond existing limits—played a central role in official assertions about the right to rule. This is reflected in the assumptions made by government officials about the population they sought to animate. Officials assumed that there was a vast field of idle peasant labor on hand that was simply waiting to be put to work for the good of the nation. As was the case with the military's plans, once again it is the numbers that tell the story.

By regional standards, the Chachapoyas-Cajamarca-Bagua Highway was a mammoth undertaking. Indeed, in terms of its impact on the regional population, this modernization project overshadowed all the rest. During the *oncenio* of Augusto Leguía (1919–1930), plans had been drawn up to build an important new highway through the department of Amazonas that would be suitable for motor vehicles. To the west, the highway was to link Chachapoyas to the city of Cajamarca, which was already fully connected by road to centers of international export production on the coast, and to the national capital (Deere 1990; Taylor 1986). To the east (and north), the highway was to connect Chachapoyas with the fertile zone of Bagua. Still a frontier region in the 1920s, Bagua was seen as having great potential for large-scale commercial agriculture and livestock production.

Although the section of the highway between Chachapoyas and Cajamarca covered a relatively short linear distance (about 75 kilometers), it traversed exceptionally rugged terrain. From the city of Chachapoyas (at 2,334 meters above sea level [ASL]) it dropped precipitously, over 1,500 meters, into the malaria-ridden valley of the tempestuous Utcubamba River (at less than 1,000 meters ASL), only to rise gradually to the crest of a frigid cordillera (at 3,500 meters ASL) located approximately 60 kilometers to the south, near the village of Leimebamba (see Map 1). From there the highway route rose somewhat before plunging almost 3,000 meters to the floor of the Marañon River canyon (at about 850 meters ASL), only to cross the river and rise up again rapidly, this time over 2,000 meters, on the other side (to 3,060 meters ASL).

Work on the Chachapoyas-Cajamarca-Bagua Highway had begun in the late 1920s, during the period of *casta* dominance, as part of president Augusto Leguía's extensive road construction program. Little real progress, however, had been made. In fact, the Leguía government had made very large sums available for the highway, but most of these monies had disappeared into the pockets of the leaders of the Pizarro-Rubio power bloc. Indeed, these and other irregularities were the cause of considerable scandal and an extensive, official investigation after Leguía and his local allies were driven from power in August 1930 (Nugent 1997).

In the early 1930s work on the highway began anew, under transformed conditions of political rule. The Ministry of Development's Office of Highways (the Ministerio de Fomento's Oficina de Caminos) was in charge of building the highway, but the office had little in the way of machinery with which to carry out such an imposing project. At the same time, government planners could not help but notice the large numbers of Indian peasants living in the immediate vicinity of the proposed roadway—people who were regarded as idle or underemployed for much of the year. Planners in the Oficina de Caminos were quick to cast their eyes upon these peasant cultivators as a potential labor force, and to devise a plan for putting them to work for the good of region and nation.

The plan devised by the Oficina de Caminos identified a catchment area that included all the rural districts that bordered the Utcubamba River, along which the highway was to run. There were twelve such districts in the province of Chachapoyas and twelve more in the province of Luya.[1] All of these districts were expected to provide labor conscripts for the highway project. Men between the ages of eighteen and sixty from each district were to be pressed into service, and were expected to work for a period of fifteen to twenty days before being relieved by workers from other districts.

The number of districts called upon to provide conscripts, and the number of conscripts called, depended on the labor demands of the work being done at any given point in time. Typically, however, six (three from each of the two provinces adjoining the highway) were asked to participate at any one point in time. Whenever possible, the Oficina de Caminos drew on laborers from districts located close to the construction site. When sufficient numbers of workers could not be found in these districts, planners from the Oficina de Caminos were forced to go further afield.

The Office of Highways also devised a system of rotation for the districts in the catchment area, so that each district would be called to service every three months.[2] As we will see, however, in practice, labor conscription demands diverged considerably from these plans. Because of the heavy labor demands of the Chachapoyas-Cajamarca-Bagua Highway project, and the scarcity of workers that resulted from the military's new conscription procedures, the Oficina de Caminos was often forced to return to the same communities repeatedly throughout the year—more frequently than every three months.

The precise number of men forced into government press gangs at any given point in time varied according to the nature of the tasks to be completed. It was not uncommon, however, for the plans of the Office of Highways to call for five hundred to one thousand individuals to be at work on the project.[3] It is instructive to compare the number of laborers sought by the Oficina de Caminos with the number of rural households available to provide these workers, for such a comparison provides some sense for just how idle central planners considered the (imaginary!) rural work force to be. This comparison also reveals just how delusional the plans of this office of government were.

In July 1942, for example, the six rural districts that were the focus of official labor impressment efforts included three in the province of Chachapoyas and three in the province of Luya.[4] There were a total of 1,342 households in these six districts (MHC 1942, 5–6). The plans of the Oficina de Caminos called for over 1,000 men to be at work on the highway project at this time.[5] The labor demands of the Office of Highways thus meant that each household in these districts was expected to sacrifice close to one full productive member, for a period (in this case) of twenty days.

As onerous as were the demands suggested by these figures, they underrepresent the hardships imposed on rural cultivating families by the highway project. The individuals sought by the Oficina de Caminos—adult males between the ages of 18 and 60—played a crucial role in the reproduction of agrarian households and communities. According to the national census of 1940, the mean number of men in this age category per household in the province of Chachapoyas was .90. The mean number in the province of Luya was 1.12 (MHC 1942, 9–10).[6] In effect, the Office of Highways sought to deprive these six districts of their entire adult male work force (for a period of twenty days). The system of rotation devised by the Oficina de Caminos called for each district to provide laborers every three months.[7]

A labor tax of this magnitude was an enormously debilitating imposition on the households in question—one they could not possibly sustain. As a result, they resisted in whatever way possible. There was simply no way that the rural peasantry could do without its entire male work force, at repeated intervals, over such an extended period of time. Peasant resistance to sacrificing so much in the way of labor to this project contributed in major ways to the endless labor shortages associated with the government's modernization scheme. Delusional though the labor demands associated with the Chachapoyas-Cajamarca-Bagua Highway project were, however, they were only part of the problem faced by peasant cultivators. In addition to being called upon to satisfy the labor demands of the Office of Highways, the households of these same districts were also subject to the conscription demands of the military. As we saw in the previous chapter, the plans of the army *also* threatened to deprive rural society of its entire male workforce—and for an even longer period of time (typically, about five years).

For the present purposes, two points about the many schemes and projects associated with the modernization process are of special relevance to the present discussion. The first has to do with the way that modernization created conditions of artificial labor scarcity. In their zeal to carry out modernization schemes that were intended to redeem the country from its unfortunate past/present, the officials who were in charge of these two initiatives alone conjured into being a labor force that was roughly twice the size of the actual (adult male) population! But these were only two of a great many modernization schemes. Because each new scheme relied upon additional quantities of conscripted labor, each one further increased the size the imaginary workforce. And in increasing the size of the imaginary workforce, each additional scheme deepened the real labor deficit. This was because government functionaries were expected to produce the worker imagined into being by government planners.

The second point about the modernization process that is relevant here concerns the role of categories of rule in concealing the delusion that was inherent in state projects and plans. Based on what is contained in the documentary record, one would never know that delusion, fantasy, or even coercion played any role whatsoever in the processes under consideration. Based on the state's relentless strategy of overstatement, one would assume that what is described in the documentary record is an entirely ordinary, mundane process of administration. This applies with special force to the seemingly neutral use of numbers. Rather than serving as a neutral description of the scale of labor conscription, the numbers of conscripts solicited in official documents provide a rough measure of the magnitude of state delusions about labor abundance.

But even these figures do not fully capture the ways in which the Oficina de Caminos's corvée labor program disrupted rural social life. Work on the highway press gangs also imposed a heavy burden on women, on the households of which they were a part, and on the interhousehold networks in which women and men alike participated. This was because most men who were forced to labor for the Office of Highways were accompanied to the work site by a female relative (often, their wives). Female kin accompanied conscripted men because the Oficina de Caminos had not made adequate provisions for feeding or housing its workforce. As a result, these women were compelled to travel to the construction site, set up makeshift accommodations adjacent to it, and care for their conscripted relative or partner throughout their period of forced labor (thus further subsidizing the construction of the highway).

In addition to representing an enormous drain on the labor supply of the peasant population as a whole, the fact that adult men were regularly pressed into service on the highway project was very disruptive to the individuals themselves, and to the families and communities from which they were taken.[8] Because peasant households resisted serving on the press gangs of the Oficina de Caminos in whatever way they could, the authorities generally found it necessary to employ the services of the Guardia Civil to breathe life (and put teeth!) into their plans for coercing labor.

The Guardia Civil became involved in labor impressment in the following manner: once the planners in the Oficina de Caminos had targeted a particular set of districts in the project's catchment area, they would send an official request (an *oficio*) to the departmental prefect, and would ask for his assistance in conscripting the laborers. The prefect would in turn send his own *oficio* to the governors of the districts in question, informing them of the plan and instructing them to work together with the other functionaries of their district (the justice and the mayor) to procure the laborers. At the same time the prefect would send an *oficio* to the comandante of the Guardia Civil, advising him of the plan and asking him to take whatever steps were necessary to ensure that the conscripts from each district arrived in a timely fashion at the work site.

The head of the police force would then send a pair of *guardias* to the districts in question. A pair of police officers was considered the minimum necessary for such assignments because each could help "watch the back" of the other. A single policeman traveling alone on such a mission would have been in peril of his life.

In theory, the governor was to work in concert with the mayor and the justice to ensure that the conscripts sought by the Office of Highways had been assembled prior to the arrival of the police. If these district functionaries had been unable (or unwilling) to find a sufficient number of workers prior to the arrival of the *guardias* (which was almost inevitably the case), the process of procuring laborers became more protracted. In cases such as these, district functionaries were to use their detailed knowledge of the terrain and the population to actively assist the police in locating the required laborers (under the assumption that many people had concealed themselves in places that the police would be unlikely to know).

Once the conscripts had been assembled, the *guardias* were to escort them to the construction site. To prevent conscripts from escaping during the journey, the *guardias* generally found it expedient to bind the hands of each man, and then tie the whole group together with a long rope. Once they arrived at the work site, other *guardias* were on hand on a round-the-clock basis to prevent highway conscripts from fleeing.[9]

It proved impossible to procure the number of workers the Oficina de Caminos sought for the Chachapoyas-Cajamarca-Bagua Highway. Indeed, the archives are littered with documents attesting to the obstacles that members of the state bureaucracy encountered in seeking to conscript labor from the rural populace. The problems that government functionaries experienced were in part a function of the extremely disruptive nature of the work demands. Government planners were under the misperception that the peasantry was idle for much of the year, and that new work opportunities would therefore be welcomed. They also believed that labor of this kind would have a positive, redemptive influence on the rural Indian population—would help them develop modern work habits and forms of discipline (Drinot 2011).

In fact, however, work on the highway project threatened rural cultivating families in major ways. It meant that they had to sacrifice their most productive members—male and female alike—who were forced to work for extended periods of time in difficult and often dangerous conditions (the use of dynamite in highway construction was commonplace). Although conscripted men earned a money wage, cash earnings were of minor importance to this subsistence-oriented peasantry, who in any case had far less onerous ways of earning the money they needed for household reproduction.[10] Furthermore, the wage offered by the Oficina de Caminos was almost invariably substandard. Finally, men who found themselves pressed into labor gangs were forced to neglect important household and community obligations. As a result, the prospect of work on the highway project filled most people with dread.

Because labor conscription was so highly disruptive of their lives, rural cultivators resisted being pressed into service in whatever ways they could. For this reason alone it was virtually inevitable that district functionaries would fail to capture the number of conscripts sought by the Oficina de Caminos. Adding to their difficulties in finding enough workers for the highway project, however, was the fact that other branches of government were simultaneously competing for control of the same supply of labor. Most notable in this regard was the Peruvian military. As we saw in the previous chapter, the armed forces' military conscription program threatened to deprive rural society of virtually its entire adult male work force. The efforts of the Oficina de Caminos to conscript labor for the Chachapoyas-Cajamarca-Bagua Highway were *in addition to*, and in competition with, those of the military. These multiple demands on the peasantry meant that district functionaries were faced with an inevitable deficit of imaginary laborers—a deficit that their superiors expected them to make real.

Whenever governors, mayors, and justices were unable to capture the number of conscripts sought by the Office of Highways, it was up to the prefect to attempt to resolve the problem. There were two reasons that the prefect was forced to take such a prominent role in these disputes. First, he was the president of the departmental Council of Public Works (the Junta de Obras Públicas), the body that was responsible for overseeing all development projects in Amazonas. In addition, however, the prefect was the highest-ranking government official in the department. The district functionaries who were responsible for organizing press gangs for the

Oficina de Caminos were therefore directly answerable to him (although the justice and the mayor were also answerable to their superiors, respectively, in the judicial and municipal branches of government). Whenever they failed to perform any of their duties, it was the prefect's responsibility to correct the problem.

The prefect would become of aware of problems with labor conscription for the highway project in several different ways. It was often the departmental engineer in charge of overseeing the construction of the highway (and employed by the Oficina de Caminos) who would inform the prefect that there were difficulties that needed to be resolved. In light of the fierce resistance to conscription offered by flesh-and-blood cultivators, and the fictive nature of the labor pool that the engineer sought to mobilize, it was inevitable that the number of conscripts he expected from a particular district would fail to appear at the construction site—despite the fact that the Oficina de Caminos had worked out a careful plan, complete with rotation schedule for the districts concerned, to ensure that the required workers would be forthcoming. When the number of laborers who were expected did not arrive, the engineer would send an *oficio* to the prefect to explain the problem. The engineer would also ask for the prefect's assistance in resolving the matter (see chapter epigraph).

Having been informed of problems such as these, the prefect would then write to the governors of the districts in question (or to the subprefect, or to all of these officials), and would demand an explanation. Being unable to state the real reasons that they were unable to procure the labor in question, the governors would seek to displace the problem onto an alternative source. Upon first being queried by the prefect, it was very common for functionaries in this position to invoke the region's rains as the source of their problems. It was equally common for them to argue that the peasantry was involved in important agricultural tasks, which could not be interrupted:

Sr. Prefect of the Department.

This office has received the following *oficio* from the Justice of the Peace of the District of La Jalca:

"The citizens [of] this district request that they not be compelled to work on the Chachapoyas[-Cajamarca-Bagua] Highway on the date indicated by . . . the Sr. Engineer. In the first place, they explain, it is currently the rainy season, which impedes work on the . . . project, and in the second place they have their own agricultural tasks [*faenas*] [to attend to]. . . . As an alternative, they suggest the month of June, and state that at that time the community will be able to devote itself fully to this important task." (ASC39, 7 de Abril de 1934)

Although invoking the rains and the agricultural cycle was little more than a delaying tactic, district functionaries used it to very good effect. As in the example above, they were often able to propose an alternative later date when the inhabitants of the district would (in theory) appear to work on the highway project. The prefect would generally accede to such a proposal. The alternative date would generally come and go, however, and at best only a portion of the conscripts would appear at the work site. The engineer would again inform the prefect of the problem, and the prefect would contact the governor, once again demanding an explanation, but this time employing a more threatening tone. He might even threaten the governor with dismissal or legal action:

Sr. Governor.

I reiterate to you the orders contained in my *oficio* No. 605, of the 25th of October of the present year, to which this Office has yet to receive a response.

I warn you that if you continue to ignore the commands of this Office you will be dismissed, and will be subjected to legal action, whether for intentional or unintentional negligence, because you have yet to provide the witnesses called to testify by the [provincial] Judge, nor have you produced the conscripts from your district called to work on the Chachapoyas[-Cajamarca-Bagua] Highway. It is difficult to avoid reaching the conclusion that the Governorship of your District has chosen to disregard my orders, which this Prefecture will not tolerate. (ASC6, 14 de Noviembre de 1933)

In addition to threatening the governor, it was not uncommon for the prefect to devise some kind of punishment for the district population. Most commonly, he would impose additional work obligations on the entire district:

Sr. Subprefect of Chachapoyas.

According to reports that this office has received from the Head of the Guardia Civil, the citizens of Chiliquín have not complied with their agreement to work on the Chachapoyas[-Cajamarca-Bagua] Highway [project] . . . and therefore I order that they be made to work double the time of the [original] contract, at the orders of Foreman, Arturo Zaavedra Tuesta, at the Calo-Calo construction site. . . . This office will not except excuses or delays of any kind. (ASC8, 13 de Agosto de 1943)

In some instances, the prefect would seek to preclude resistance to highway conscription by threatening in advance to impose double work obligations on all workers who failed to appear when first called:

Sr. Subprefect of the Province of Luya.

The Head of the Office of Caminos for the Department of Amazonas, Engineer Justo Paz, has written to this office to ask that the *obreros* from Luya, Lámud, Conila, Cuechán, Olto, Paclas, Chosgón, San Jerónimo, and Luya Viejo be ordered to the . . . construction site . . . to work on the Chachapoyas[-Cajamarca-Bagua] road. He . . . requests that they be made to appear on January 1st . . . which will give them the opportunity to finish their agricultural labors. Each *obrero* will work for a period of fifteen days [*una quincena*]. Those who do not appear when called will be made to work two consecutive periods of fifteen days. . . . The Guardia Civil will supervise the [project]. (ASC8, [illegible] de Diciembre de 1943)

Unless the governor was able to produce the required number of conscripts (which almost never happened), he would seek to displace the problem onto some alternative source. In addition to the vagaries of climate and the rural agricultural cycle, among the most common of these forms of displacement was interference from other district functionaries. The latter were said to be corrupt, and to be diverting to some other purpose labor that would otherwise have been available for highway construction. Some of this diversion of labor was technically extralegal but nonetheless customary, and reflected longstanding obligations stemming from the region's hierarchical, agrarian social order:

Sr. Prefect of the Department of Amazonas.

Having received your *oficio* No. 9, in which you order me to send 30 *obreros* to be placed at the disposition of Sr. Solís, Engineer of the Chachapoyas[-Cajamarca-Bagua] Highway, I have left this assignment in the hands of my Lieutenant Governor, don Demetrio Torrejon, because I have been called to the capital of this province by the Sr. Provincial Judge, to testify . . . concerning allegations that the Justice of the Peace of [Colcamar] has sent an equal number of men to work at Tincas [a nearby hacienda], because of which there is a shortage of *obreros* in this District. (ASC41, 18 de Enero de 1936)

It is not at all surprising that district functionaries were involved in diverting labor away from the Oficina de Caminos's road-building project. As we have seen, in addition to being in government service, governors, mayors, and justices were also beholden to political patrons, who counted on district personnel to provide them with the labor they needed for the success of elite enterprises.[11] As the *oficio* above suggests, these extralegal obligations to the landed elite were interfering with the ability of district functionaries to fill the conscription quotas for the highway project.

It was not just the representatives of landed power, however, who were accustomed to drawing on the labor of the rural peasantry, and in ways that interfered with highway construction. The same was true of influential members of the Catholic Church:

Sr. Lieutenant Governor of Sonche:

With this *oficio* you are ordered to have the *comuneros* at your command appear . . . without delay . . . to fulfill their obligation to work . . . on the Chachapoyas Cajamarca Highway [project]. This Prefecture is aware that almost the entire community is currently occupied in putting a roof on the house of *canónigo* Ocampo, in Pipos. This is illegal, and will not be tolerated. (ASC6, 25 de Setiembre de 1933)

But the boundary between legal and extralegal uses of labor was often a fine one. It was not just district functionaries who were beholden to members of the old, landed elite. So too were high-ranking government officials like the prefect. It was not at all uncommon for these officials to order that the labor of rural cultivators was to be made available to estate owners. According to the law, however, labor drafts were expressly *not* to be used for such purposes. They were only to be employed on projects that advanced the well-being of the public as a whole. As a result, whenever high-ranking officials decided to break the law, and to make peasant labor available to estate owners, they were compelled to transform the nature of those labors—at least in discourse. They were forced to represent the labor needs of individuals like hacendados as if they were part of some general, unspecified common interest:

Sr. Governor.

Please notify the citizens of your jurisdiction that on Monday, the 13th of the present month they are to appear at the Hacienda called "Burgos," in the valley of the Utcubamba [River], to labor for a period of twelve days, without excuses or pretexts of any kind, in order to contribute to the public and collective good, for FIFTY CENTAVOS a day. . . . (ASC5, 2 de Agosto de 1934)

As discussed earlier in the chapter, in addition to their extralegal obligations to members of the landed class, district functionaries also had entirely legal, administrative duties that called upon them to maintain the region's infrastructure. In order to do so, they were compelled to utilize the labor of the district population that had been entrusted to them. Because work on the Amazonas highway was so labor intensive, however—and because the demands of the Oficina de Caminos were in addition to the conscription needs of the military authorities—the Office of Highways and the Army Conscription Office threatened to deprive district functionaries of all the labor they needed to carry out their administrative duties.

The archives are literally overflowing with communiqués from district officials to their superiors in government, in which the former explain to the latter that the district population is already engaged in some other project and therefore cannot attend to work on the Amazonas highway. Some of the activities that competed with forced highway labor were organized by governors and mayors, who were seeking to maintain the infrastructure of their own districts:

Sr. Prefect of the Department.

In view of your orders that we proceed to the [construction] site of the Chachapoyas[-Cajamarca-Bagua] Highway, the citizens of this district respectfully request that they be exonerated from their obligation to contribute to the aforementioned work, [because they are] already involved in a local project, the reconstruction of the temple. . . . It has been only a few days since the rains have finally stopped, and as a result it has not been possible until now for me to convince my citizens to dedicate themselves to the repair of the Church. (ASC41, 20 de Abril de 1936)

Other activities that competed with work on the Amazonas highway were organized by the provincial authorities (the subprefect and the provincial mayor), who were attempting to mobilize the citizenry of multiple districts to undertake projects of a larger scale:

Sr. Subprefect of the Province of Chachapoyas.

The Departmental Engineer [in charge of] Public Works would like to speed up work on the repair of the sewage system for the City [of Chachapoyas], and as the scarcity of [wage] workers in this locale is well known, and as the project is one that is of benefit to all the people, you are to notify the communities of Chiliquin, Asunción or Gonche, Yambajalca, Diozan, Quinjalca, Olleros, Molinopamba, Cheto, Soloco, Huancas, Sonche, and Daguas that they are to provide approximately 300 men who will provide their services for a minimum of three days, until the project is completed. (ASC8, 28 de Octubre de 1943)

Such a sudden and unexpected assault on the labor supply of so many districts would have been resisted in the best of circumstances.[12] Indeed, in the days and weeks after the prefect issued these orders, the subprefect found it impossible to locate the workers requested by the departmental engineer. The subprefect's problems, however, stemmed in no small part from the fact that these were not the best of circumstances. Within just a week, at the request of the same engineer, the prefect also issued an order that over four hundred men from these same districts were to come to labor on the Chachapoyas-Cajamarca-Bagua Highway. The response from one district governor typifies the response of all, and was quick in coming:

Sr. Prefect of the Department.

The subprefect of the province of Chachapoyas has informed me that your office has ordered that 120 *obreros* [from Quinjalca] are to proceed to . . . the construction site at Caclij . . . [where they] are to work on the Chachapoyas[-Cajamarca-Bagua] Highway for a period of fifteen days. . . . As you know, Sr. Prefect, many citizens of Quinjalca have been called to the city of Chachapoyas to work on the repair of the sewage system, [also] at the orders of the subprefect, [and] until they return I have no one available to send to Caclij . . . to work . . . on the highway [project]. (ASC33, 5 de Noviembre de 1943)

In addition to creating tensions between district personnel and their superiors, the scarcity of labor that resulted from government efforts to conscript so much of the population also generated conflicts between the functionaries who were responsible for administering the same district. As they went about carrying out their administrative duties, governors and mayors were forced to fight with each other to control the same, limited labor force. As we saw earlier, in an effort to prevail in this competition, they took to denouncing one another to their superiors, each arguing that his corrupt counterparts were interfering with his ability to carry out the orders of his superiors.

But more was at stake than simply the ability of each functionary to perform his own duties. It was very common for these personnel to misuse their administrative positions. Having been given the responsibility of calling out the population to perform public works, governors and mayors would often "privatize" the labor of their district. Rather than direct that labor toward the maintenance of infrastructure, they would use it, in whole or in part, to develop their own enterprises.

The drain on the district labor supply represented by large government projects like the Chachapoyas-Cajamarca-Bagua Highway threatened to deny district functionaries the ability to perform their administrative duties as well as to privatize public labor. As a result, the competition between governors and mayors to prevail over their counterparts, and to control the local labor supply, at times became fierce:

Sr. Prefect of the Department of Amazonas.

On the 9th of January, in [*oficio*] #17, I sent to your . . . office a denunciation of the . . . Sr. Mayor of this district, who insulted me in my office, and later was guilty of showing contempt for my authority, and I asked [at that time] that my denunciation be sent to Judiciary, so that abuses of this nature be sanctioned, and so that morality and respect may be maintained among all my citizens.

I also report to you that I have ordered the inhabitants of this district to repair the road that runs through Chiliquin, which is currently in very bad condition, and have asked for the assistance of the municipal council, which refuses to collaborate, [and so] I have imposed a fine of one sol on every citizen for every day of work that they miss. . . . (ASC41, 27 de Febrero de 1936)

A communiqué that was sent to the prefect just two days prior to the governor's *denuncia* of January 9, however, suggests that this conflict was not strictly about morality, respect, and working for the common good. Rather, it appears to have been generated by competition between the mayor and the governor over the district labor supply:

Sr. Prefect of the Department of Amazonas.

Yesterday the Governor of this district . . . dishonored the Mayor, and completely without cause dragged him by force to jail, where he remains, his clothing ripped, and only because the Mayor objected to the efforts of the Governor to force all the citizens of this [district] to provide him with personal labor on his own lands, and to fine those who refuse the sum of one sol per day, [while] claiming that his demands are for the good of the District. . . . We ask that you free us from this situation, which is completely lacking in justice.

Francisco Salazar, Alderman of the Municipal Council (ASC41,
7 de Enero de 1936)

Struggles between the functionaries that administered the same district were not limited to disputes between governors and mayors. They extended to justices of the peace as well. Governors were under sufficient pressure from their superiors to find the laborers required for work on the Chachapoyas-Cajamarca-Bagua Highway, and had such conflictual relations with their district counterparts that they resorted to extreme measures. They took to conscripting justices of the peace—their fellow government functionaries, who in theory worked closely with the governor to ensure that sufficient numbers of laborers could be found:

Sr. Prefect.

This Office has received numerous complaints from the Justices of the Peace of the Districts of Chachapoyas, Luya and Bagua Provinces . . . that the governors of their districts . . . consider them part of the [population of] citizens who are eligible for conscription, and . . . seek to force them to . . . work on the Chachapoyas[-Cajamarca-Bagua] Highway. . . . As the Judge for this Province, I object to this abuse in the strongest possible terms . . . as it is a violation of the law and an insult to the dignity of the Judicial Branch of Government. (ASC8, 30 de Junio de 1944)

The efforts of governors to conscript justices of the peace may in part have been retaliatory. For justices, under pressure from their own superiors, had been compelled to denounce the governors and lieutenant governors of their districts. These functionaries, it seemed, had failed to help the justices apprehend individuals being sought by the courts. As the following *oficio* makes clear, this was a criminal offense. The fact that governors and their lieutenants were being threatened with criminal sanctions for not assisting the justice of the peace of their district meant that the latter became a significant threat to his counterparts:

Sr. Subprefect of the Province of Chachapoyas.

The President of the Superior Court of Amazonas has sent the following *oficio* to this Office:

"Chachapoyas. August 4, 1944. Sr. Prefect of the Department of Amazonas. . . . This Tribunal has received numerous complaints from the justices of the peace . . . of this Department . . . that the Governors and Lieutenant Governors . . . are not complying with the orders of the Court to detain suspects nor to compel witnesses to appear before the Court. . . . Such negligence on their part will not be tolerated, and is in direct violation of Articles 338 and 361 of the Penal Code. . . . Sr. Prefect, the Members of this Tribunal ask that you take the steps necessary to correct this problem . . . as soon as possible."

Please . . . ensure that the Governors and Lieutenant Governors of your Province are in strict compliance with the orders of the Superior Court. Their continued negligence . . . will result . . . in them being placed before the Superior Court . . . and [being] subject to the sanctions of the law. (ASC8, 4 de Agosto de 1944)

These struggles between governors and justices within the rural districts reflected broader tensions between members of the political and judicial branches of government—tensions that were ongoing. Indeed, the subprefects of the provinces of Amazonas had already been threatened by the courts with jail time for having failed to comply with requests to assist the judiciary in apprehending suspects and witnesses:

Sr. Subprefect of the Province of Chachapoyas.
This Prefecture has received the following *oficio* from the Superior Court of Amazonas:
"Chachapoyas, October 2, 1943. Sr. Prefect of the Department of Amazonas . . . Oficio No. 663. . . . In the course of reviewing the cases brought before this court by the Provincial Judges, one notes that it is very common that the Subprefects do not reply to the *oficios* that are sent to them by the Judges, requesting that suspects be captured or that witnesses be made to appear before the Court, which makes it impossible to proceed with the cases according to the procedures set out in the Penal Code. This failure does grave damage to the ability of the Court to bring cases to a successful conclusion, and makes the negligent authorities subject to the sanctions of Articles 338 and 361 of the Penal Code, and other sanctions even more serious. . . . If any political authority is prevented from capturing an individual sought by the Court, whether due to being related to that person, or for any other reason, he should inform the Provincial Judge . . . who will take the appropriate measures, but never should he remain silent [on the matter]."
I relay this [*oficio*] to you . . . to ensure your compliance, because . . . public functionaries . . . who interfere with the prosecution of official orders will be punished with a jail term of *three to ninety days*, and will be disqualified from returning to their posts. (ASC8, 5 de Octubre de 1943)

These conflicts between public officials contributed in important ways to disordering the operation of the state apparatus, and made it difficult to embed the remarkable in the routine. Indeed, they were but symptoms of deeper problems with the government's entire program of forced modernization. It was the competing demands of the region's two main forms of conscription that created the deficit of labor that pitted functionaries against one another. Just as the military sought to induct large numbers of men into the army, the Oficina de Caminos attempted to conscript those same men to work on the Chachapoyas-Cajamarca-Bagua Highway. At times the military and civilian officials who were responsible for conscription managed to stay out of each other's way. At other times, however, they would come into open conflict for control of the rural labor supply:

Sr. Assistant to the Engineer of the Chachapoyas[-Cajamarca-Bagua] Highway.

The Sr. Lieutenant Colonel, Territorial Commander, in *oficio* No. 1, dated today, informs me of the following:

"I have the honor of writing to you to register the following complaint: The Governor of La Jalca Grande, Don Francisco Culqui, complying with the . . . orders of the political authorities of the Department, attempted to gather together the . . . conscripts for the [army's] contingent [of blood] for his District, but at the very moment he attempted to put his plan into action, as a diligent and patriotic official, he ran up against the erroneous conception of how to comply with the laws of the land that is held by Don Manuel Flores, Assistant to the Engineer of the Highway from Cajamarca to Chachapoyas [the Chachapoyas-Cajamarca-Bagua Highway]—who has placed more importance on these individuals working a few days more [on the highway project] than on them complying with the civic duty that the law and their patriotism imposes upon them.

As a result of the defeatist behavior observed by this bad citizen, those who are called upon by law to serve their country have not presented themselves for military duty, and have fled scandalously to the *montaña*, so that [the Assistant to the Engineer] is also without the benefit of their labor.

In my capacity as Territorial Commander of this [military] Region, currently on special assignment in this Department, I denounce this act, and place it before the consideration of your office with the hope that you will dictate the measures necessary to ensure that grave offenses such as the one that I denounce not be repeated, and [likewise] to ensure that this same individual be made to capture the men who form the contingent [of blood] for La Jalca, and to conduct them to this Capital [Chachapoyas] in the least time possible."

Sr. Assistant to the Engineer, I relay this [*oficio*] to you so that as soon as possible, you will bring the contingent that corresponds to the District of La Jalca to Chachapoyas, as requested by the Sr. Territorial Commander. (ASC6, 10 de Noviembre de 1933)

Several days later the prefect received a response, but not from the assistant to the engineer, who was mysteriously taken ill. Instead, the engineer himself answered the charges made against his assistant. Once he had done so, the prefect passed the engineer's response directly to the territorial commander:

Sr. Territorial Commander.

I relay to you the *oficio* that this office has received from the Departmental Engineer in charge of the Chachapoyas[-Cajamarca-Bagua] Highway, who responds . . . on behalf of his Assistant, who is currently recovering from an illness he contracted while working on the highway.

> "I have read the contents of the *oficio* of the Sr. Territorial Commander with great care, and being greatly alarmed at what I read, made enquiries about what actually occurred, and have concluded the following; contrary to the claims of the Governor of La Jalca, my Assistant, Sr. Flores has never prevented the Governor from assembling the men he required for the contingent [of blood]. Because the Governor clearly exercises authority over all the citizens of his own district, Sr. Flores could only have succeeded in opposing the Governor if he had used force. Never has Sr. Flores been in a position to exercise force to make the residents of La Jalca work for him, and never has he invoked Executive Authority in order to oppose the wishes of the Governor. It is my belief that, for reasons I do not understand, the Governor did not want to capture the men who had been called to serve in the contingent of blood, and that he sought to conceal this fact by blaming Sr. Flores. Sr. Prefect, it is impossible to accept the assertion that don Manuel Flores, acting entirely on his own, while in the jurisdiction of the Governor, was able to overcome the Governor's authority, and to force a large number of people to obey him. . . .
>
> Sr. Flores does not have men at his disposal to capture the contingent [of blood] for La Jalca. He has only men for [work on] the highway, and these cannot be employed in any other way except by direct order of the Ministry of Development."

Sr. Territorial Commander, in light of this response to your complaint, I am ordering an investigation of what has occurred. (ASC6, 14 de Noviembre de 1933)

In sum, the efforts of the central government to implement a series of forced modernization programs in the Chachapoyas region put enormous strain on rural cultivators—and on the district functionaries who were responsible for conscripting the labor upon which these programs depended. Among the most onerous of these programs was the Oficina de Caminos's highway construction project. There were clear risks involved for government functionaries who refused to assist with conscription efforts for this project. Even so, there were times when the combined weight of the multiple obligations that these functionaries were compelled to honor left them unable, or unwilling to lend their support:

Sr. Prefect of the Department.

 . . . on the 9th day of the present month a pair of *guardias* from the police post at Leimebamba was sent on assignment to the districts of San Pedro, Jalca Grande, and San Ildefonso, with the goal of gathering together the braceros who are obliged to work on the Chachapoyas[-Cajamarca-Bagua] Highway [project], according to the agreements already established with the Governors of the respective districts, but said pair has encountered resistance from these braceros, as well as from the Governors, who allege that their citizens are currently at work planting their crops, and refuse to interrupt their [labors], even though the Subprefecture of the Province has imparted the same orders to the district political authorities. The Governor of San Ildefonso has declared that the braceros of these districts have worked [as recently as] the month of October, and [therefore] are not due to work again until the month of January [i.e., every three months], and as a result only the eight braceros from San Ildefonso, the sixteen from Jalca Grande, and the eight from San Pedro who were absent during [October] have left for the [construction site]. . . .

Rather than offer their full collaboration with the police so that their mission has the best possible outcome, the Governors of the districts previously referred to are the first to interfere with the work of the *guardias*, who have been charged with gathering together the braceros who are to appear at the construction site to work on the Highway [project], as a result of which the police are unable to carry out their duties, a fact that I place before the Prefecture so that, taking into consideration what I have declared, you may take the measures you consider most appropriate to correct this problem. (ASC18, 30 de Diciembre de 1943)

As the foregoing suggests, government officials attributed the difficulties they encountered in conscripting the peasant population to an entire range of displaced, phantom causes. These included the region's heavy rains and the needs of the peasantry to perform important agricultural endeavors. They included as well the self-serving behavior of corrupt individuals like district mayors and district governors. The inability of rural cultivators to understand the importance of key nation-building activities was also cited as a reason that it was so difficult to procure the laborers sought for the modernization of the Chachapoyas region. So too was the greed of members of the old landed elite, who would at times interfere with conscription efforts. Finally, as we will see in the next chapter, public servants also attributed their inability to procure the labor needed to redeem region and nation to APRA. According to government functionaries, the party's fanatics were roaming the countryside and were systematically attempting to interfere with the efforts of government functionaries to modernize Peru.

Government planners took steps to deal with as many of these phantom causes as possible. They did so by seeking to expand the reach of the state. They passed laws and tightened existing regulations. They issued threats and made appeals. Never once, however, did they confront the actual sources of their difficulties. As we have seen, these were threefold. First, government efforts to modernize the highlands of Amazonas were based on brute force, because of which the subaltern population had to be coerced against its will to labor for members of the elite. Second, the government's modernization projects were added to an existing set of coercive practices of labor extortion in which virtually all of regional society was implicated. Third, the government's entire modernization effort was based on delusion. Indeed, as the various offices of the government that were involved in the modernization effort estimated the number of laborers they needed to complete their particular projects, they imagined into being a labor force of fictive proportions.

As a result, at the end of the day government officials remained baffled by their inability to conscript the labor they required for the Chachapoyas-Cajamarca-Bagua Highway. This convinced them to launch investigations that were intended to shed light on and also to resolve this difficult problem:

Sr. Subprefect of the [Province of Chachapoyas]

This Office is deeply puzzled about why the braceros of your province refuse to appear as called upon to work on the Chachapoyas[-Cajamarca-Bagua] Highway [project], despite the fact that the highway is in the direct interest of the Department and [is crucial to] the defense of the Nation. I therefore order you to tour all the districts of the Province, accompanied by two *guardias*, during the summer months in order to investigate the causes of this problem, and to bring the problem to a rapid conclusion. (ASC8, 20 de Julio de 1944)

As one might have guessed, however, investigations of this kind did little or nothing to facilitate government efforts to impress labor, for the officials that undertook the investigations could not name the true sources of their difficulties. Rather, they were compelled to displace their problems onto a series of alternative, phantom sources that could be named in political discourse. The result of this process of displacement was that government functionaries systematically misconstrued the nature of the problems they themselves sought to address as well as the solutions that were best suited to deal with these problems. This in turn meant that what they would be able to report upon based on their investigations had been carefully circumscribed in advance—and in a way that ensured that they would be unable to identify the reasons that they faced such intractable problems.[13]

In this chapter, we have examined the efforts of government officials to transform conscription from a violent, delusional, and disordering process into an ordinary act of administration. Furthermore, we have done so during a period of relative calm—a period when the phantom forces to which the authorities attributed their difficulties in transforming the region were not considered a serious threat to the modernization process. Throughout this entire period, the problems that the government faced did indeed seem to consist of the ordinary, mundane, practical challenges of rounding up rural cultivators. Indeed, on the basis of what is contained in the documentary record, one would never know that the authorities were in pursuit of a largely imaginary workforce.

What is so very striking about state documentary practices is the difficulty of seeing *anything* through the veil of the ordinary and the routine in which these practices enshroud themselves. Through the use of a particular kind of overstatement, documentary practices act as (anti-)rites, which seek to purge the state of what it is not allowed to be. They also attempt to displace responsibility for what the state does onto phantom forces that are said to be alien to the state, but are actually of the state's own making. By means of displacement, state documentary practices also invert the ordinary and the extraordinary, and attribute to the forces of order an indispensable role in protecting the former from the latter. In many circumstances, so effective are these cultural practices of rule that it is virtually impossible to recognize just how delusional official projects and plans are. Instead of appearing as remarkable—as violent, delusional, and coercive—these projects and plans seem entirely ordinary and mundane—so much so that there is no reason to give them a second thought.

But not in all circumstances! As we saw in Chapter 2, there are situations in which the state descends into a kind of madness. During periods of political crisis—when the barriers erected to separate purity from danger have been overrun—what characterizes the official response to state phantoms is paranoia. In such situations, government officials treat their phantoms as Third Order Standard Deviations. The authorities become almost hysterical about the dangers represented by these phantom forces, to which they attribute great power and potency. The authorities are also possessed of a burning desire to resolve their fears—to gather the intelligence necessary to convert anxiety into control. They seek to collect information that would break through the wall of secrecy behind which their enemy lurks, to make the enemy visible, transparent, and knowable.

But there is an intermediate stage between First and Third Order Standard Deviations, between denial and paranoia. There are circumstances in which the authorities come to believe that the phantoms of state are threatening to overrun the boundary between order and disorder but have yet to do so. Government officials respond to these fears with a strategy of surveillance. They seek to shore up the boundary between purity and danger, in order to ensure that the former is safe from the latter. In these circumstances, government officials treat the phantoms of state as Second Order Standard Deviations.

The next chapter deals with just such a period. The focus of that chapter is the Party of the People. Chapter 8 explores a time when the authorities came to fear that APRA was surreptitiously seeking to climb out of the shadows, and to cross over into the most important domains of social life. The authorities responded to their fears with a strategy of containment. Their goal was not so much to know the party as to monitor and control it. They sought to ensure that APRA was not able to spread into the public sphere, or into the institutions of civil society (especially labor unions) or the government (especially the armed forces). In other words, how APRA came to be known, understood, seen, and recorded as a Second Order Standard Deviation was a function of official concerns with keeping it at a distance—with maintaining the boundary between order and disorder.

8

Glimpses of Danger and Subversion

Sr. Director General of Government.

In an effort to preserve the public order, and to protect the laws
and dispositions that govern us. . . . I ask that the police who offer
their services in this department for more than two years be transferred
to other parts of the Republic, [two years] being a sufficient amount
of time for them to become completely familiarized with the region,
and to acquire the local prejudices and sympathies that oblige them
to act in a compromised manner that diminishes the prestige of the
Institution to which they belong. . . . The great part of the police force
is made up of individuals who are sympathetic to or are members of
the Popular American Revolutionary Alliance [APRA]. . . .
        —Chief Engineer, Department of Amazonas

Introduction

As we have seen, government efforts to modernize the Chachapoyas
region in the middle decades of the twentieth century were violent, chaotic, and delusional. In their sacropolitically inspired desire to redeem the
country from its unfortunate past, government officials set for themselves
a seemingly impossible task. They sought to integrate the (supposedly)
backward sierra regions of the country with the (purportedly) progressive
coast. In the process, the authorities inadvertently conjured into being a
labor force of fictive proportions. They also assumed that this imaginary
population was waiting to be put to work for the good of the nation.

The previous two chapters have examined official efforts to conscript this fictive workforce, so as to carry out the government's two most important modernization initiatives: military conscription and highway construction. Despite the delusional nature of these projects, the authorities employed a particular kind of overstatement to characterize their activities. By treating conscription as an ordinary, unremarkable part of nation building, and by repeating this framing with mind-numbing regularity, government officials sought to encrypt their violent and coercive efforts in a form that rendered them unrecognizable—that transformed them into mundane, everyday acts of administration.[1]

In this way, the documentary practices in which the authorities were so deeply involved, and the bureaucratic processes associated with them, functioned as a particular kind of (anti-)rite. They came to operate as highly ritualized procedures by means of which the state sought to purge itself of what it was not allowed to be (violent and coercive). These (anti-)rites also sought to protect the state from the phantom forces that were said to threaten the state of redemption that government officials had declared for the nation as a whole. By pursuing this strategy officials sought to create and maintain a surface appearance for the state that was contrary to its actual nature. The authorities also sought to embed the remarkable (their massive program of forced labor) in the routine (ordinary, everyday administration).

As long as these phantoms forces that the government regarded as seeking to undermine its modernizing efforts did not appear to be too disruptive, the authorities responded to them as what I have referred to as First Order Standard Deviations. That is, the government's response to these forces was to deny them any significance—to treat them as being unworthy of official attention or concern. In these circumstances, it was a relatively simple matter to maintain the illusion of the ordinariness of the state's remarkable, delusional assault on the regional workforce. From time to time, however, the government would come across evidence that suggested that these phantom forces were actually far more active, and far more dangerous, than the forces of order had been willing to concede. Government officials responded in ways that made it difficult to keep up appearances—that made it clear just how close to the surface paranoia and delusion had been all along.

The summer of 1936 was one such time. In the morning of July 4, government officials in Chachapoyas stumbled across evidence suggesting that things were not even remotely as they seemed. After treating APRA as a First Order Standard Deviation for several years, the forces of order were confronted with signs that convinced them that they had been massively deceived—that the Party of the People was operating behind a carefully constructed facade that had rendered the party invisible to the authorities. This discovery led the forces of order to reassess APRA, and convinced them to treat the party as a Second Order Standard Deviation. It also brought to the surface fears and delusions that had been there all along.

In this particular case, the concerns of government officials were provoked by the cascading series of revelations that followed upon a quite random event—the chance arrest of a small group of Apristas by a high-ranking police officer in the streets of Chachapoyas. It is to the details of that encounter, and the department-wide investigation that followed in its wake, that we now turn.

A Close Encounter with Subversive Elements

In the early morning hours of July 4, 1936, Lieutenant Miguel Collantes Rojas, a commander in the Guardia Civil, made an accidental discovery—one that was to have far-reaching consequences for the region as a whole. As he made his rounds through the streets of Chachapoyas he stumbled upon a young boy who was engaged in what seemed very suspicious behavior. Collantes related what transpired in his official report on the matter:[2]

Lieutenant Miguel Collantes Rojas, attesting to antisocial activities against the tranquility and stability of the nation.

Don Miguel Collantes Rojas, Lieutenant of the Guardia Civil, Commander of the third company of Amazonas and of the Second Mixed Command . . . attests to the following: that at 5 am today, the 4th of July, 1936, finding myself in Triumph Street of this city, I spied an underaged minor banging on the door of the house of Don José Nicolás Muñoz [Valenzuela] . . . moments later when the door opened the minor entered, followed closely by Don Francisco Torres, who had been standing nearby adopting a suspicious attitude.

Investigation:

Having witnessed these suspicious activities, I ordered Sergeant Second Class [Angel] Navarro Astete, Corporal Aurelio Ordoñez Aguilar, and Guardia Simón

Castañeda Rocha . . . to arm themselves and to gather in the aforementioned street, at the same time that I entered the house [of Muñoz] and found the underaged minor, Pedro Mauro Torres Llaja [and] Francisco Torres Santillan, together with the owner of the house, José Nicolás Muñoz Valenzuela, the latter with a file of papers in his hands demanding of the minor, "Where are the rest of my papers?" But upon noticing my presence, he immediately stopped talking, and tried to disguise his true intentions. I ordered that all [three] be detained, and at the same time seized the file that Muñoz was carrying, and upon examining it discovered that it was antisocial propaganda of a leftist character that carried the title, "Aprista Party of Peru, Manifesto of the Amazonas Action Committee, to the Department."

As the police began to escort the men from the home of Nicolás Muñoz to police headquarters, a crowd gathered. As it did so Sr. Miguel Trauco Alvarado, a neighbor and friend of Muñoz, approached Muñoz, who attempted to use the confusion created by the crowd to give Trauco a notebook. The police escort noticed that something appeared to have been passed between the two men, however, and demanded that Trauco surrender whatever Muñoz had given him. The latter denied having receiving anything, and said that he had been examining his wallet, and that perhaps the police had misunderstood. Dissatisfied, but wishing to proceed with their original suspects, the *guardias* then escorted the three to police headquarters, where they took statements from them all. On the basis of the testimony of these individuals, and of others who were implicated by the original suspects, the police concluded that they had glimpsed the outlines of an extensive network of underground subversion—one that involved a great many people, from multiple walks of life, from across the entire region.

The interrogators began by interviewing the underaged boy who police Lieutenant Collantes had observed banging on the door of the home of Nicolás Muñoz on Triumph Street in the early hours of the morning. The minor was Pedro Mauro Torres Llaja, fourteen years of age, who lived with his mother and father on Santo Domingo Street, a short distance from the residence of Muñoz, and who worked as an apprentice in his father's tailoring shop.

Statement of Pedro Mauro Torres Llaja, underaged minor.

Having been asked to explain how he came to be in possession of the file of papers that was seized early in the morning by Lieutenant Don Miguel Collantes Rojas, in the house of José Nicolás Muñoz, if he acknowledged that the file was the same as that shown him [during his interrogation], and [also] if he had been aware of the contents of the file, the *manifestante* said: that early today he was told by his aunt Carmen Cruz to go the tailor's shop of his father Don Francisco Torres, located on Triumph Street . . . where his father gave him the same typewritten papers shown to him during his interrogation, and said to him, "Take these papers and deliver them to Don José Nicolás Muñoz, once I show you which house is his," his father having said this he and [his son] made their way to the fountain that is located next to the house of Doña Melchora Angulo, from where his father indicated the house where he should deliver the papers, saying: "Deliver these, and if [Sr. Muñoz] has any others, bring them to me." Once the boy had arrived at the house indicated by his father he knocked, the owner José Nicolás Muñoz answered, and he delivered the papers, but at this same moment his father Francisco appeared, [followed by] the Lieutenant, who seized the papers that he had just delivered to Muñoz. . . . The *manifestante* said that he had no knowledge of the contents of the papers, having been unaware of their existence until his father told him to deliver them [to Muñoz], and that his father had said he had taken the papers from underneath the mattress of his bed.

Having been asked how many times [in the past] he had carried files of papers to the house of Muñoz or to other houses, he said: that the only time he had delivered papers to the house of Muñoz was today, but that on other occasions he had carried handwritten papers to the house of Don Rosendo Zubiate, and that he delivered the papers to [Zubiate] without having received any reply.

The testimony of fourteen-year-old Pedro Mauro Torres Llaja suggested the existence of a network of Aprista craftsmen and their families: Carmen Cruz, the aunt who sent young Pedro to his father's workshop, was the wife of a well-known tailor; Nicolas Muñoz Valenzuela was a prominent carpenter; and Francisco Torres Santillan, the father of the accused, was also a tailor. Some of these individuals were kin-related, and most lived in the same neighborhood. It was clear that all were involved in exchanging subversive literature among themselves, and to others outside their immediate kin and neighborhood-based networks.

It was equally clear that these individuals had given considerable thought as to how to exchange clandestine information without encountering difficulties with the police. Toward that end, they had chosen the hours of the early morning to communicate with one another. They had also elected to distance themselves from direct involvement in the transfer of the seditious materials, and instead had chosen to employ the labor of an underaged minor. This may have been because they thought that the town's *guardias* would view a child with less suspicion than an adult. The

Apristas may also have decided to use a child as their messenger because of children's legal status; should they be apprehended, being underaged, they were less likely than adults to feel the full weight of the law.

It could not have escaped the attention of the police that the subversives were not satisfied with drawing on the services of the innocent and the underaged. They were going so far as to employ the labor of their own *children* to accomplish party objectives. That is, they were using the authority of family and kin to compel their offspring to do their bidding. Furthermore, they appeared to be doing this on a regular basis. Indeed, Pedro Torres Llaja's family had told him to deliver clandestine messages on multiple occasions. In addition to the services he had provided on July 4, for which he had been arrested, Pedro had previously carried Aprista materials to interested parties in other parts of Chachapoyas. The statement of this underaged boy suggested a level of trust and regular interaction between the adults.

One such person to whom Pedro had delivered papers, Rosendo Zubiate, was neither an artisan, a neighbor, nor a relative. Rather, he was a public employee who had worked in a number of government offices and who lived in an entirely different neighborhood of Chachapoyas. Pedro's testimony thus suggested to the police that APRA's networks were quite broad—that at the very least, they extended across divides of neighborhood, profession, social class, and generation. More alarming still, APRA's networks also appeared to extend into the domain of government service.

The police also interrogated Pedro's father. This man had instructed his son to deliver the Aprista documents to the home of Nicolas Muñoz, had followed his son to the house of Muñoz (unbeknownst to his son), and had been arrested along with Pedro and Muñoz by Lieutenant Collantes. The father was Francisco Torres Santillan, who was fifty-one years old, unmarried, and living with his son and common-law wife on Santo Domingo Street, not far from the home of Nicolas Muñoz Valenzuela.

Statement of Francisco Torres Santillan.

Having been asked how he came to be in the possession of a file of typewritten papers the content of which was the manifesto of the aprista party [*sic!*] for the department of Amazonas that carried the title, "Peruvian Aprista Party. Manifesto of the Action Committee of Amazonas to the department," he said: that on the night of Saturday, June 27th the *manifestante* found himself in the cantina of Don Miguel Mendoza, where he had gone to borrow from [the owner] a newspaper . . . called "The Bell," and when he asked for it Mendoza retrieved it from a chest under the counter. It was in these circumstances that Don José Nicolás Muñoz, who was also in the bar, approached him with the "aprista" manifesto and told him: "Here, take this also, read it and return it to me afterwards," and having received both the newspaper and the manifesto he returned to his home, and during the night he read only the newspaper, until he went to sleep, at about 10:30 at night, and after having read the title of the manifesto, he did not read on, but instead stored the manifesto beneath the mattress of his bed until Saturday, July 4th, at which time he drew upon the services of his underaged son Pedro to return the manifesto to señor Nicolás Muñoz. . . .

Having been asked what position he occupied in the Aprista departmental Committee of Amazonas, he said: that in the first place he detests the party and is not a member, and as a result he occupies no position whatsoever on the [departmental] committee, and in the second place he is not familiar with its organization.

Having been asked why, if he is not a member of Aprismo [sic] he travels to the [rural] villages on trips of clandestine propaganda for that sect, he said: that on no occasion has he gone to the villages to make propaganda or anything like it.

Having been asked why, if he was not interested in the contents of the Aprista manifesto, he had kept it for a period of eight days, he said: that he had forgotten about it until [Muñoz] asked him to return it and that he had never had any intention of using it for the purpose of making propaganda of any kind.

The police found this testimony utterly unconvincing. It did reveal to them, however, aspects of the subversives' methods of conveying information among themselves that were not to be found in the testimony of Francisco's son Pedro. It appeared that the Apristas were using the town's cantinas (specifically, the cantina of Sr. Miguel Mendoza Lopez, located on May Second Street) to exchange messages and party literature. Cantinas were an ideal location for such activities because they were among the very few places where groups of men could gather at night without drawing the attention of the Guardia Civil.

This testimony also reveals that the authorities were concerned with the question of how subversives in different parts of Amazonas communicated with one another, which in turn lead them to be concerned with the Apristas' movement through the regional space. Although they had no direct evidence that Francisco's trips to the countryside were undertaken for illegitimate purposes, they were suspicious of the fact that he made these journeys at all. The questions that the police posed to Francisco show that they were convinced that the party's reach extended far into the countryside—that Apristas such as he were traveling in secret to the rural villages in order to propagandize for APRA. In addition to crossing boundaries of neighborhood, profession, social class, and generation, and in addition to extending into the domain of the state, APRA's networks also appeared to link the region's towns with its rural villages.

Finally, the interrogation of this suspect shows that the forces of order had a rudimentary understanding of the party structure.[3] They knew, for example, that there were a series of positions in the departmental command. It appears that they were trying to confirm what these positions were. They were also seeking to fill in gaps in their knowledge about who occupied these posts.

The police also felt compelled to interrogate the individual to whom José Nicolás Muñoz Valenzuela had passed a notebook in the streets of Chachapoyas, after Muñoz had been arrested and as he was being escorted to police headquarters. The individual in question was Miguel Trauco Alvarado, thirty-five years old and married, who worked as an employee in the Caja de Depósitos y Consignaciones, the precursor of the National Bank. Trauco was also a carpenter. He lived on Triumph Street near Muñoz.

Statement of Don Miguel Trauco Alvarado

Having been asked why, on the morning of Saturday, July 4th, as Don Nicolás Muñoz was being taken from his home to the barracks of the Guardia Civil, he had approached Muñoz and had taken from him a notebook and why, moments later, when the return of said notebook was demanded of him he denied having it, arguing that he had only his wallet, and with what purpose he had done this, he said: that on the morning of [July 4], seeing that his friend Muñoz was being led away by the police, he approached him to see what was the matter, and that Muñoz took advantage of the moment to give him a notebook . . . and told him: "Look after this for me," and that he had taken it home and taken care of it, and had not turned it in despite repeated demands from Lieutenant [Collantes Rojas] as well as from Corporal Ordoñez . . . and that he had done this not with the premeditated goal of covering up any crime that Muñoz might have committed, but because he could not understand the importance of handing over a notebook that he thought contained nothing more than Muñoz's personal documents, but that he had returned the notebook due to the demands of the police and of Muñoz, and that he had no idea whatsoever what the contents of the notebook were. . . .

Having been asked if he is a member of the Aprista party or if he performs any service for it, he said: that because of his job as a [public] employee, and due to the fact that he is a family head of modest means, he is obliged to have no involvement with any political party.

The police found the testimony of Miguel Trauco Alvarado to be a complete fabrication. It did suggest to them, however, the lengths to which party members would go in an effort to protect themselves. Despite his protestations to the contrary, the police were convinced that Trauco was an Aprista. His statement thus confirmed that APRA's networks extended directly into the government bureaucracy—that state employees were deeply involved in party activities. Trauco's testimony also showed that the Apristas were willing to lie, conceal, and dissimulate in order to protect the Party of the People.

The Police Investigation Broadens

The police then interrogated José Nicolás Muñoz Valenzuela, owner of the house to which fourteen-year-old Pedro Torres Llaja had delivered the Aprista documents at the orders of his father, Francisco Torres Santillan. At the time of his arrest, Muñoz was thirty-six years old, married, worked as a carpenter, and lived on Triumph Street. He claimed not to remember his address.

Statement of José Nicolás Muñoz Valenzuela.

Asked if, on the night of Saturday, June 27th, while in the cantina of don Miguel Mendoza, he had given don Francisco Torres Santillán a file of papers so that [Torres] could read them, and if he knew the contents of the papers, and in whose presence he had delivered them [to Torres], the *manifestante* said: "On the night . . . of the 27th I was in the cantina of Mendoza watching a game of billiards, when don Francisco Torres arrived at the cantina, and after drinking a few glasses [of cane liquor] approached me and asked me what was new with me, and I responded by saying, "This is new, read it," and [at this point in the account, the narrative changes from the first to the third person], [Muñoz] gave [Torres] a piece of newspaper that he always carries with him for whatever purpose, and that it was not a file of papers, and that he did not know the content of the piece of paper that he gave to Torres, and that he did this in the presence of various other people who he doesn't know and whose names he doesn't remember.

Asked how it was that he came to be in the possession of a file of papers that contained the manifesto of the Aprista departmental committee, Muñoz said: that it was not a file of papers that contained the aprista [*sic!*] manifesto that he gave to Torres but a piece of newspaper, as he stated earlier.

Asked if he had been affiliated with "Aprismo" and what post he occupied in the department, he said: that he is not a member of this sect and occupies no role [for the party] whatsoever in this department.

Asked why, if he had not given [Francisco] Torres the Aprista manifesto he asked Torres to return it on the morning of Saturday, July 4th, he said: that [this claim] is completely false and that he never asked Torres to return any manifesto, and that since the night that he had encountered [Torres] in Mendoza's cantina he had not seen him except for encountering him [briefly] in the office of the Prefect of the department, and that it is possible that Torres was so drunk that night that he does not remember who gave him the manifesto.[4]

Asked why on the morning of the 4th of the present month, after being detained, as he was being led from his house on Triumph Street to the police station, taking advantage of the crowd that had gathered, he gave a notebook of his to Miguel Trauco, employee of the Caja de Depósitos y Consignaciones, and what confidential notes are contained in this notebook, he said: that it is true that while he was being escorted from his house to police headquarters he gave a notebook to Miguel Trauco when [Trauco] approached him so that Trauco could give the notebook to his family, because he was afraid that the police would confiscate the notebook, and that it contains no confidential information whatsoever.

Asked if he recognizes as his, the notebook . . . shown to him [during his interrogation], he said: that it is the same, and that he recognizes it as his own, as well as the observations that appear in it, which have been entered by him.

Asked to explain the meaning of the terms, initials, and other symbols as well as the amounts of money that are recorded . . . in the aforementioned notebook, he said: that they are the names of the members . . . of the "Society of Artisans" [the Fraternal Assembly of Artisans and Laborers of Amazonas], which ceased functioning in July 1935.

Asked why, if the [Society of Artisans] had not been in operation since the date cited, in the notebook there is an entry that says: M. Gordo, March 2nd, 1936, five soles," after the date that the Society ceased to operate, he said: that as he recalled, on that date M. Gordo, that is to say Victor Manuel Cabañas, had given him the sum of five soles from the funds of the "Harmony Society of Chachapoyas" [Armonía Chachapoyana, an organization devoted to sports and music], of which Cabañas is Treasurer, so that the [former] members of the "Union [sic!] of Artisans" could organize a fiesta in honor of the members of the "Harmony Society."

Asked in what typewriter he had used the ribbon and the transport papers he had recently bought, and that are recorded in . . . the same notebook [mentioned earlier], he said: that the ribbon for the typewriter and the transport papers he had bought on credit at the store of the son of don Fidel Ampuero, that he had not used them in any typewriter, but had sent them to the hacienda "Llajen," which belongs to don Tomás Horna, located in the province of Celendín [in the neighboring department of Cajamarca], so that they could be delivered to the representative of the hacienda, whose last name is Guzmán. . . .

As was the case with the testimony of Francisco Torres Santillán, the police found the statement of José Nicolás Muñoz Valenzuela to be utterly unconvincing. Together with the notebook they managed to retrieve from Muñoz's neighbor Miguel Trauco, and the information they gathered about Muñoz's purchase of a typewriter ribbon and transport papers, however, the testimony suggested to the authorities the existence of an extensive network of subversive individuals, organizations, and activities. Muñoz appeared to the police to be at the center of these.

Muñoz's testimony confirmed in broad outline the statements made by fourteen-year-old Pedro Torres Llaja, his father Francisco Torres Santillán, and Muñoz's neighbor Miguel Trauco Alvarado. It seemed clear that networks of kin-related artisans were employing the early morning hours, when most people were asleep, to exchange subversive literature among themselves. It was equally clear that the Apristas were using the town's cantinas, where people could gather at night without raising the suspicions of the authorities, as a cover for their underground activities. Muñoz's statement also suggested that APRA's networks were not restricted to artisans, but extended into the government bureaucracy and the organizations of "civil society," like the Society of Artisans and the Harmony Society of Chachapoyas.

But the statement of Nicolás Muñoz did not simply confirm what other suspects had already said. His testimony also supplied crucial information that implied additional aspects of party organization and activity that the authorities found very alarming—especially the "terms, initials, and other symbols as well as the amounts of money that [were] recorded . . . in the notebook." For as we will see presently, and despite Muñoz's claims to the contrary, the police concluded that the Apristas were making extensive use of pseudonyms in order to protect the identities of their members. The forces of order also surmised that party members were contributing significant sums of money to the departmental command to support the activities of their party. These were both issues that Lieutenant Collantes took up in greater detail in his final report to the prefect (see below).

In addition to their preoccupation with pseudonyms and money contributions, the police pursued two additional matters in their questioning of this subject. Toward the end of the interrogation, the police broached an issue that was clearly of great concern to them—how it was that the Apristas had managed to produce the party manifesto that Lieutenant Collantes had confiscated from Nicolás Muñoz. Throughout all the interrogations, of all the suspects, the police returned repeatedly to the fact that the Aprista manifesto was typewritten. There were a limited number of typewriters in Chachapoyas, and the authorities had been laboring under the illusion that they had accounted for all of them. They were therefore especially disturbed to discover that the subversives appeared to have secreted one away somewhere in some undisclosed location, and were using it to produce antisocial propaganda. Having discovered evidence in Muñoz's notebook that he had recently purchased a typewriter ribbon, and having confiscated from his own hands a freshly typed Aprista manifesto, the Guardia Civil hoped that their interrogation would lead them to the typewriter that had been used to produce the seditious document. That is, the authorities were intent upon reconstructing the networks that had allowed the party to challenge the government's monopoly on the printed word.

Rather than leading them to the typewriter, however, and through the party networks that had been involved in producing the manifesto, Muñoz steered the authorities in a different direction altogether. According to his narrative, there was no subversive network of Apristas who had conspired to provide the funds and other resources needed to produce antisocial propaganda. Rather, Muñoz's purchase of the ribbon had been an entirely innocent act. No one, it seems, had provided him with the funds. Rather, he had purchased it by means of the impersonal mechanism of "credit," at a store in Chachapoyas whose owner is not even mentioned by name. The owner was in fact Alberto Ampuero, who was, unbeknownst to the police at the time, one of the key members of APRA's departmental command. Rather than refer to the store owner, however, Muñoz named the father of the owner, Fidel Ampuero, who was known to be a staunch defender of the government.

Not only was there no criminal trail to follow with regard to the purchase of the ribbon, neither was there any subversive network to reconstruct with respect to its use. Muñoz claimed that the ribbon had not been employed for any purpose whatsoever in Amazonas. Rather than use it, he had sent it out of the region entirely, to the neighboring department of Cajamarca (specifically, to the town of Celendín).

The implication was clear. Muñoz's story had a clear, unambiguous, and innocuous beginning and end. It implicated no one but himself and individuals who were of no concern to the police. According to his testimony, there was no missing typewriter to be found. Nor were there networks of Apristas who were devoting their time, energy, and money to the task of producing seditious literature. The only difficulty, however, was that the police had in their possession the very freshly typed manifesto that Muñoz's testimony could not account for. Furthermore, they had seized it directly from Muñoz. His statement therefore came across as an elaborate and unconvincing ruse. Indeed, it ended up implicating the very people it was intended to exonerate, and confirmed the existence of the very networks the existence of which it denied.

Even so, unconvincing though it might have been, Muñoz's testimony did succeed in preventing the authorities from reconstructing the networks that would have led them to the clandestine typewriter that the Apristas had in fact used to prepare their manifesto. His statement also kept the police from identifying the individuals who had actually been involved in helping to produce the manifesto. The police were also prevented from investigating when and where the document had been prepared, and under whose auspices. While the Guardia Civil were not so naïve as to believe what Muñoz said, they appear to have been uninterested in investigating beyond the parameters of the account he had provided. For at the time the police stumbled across Muñoz and his small band of confederates, the authorities were accustomed to treating the Party of the People as a First Order Standard Deviation. The chance discovery that they made in the early morning hours of July 4 certainly put government officials on guard. But it was not enough to provoke the kind of full-blown paranoia associated with Third Order Standard Deviations.

In addition to the problem of the typewriter, Nicolás Muñoz's testimony raised a second issue of concern to the police, above and beyond APRA's use of pseudonyms to conceal the identities of its members and the Apristas' money contributions to support party activities. Muñoz's statement also implied to the authorities that the influence of the Party of the People extended into organizations that appeared on the surface to have no connection to politics whatsoever. Organizations such as these went out of their way to present themselves to society at large and to the authorities as being concerned solely with wholesome and healthy activities like sports and music. The possibility that organizations such as these—of which there were a considerable number in Amazonas—were actually fronts or covers for Aprista subversion was very disturbing, indeed.

The specific organization that Muñoz's testimony caused officials to question was the Harmony Society of Chachapoyas. When asked to account for the coded entries in his notebook, the suspect had claimed that one of the pseudonyms referred to Sr. Víctor Cabañas Santillán, who was treasurer of the Harmony Society. Muñoz also asserted that the "5 soles" entered opposite Cabañas's pseudonym ("M. Gordo") referred to monies that Cabañas had provided to Muñoz from the funds of the society so that the former members of the Society of Artisans could throw a party for the members of the Armonía Chachapoyana. Muñoz provided no rationale that could account for this tortured story. Predictably, when the *guardias* interrogated Víctor Cabañas Santillán, he denied all aspects of Muñoz's account—other than the fact that he was a member of the Harmony Society.[5]

There was a simple reason that Nicolás Muñoz's testimony raised official concerns that the Harmony Society of Chachapoyas might be a cover for seditious activities. The year before the society had been investigated by the police for precisely the same reason. In July 1935—in the aftermath of one of APRA's failed civil-military uprisings, the prefect of Amazonas instructed the police to investigate several organizations in Chachapoyas for possible Aprista leanings. One of these was the Fraternal Society of Artisans and Laborers of Amazonas, which Muñoz refers to in his statement. The Society of Artisans was closed down when officials came to the conclusion that a number of its members were Apristas.[6]

Another organization that officials investigated the year before (in 1935) was the Harmony Society of Amazonas. By the end of July, the prefect had informed the president of the society of the results of the authorities' investigation:

Sr. President of the Harmony Society of Chachapoyas.

I am pleased to reply to your *oficio* No. 1 of the 27th of the present month, in which you enquire about [the status of] your efforts to clear your name and those of the other members of the Harmony Society, and [about] the results of the investigations carried out by the police with respect to the suspicions that have fallen upon your Society for having been the authors of the subversive Aprista propaganda that appeared on the morning of the _2 [illegible] of this month on the walls of this city.

With respect to this question, I am very pleased to be able to report that the investigations carried out by my Office as well as by the Police have led us to the conclusion that the members of Harmony Society had no involvement in these acts whatsoever, and [furthermore] that according to all the information we have received the members of the Institution over which you . . . preside have the best of reputations. . . . (ASC5, 31 Julio 1935)

The fact that Nicolás Muñoz mentioned the Harmony Society in his statement made the police wonder whether they had come to the right conclusion about the society the year before. Muñoz apparently sought to trade upon the Armonía's excellent reputation, which had been previously confirmed by the prefect, to demonstrate the nonseditious nature of his activities. Because the authorities regarded Muñoz as a dangerous subversive, however, their views of him ended up raising doubts in their minds about the Harmony Society. As a result, they launched a new investigation into the political sympathies of its members. As we shall see, the second time around the forces of order reached a quite different conclusion—one that raised questions in their minds about the judgment they had made the year before. The revised conclusion of the police regarding the subversive nature of the apparently apolitical Harmony Society also caused them to wonder about the inclinations of other seemingly wholesome and healthy organizations (see below).

Having interviewed a number of people, and having collected a range of evidence based on the police interrogations, the chief of police issued his final report to the prefect. The document is worth quoting at length despite the fact that it repeats some of the earlier testimony. On the one hand, it provides new information gleaned from the interrogations of the prisoners. On the other, it shows the official police interpretation of the information they had gathered. That is, it shows which facts they considered most salient, and how they aggregated those important facts into a broader pattern. In other words, the final report shows what inferences the police made about APRA on the basis of this investigation.

Sr. Prefect of the Department.

At 5 am on the fourth of July of the current year, finding myself [patrolling] the street[s] . . . of the city, I detained the underaged boy Pedro Mauro Torres Llaja, his father Francisco Torres Santillan, and Don Nicolás Muñoz Valenzuela, in the home of Muñoz, and at the same time confiscated from [Muñoz] a file of typewritten papers containing the Manifesto of the Aprista Party of the department of Amazonas, written by the individual Manuel Chávez Várgas, presently a fugitive. . . . Sergeant Angel Navarro and Guardia Simón Castaneda then appeared, and they escorted the three subjects to police headquarters, and took their statements, which suggest the following: on the night of June 27th of this year, the individual Nicolás Muñoz Valenzuela was watching a game of billiards in the cantina owned by Don Miguel Mendoza López that is located on May 2nd street. . . . [Muñoz] gave to Francisco Tórres the manifesto of antisocial character . . . and said to him: "Here, take this . . . read it and return it to me afterwards." . . . Despite the fact that the testimony of others confirms that Muñoz delivered the manifesto to Torres, Muñoz denies this, and alleges that it was a piece of newspaper the content of which he did not know. . . . But in reality Muñoz is a permanent member of the Aprista Committee in this department, and at present occupies the post of Secretary General (in an interim capacity);[7] this assertion is confirmed by the nocturnal activities in which he engages in support of the antisocial aprista sect . . . and even more so because I recovered a notebook that is the property of Muñoz that contains the *key to aprismo* [emphasis added], which includes the pseudonyms that the party members in this region utilize and the amounts of money that they contribute and the villages that support the party. At the same time the individual Torres is also a member of the same sect [and is equally] involved in clandestine activity in support of [APRA]. It is likely that he is the secretary of information, because it has been verified that he makes frequent trips to different districts of this department under false pretexts.[8] The fact that he accepted the aprista manifesto, and kept it for eight days, is conclusive proof that Torres is a member . . . even though he claims not to be an aprista. . . . It is possible . . . that men like Muñoz and Torres use the services of minors, corrupting them from an early age, in order to disguise and provide a cover for their own activities. Such seems to be the case here, as the minor Pedro Mauro Torres was the one who carried the clandestine documents.

In his final report to the prefect, Lieutenant Collantes included several facts only alluded to in the previous testimony. First, it appears that the notebook that Nicolás Muñoz passed to Miguel Trauco in the streets of Chachapoyas—and that the police subsequently confiscated from Trauco—contained a list of the pseudonyms of a significant number of party members. Although it is impossible to be sure of the precise number, in his original statement Muñoz claimed that the names were those of the members of the Fraternal Assembly of Artisans and Laborers of Amazonas. The founding document of this well-known organization, which was sent to the prefect in 1931, lists 208 members (Nugent 1997, 291). The organization had grown in size since then, until it had been closed by government officials in 1935 (due in part to official fears of Aprista influence). It is thus not at all unlikely that the list of pseudonyms that the police encountered in the notebook of Nicolás Muñoz was a long one.

Unfortunately for the police, the notebook contained *only* the pseudonyms of the Apristas and not their actual names. As a result, while the notebook seemed to offer conclusive proof that there was a sizeable number of party members, it left the authorities unable to tell who these individuals actually were. In other words, as was the case with much of the evidence the police collected as a result of this investigation, the list of pseudonyms raised more questions than it answered. Government officials were afforded a glimpse of the party's inner workings, but they were unable to penetrate the barrier of anonymity that the Apristas had erected to protect themselves from government scrutiny. Indeed, the list makes it clear that there was an active and extensive APRA underground. But it leaves the authorities keenly aware of the fact that they had no way of entering the party's subterranean realm.

Second, Lieutenant Collantes's final report to the prefect made it clear that the use of pseudonyms by the Apristas was generalized. Not only did all party members appear to have a pseudonym, but it seemed to be a security matter of the utmost importance that only pseudonyms be used. Indeed, even clandestine party records like the notebook seized from Nicolás Muñoz by the authorities, which were *never* intended to be viewed by anyone other than party leaders, included only pseudonyms. The police were never able to discover whether there was an equivalent list of proper names, although they never abandoned their efforts to find one. It seemed, however, that only high-ranking party secretaries like Muñoz (if indeed he was such a secretary; the police could not be sure) understood the meaning of the pseudonyms. In other words, the only permanent record of the true identities of the Apristas appeared to be found in party leaders' heads.

The Key to Aprismo

In his final report to the prefect, Lieutenant Collantes claimed to have found the "key to Aprismo" (see above). This was a key, however, that unlocked surprisingly few doors. Indeed, it appears that the authorities never succeeded in deciphering most of the information they encountered in the notebook. In their interrogation of Nicolás Muñoz, the police were forced to ask the suspect "to explain the meaning of the terms, initials, and other symbols . . . that are recorded . . . in the . . . notebook." Muñoz never complied with this request. What the authorities encountered in the notebook thus indicated that APRA had developed an entire language of its own—one that the police never succeeded in translating.[9]

Lieutenant Collantes also mentions other information that the police encountered in the notebook that undoubtedly raised additional concerns on the part of the forces of order. It seems that opposite each pseudonym in the notebook was an amount of money and a date. Collantes interpreted these figures as referring to the amounts of money that the various party members had contributed to APRA, and the dates on which they had made these contributions.

It must have been very disturbing for the authorities to learn that significant numbers of Apristas were in effect tithing, and in the process, were apparently transferring sizeable sums of money to party leaders (the only example mentioned in the testimony—5 soles, contributed by M. Gordo, on March 2, 1936, represented about a week's pay for a day laborer). As we have seen, during this period government officials experienced enormous difficulties in extracting either labor or wealth from the regional populace. Generally, they could do so only at the point of a bayonet. The notebook of Nicolás Muñoz, however, suggested that the Apristas had a far different attitude toward the party than most Peruvians did toward the state. The notebook pointed to the existence of an entire cohort of underground citizens who *voluntarily* surrendered their wealth and their labor to the Party of the People.

Lieutenant Collantes's final report to the prefect also mentioned an additional piece of information found in the notebook. This information added a spatial dimension to the way the authorities were compelled to imagine the Party of the People. It appears that the Apristas had classified the many rural villages in the department of Amazonas according to the degree and nature of their support for the Party of the People.

This list was important for two reasons. On the one hand, it suggested that APRA had developed the surveillance capabilities necessary to subject all of Amazonas to a unified party gaze. The Apristas, it seemed, had been able to gather information about the specific political conditions that prevailed in each of the region's multitude of rural villages. Furthermore, they had been able to aggregate these data in some central location, and had subjected the information thus assembled to the scrutiny of some person or group of persons who the party considered qualified to arrive at general conclusions about issues of great significance to the party. These people had assembled the disparate bits of data about each of the region's rural villages into a composite picture. On this basis they had come up with a kind of map of the political sympathies of the department as a whole.

It was unclear from the material in the notebook precisely how the Apristas had gathered the information—although the authorities' belief that party members like Francisco Torres made regular trips to the countryside to organize among the peasantry was certainly suggestive of one possibility. It was equally unclear who aggregated and evaluated these data, where and when the assessments took place, and what decisions were made on the basis of these evaluations.

The experience of the doggedly anti-APRA governor of the rural district of Colcamar, however, offered the police one example of how the Apristas could have been using the political intelligence they were gathering. Indeed, the experience of this governor suggested that the Party of the People was actively seeking to shape the political geography of Amazonas. That is, it appeared that the Apristas were attempting to eliminate from the state bureaucracy individuals who were hostile to APRA, and to replace them with people who were sympathetic to the party's aims.

The most effective way of removing a functionary who was especially hostile to APRA was to accuse him of some crime. The worst crime one could be guilty of was to belong to the Party of the People. Thus, a very curious situation emerged in which real Apristas would falsely accuse other people of being subversives in order to make it easier for the party to go about its affairs. The abovementioned governor of Colcamar discovered just how effective the party could be in eliminating individuals who sought to interfere too strenuously in party affairs:

Senior Prefect of the Department.

By the decision of the Superior Court of Cajamarca, I have been placed at liberty. I was imprisoned unjustly, [due to] the denunciations made by don Guillermo Bustos [and] don Demetrio Guimac that I was a member of APRA, and [due to] the influence of someone who intervened in the judicial proceedings. . . . I also write to inform your . . . office that I will not allow [these men] to propagandize against the President of the Republic, and . . . that I have never allowed this to happen. (ASC41, 13 de febrero)

Senior Prefect of the Department.

Yesterday evening at 7 pm I went to the house of don Manuel R. Pingus together with . . . Victor Latorre and Mercedes Visalot, and as we passed by the door of

don Demetrio Guímac we were stoned by this man, with one of the stones hitting . . .
Visalot in the back. . . . With complete sincerity I can say to you, Senior Prefect, [the
following]: This individual truly hates me and slanders me at every step, because [dur-
ing my former term as] Governor I confiscated all Aprista identity cards [in Colcamar]
and gave them to the Prefect . . . and up to the present will not allow [Guímac] to hold
his Aprista meetings, nor did I permit nor will I permit him to deceive the innocent
inhabitants [of Colcamar] with his propaganda. (ASC41, 15 de febrero)

As the first of the two *oficios* quoted above indicates, the anti-Aprista
mayor of Colcamar had been falsely accused of being an Aprista by real
party members. This alone suggested just how nefarious the party could
be. But it appeared that the influence of APRA made it possible for the
party to do more than simply (falsely) accuse people of crimes. It also
seemed that the party could determine the outcome of judicial proceedings. As the ex-governor of Colcamar explains, as a result of the influence
that "unknown individuals" exercised in the judicial process, he had been
removed from his post and thrown in jail. The implication was that influential individuals within the judiciary, or close enough to the judiciary to
influence its decisions, were sympathetic to the Aprista cause. This was an
alarming possibility, indeed.

While the information that the authorities had gathered was suggestive, they could do little more than wonder about the mechanisms
by which the party carried out its department-wide surveillance tasks.
They were also left to speculate about the actions the Apristas took on
the basis of the assessments they made. What the notebook made clear to
government officials, however, was that they and their department were
being "watched." It appears to have been this revelation that convinced
the authorities that they had to be far more careful than they had been
about watching in return (see below). Indeed, as we will see, it was at this
point that government officials started to treat APRA as a Second Order
Standard Deviation.

The list that Lieutenant Collantes found in the notebook of Nicolás
Muñoz—which showed the villages that did and did not support APRA—
was important for a second reason. In addition to demonstrating to the
authorities the surveillance capabilities of the Party of the People, it also
made them aware of a fact that their own state apparatus had failed to
detect—that there was a region-wide geography of Aprismo. It is not clear
from the lieutenant's report whether the proper names of the pro-APRA

villages were entered in the notebook, or whether the names appeared in some kind of code. Considering the precautions the Apristas had taken to protect party members from official scrutiny, however, it would be very surprising if the pro-APRA villages had not been provided with pseudonyms. Furthermore, the recommendations the prefect makes for extra surveillance based on Collantes report (see below)—surveillance intended to protect against the "APRA threat"—makes no mention of specific villages.

Thus, it seems safe to assume that the authorities remained as confused about which villages supported the party as they did about which individuals did so. As we will see, rather than calming the fears of government officials—by providing them with intelligence that they could use to understand and control APRA—the references to villages that supported the party provoked new anxieties on the part of the authorities. These references made the authorities aware that parts of the countryside had turned subversive but remained silent on the question of specifically which sections these were. And because the police were unable to distinguish loyal from disloyal sections of the countryside, they were compelled to look with suspicion upon the countryside as a whole. Indeed, once the prefect had read Lieutenant Collantes's report, and on its basis called for the adoption of a range of new security measures (see below), he recommended greater scrutiny of *all* of the countryside rather than specific villages. He also called for careful surveillance of all those who traveled to and fro.

Finally, Lieutenant Collantes's report to the prefect raised another very disturbing possibility. In the case at hand it was clear that the Apristas had employed the services of an underaged minor to provide a cover for their nefarious activities. Toward the end of his report, the lieutenant considers the possibility that this may have been a widespread party practice. In other words, the authorities began to ask themselves how many other children besides Pedro Torres Llaja were being misused by the subversives. Government officials began to wonder how many additional innocent youths were being corrupted from an early age, so that the Apristas might remain invisible to the forces of order, and so that the party might reproduce itself through the generations. Government officials could do little more than speculate about this question.

The fact that Lieutenant Collantes's final report increased rather than decreased official anxieties about the extent of Aprista activity in the Chachapoyas region—that the discovery of a "little bit" of Aprismo led the authorities to fear that there was a great deal more going on that they could not see—is reflected in the following. Having read the lieutenant's report, the prefect called for an entire range of new security measures to be established, in town and country alike. In a series of communiqués—sent to the departmental chief of police and the head of Caja de Depósitos, to the subprefects and the heads of the provincial police posts, to the director of the national high school and also to the directors of Chachapoyas's two elementary schools, and even to the district governors—the prefect called upon everyone to collaborate in a department-wide effort to control Aprismo, which he characterized as a grave threat to Amazonas. He asked his subaltern officials to be on the lookout for any and all signs of subversion, which they were to report to him with all possible haste.

The prefect appealed to the chief of police to have his men take extra care in making their nightly rounds through the streets of Chachapoyas, and to pay special attention to public gathering places (i.e., cantinas).[10] There being evidence that the party had previously established itself in the national high school, the prefect appealed to his director to watch for any suspicious activity on the part of the students, and to advise his staff to do the same.[11] When the prefect wrote to district governors, in addition to ordering them to be on general alert for seditious activity of all kinds, he also told them to be on the watch for people who seemed to come and go without having any legitimate business in their districts.[12]

The following circular, sent by the prefect to government functionaries throughout the department in the aftermath of the discoveries of July 4, captures the growing attitude of fear on the part of the authorities toward the Party of the People:

Circular No. 7.

As recent events have shown, the followers of the antisocial political sect known as the "Party of the People" are seeking to spread their influence to every corner of the department of Amazonas. This Prefecture is determined to prevent them from undermining the public order, and [therefore] calls upon you to use every means possible to identify all subversive elements . . . in the jurisdictions under your command . . . remembering at all times that the members of this sect disguise their true intentions . . . [even as they] work tirelessly to find new members and to bring down the current Regime. (ASC51, 13 de Julio)

In the weeks that followed the arrests of July 4, 1936, the authorities were confronted with mounting evidence that the influence of the Party of the People was far greater than they had previously imagined. The first indication that they had underestimated the importance of APRA came in late July 1936. At that time the authorities completed their new investigation into the political leanings of the Harmony Society of Chachapoyas. The results of this second enquiry led them to believe that they had been mistaken the year before—that the Apristas were in fact using the society as a front for their own activities. The society was shut down shortly thereafter.[13] This discovery led the prefect to instruct the chief of police to investigate the political leanings of the approximately two dozen similar organizations in operation at the time. By the end of the year, by which time the party's national leadership had launched yet another abortive civil-military uprising, most of these "Sport-Culture Clubs" had been closed.[14]

By early August 1936 it was becoming clear to government officials that there was indeed a regional geography of Aprismo—that the party had established a strong presence in a number of rural villages. In some, state functionaries like the governor were able to identify the leaders of the terrorists:

Sr. Prefecto: Guimac, the old Caudillo of Gamonalismo, who has [long] dominated this district and who continues to dominate it, has managed once again to become the employee of the Caja de Depósitos y Consignaciones. This individual is disparaging the dignity of [all] the higher authorities, saying: "That in a few days the Aprista Party will rise above the [current regime]," and in this way terrorize the poor Indians of [Colcamar]. . . . Sr. Prefect, I know that you are a just official who desires the advancement of the Department of Amazonas, and therefore hope that you will punish this . . . traitorous and hypocritical man. . . . (ASC41, 4 de Agosto)

It was more common, however, for government functionaries writing to the prefect from the rural districts to claim not to know the identities of the individuals who were causing them such difficulties—to complain that "outside elements" were seeking to undermine the public order:

Sr. Prefect of the Department.

In this village, being located so far from the capital of the Province, there is an almost complete lack of Constitutional protections. . . . I am unable to make people comply with my orders. . . . Sr. Prefect, I ask that you have a pair of the Guardia Civil sent to this place for at least thirty days. Dangerous individuals who are followers of the Aprista political party have appeared here unexpectedly from elsewhere . . . and they have induced the simple people of this village to disobey the authorities. . . . I hope, Sr. Prefect, that you are able to assist me by sending the pair of *guardias* previously indicated . . . with the goal of establishing a precedent . . . [and] of restoring public order. (ASC41, 18 de Agosto de 1936)

In October 1936 another national political crisis began to unfold. General Oscar Benavides, who had ruled Peru since 1933, had sought to engineer the presidential elections of that month so that his hand-picked choice, Jorge Prado y Ugarteche, would succeed him. Much to Benavides's surprise, however, Luís Antonio Eguiguren, an opposition candidate who had the backing of APRA, took the early lead in the voting. When it seemed certain that Eguiguren would win, General Benavides annulled the elections and refused to relinquish control of the presidential palace.

The response of the Party of the People was swift. In late October the national leadership conspired with Air Force personnel in an attempt to seize control of the government—an attempt that failed (see Nugent n.d.). The crackdown against APRA that followed was just as rapid, both nationally and regionally. In Chachapoyas, the authorities sought to cripple the party by striking at its nerve center, and drew upon the new intelligence they had gathered since the revelations of early July in an effort to arrest the entire departmental command. When the police arrived to detain the various secretaries, however, they found that some of the subversive leaders had known of their plans in advance and had managed to escape. Furthermore, it appeared that at least some had been warned by none other than Sr. Ramón Villavicencia—subprefect of the province of Chachapoyas and the prefect's right-hand man and close confidant:

In reply to your *oficio* No. 170, dated yesterday, I have the honor of informing you that in response to *oficio* 159, PERSONAL. ABSOLUTELY RESTRICTED, I arranged for the capture of various Apristas who have been placed at the disposition of the señor Subprefect of the Province; but I have not been able to capture the principal leaders, such as Manuel Chávez Várgas, Secretary General of the Aprista Departmental Committee, nor those of which [the Departmental Committee] is composed, [such as] Porfirio Pizarro, Alberto Ampuero, and others, the former [Chávez Várgas] because he is currently a fugitive and the two latter because according to what I have been told by the woman Ernestina Mory, they had been warned to hide themselves or to flee, by the señor Subprefect of the Province don Ramon Villavicencia, the very same day that your office imparted to the orders for their capture.

With respect to this treason committed by Señor Subprefect Villavicencia, and his obstruction of administrative labor, in support of antisocial elements [that have been declared] outside the law, I will be initiating the most severe and careful investigation, taking the statements of those people who are knowledgeable about the case and the result of which I will inform you in the most detailed of manners.

This is the reason, señor Prefect, that I have not complied immediately and strictly with the dispositions of your Office, which was my most fervent desire.

May God protect you,

Lieutenant Miguel Collantes Rojas

(ASC18, 5 de Diciembre de 1936)

As this *oficio* suggests, the discovery that a high-ranking member of the government bureaucracy had leaked the government's arrest plans to the very Aprista fugitives being sought by the police produced something a political crisis of its own.[15] It also made the authorities realize that APRA was much "closer" than they had realized, and that it had been all along. But the political crisis extended far beyond the actions of any one individual. As the presidential elections showed, the government had seriously underestimated the degree of support the party enjoyed nationally. Having heard virtually nothing from party members for several years, the Benavides government appears to have thought that they no longer had anything to fear from the Party of the People—that APRA could be treated as a First Order Standard Deviation.

Indeed, it was for this reason that Benavides had been willing to call new presidential elections. But he was to have a rude awakening. Despite the party's proscribed status, despite the repression to which it had been subject at the hands of government officials, it appeared that APRA had been anything but acquiescent. Despite the dangers associated with party membership and the sacrifices Apristas were forced to make, after two years "in the catacombs" (to use the Apristas' phrase) the Party of the People still had enough underground support to determine the outcome of presidential elections.[16]

Conclusion

In a pattern that was to repeat itself over and over again during the period under consideration, government officials made the mistake of confusing the absence of visible party activity and opposition with the absence of party activity or influence. During such times, the authorities were led to treat APRA as a First Order Standard Deviation—as being unworthy of attention or concern on the part of the government. The developments of the second half of 1936, however, led government officials to conclude that the Party of the People could exercise very broad influence even when there were no visible signs that this was the case. All the more reason, then, to take any and all signs very seriously, whenever they were forthcoming.

Signs of this nature were abundant in 1936. Having been confronted with these signs in the most forceful of manners, the authorities were disabused of the misperception that APRA could be treated as a First Order Standard Deviation. Despite appearances to the contrary, it seemed clear that the Party of the People was surreptitiously seeking to climb out of the shadows, and to rally people broadly to the party cause. Indeed, APRA had become uncomfortably "close" to the state and to society. In these circumstances, the forces of order felt compelled to contain the Apristas, to shore up the boundaries upon which their conventional political topography depended. Once again, they became determined to drive the party back into the shadows. Once again, the Party of the People came to be treated as a Second Order Standard Deviation.

Conclusion
Behind the Mask of the State

IN "NOTES ON THE DIFFICULTY of Studying the State," Philip Abrams (1988, 58) famously argues that the "state is not the reality which stands behind the mask of political practice. It is itself the mask which prevents our seeing political practice as it is." In this volume I have explored the processes by which the mask of the state is made and unmade. I have done so by examining two qualitatively different and seemingly unrelated masks of governance—the rational and the delusional—and have demonstrated that they are alternative expressions of the same underlying project of rule.

To show the interconnections between these two facades of order, I have provided a genealogy of political conflict and contestation in which the remarkable (in the form of fear and fantasy) is ever present but is not visible to the naked eye. Rather, the remarkable is carefully and systematically misconstrued as the routine—as the rational plans and legitimate concerns of a modernizing polity. In the process of making these interconnections, I have developed an argument about how the remarkable can emerge out of the routine.

I have also sought to identify the techniques that make it so difficult to see beyond the state's carefully crafted exterior of the rational, the routine, and the ordered. Prominent among these techniques are (anti-)rites of purification, overstatement, and standard deviations. The commitment of governing regimes to what I have called an "antiepistemology of the everyday"—and the elaborate mechanisms of dissimulation and concealment that such a commitment suggests—speaks to something important about states.

I have argued that scholars have yet to understand the full extent or significance of the role of antiepistemological processes in creating a legitimating veneer of rule. Nor have scholars investigated in sufficient depth the mechanisms by which modern states produce the appearance of legitimate order. To support this claim, I bring to light what official government practice so consistently sought to obscure—the role of the remarkable and the delusional in the routine activities of state. And I suggest that the ability to look past the state's production of a domain of the ordinary and the routine is essential to understanding what states are and do.

In pointing to the concealed presence of the extraordinary in ordinary processes of state formation, I also seek to address a second set of questions. My point of departure for doing so is the desire to understand how the paranoia of the Odría regime circa 1950 could emerge out of the seemingly mundane activities that preceded it. Existing state theory, I suggest, is ill equipped to explain such developments. There are most certainly conceptualizations of the state that focus on issues of fantasy, fear, anxiety, and delusion. There is also a long and distinguished tradition of more utilitarian state theory, which focuses on mundane, pragmatic problems and dynamics of domination and control.[1]

To my knowledge, however, there is little that would help us understand both utility and paranoia as alternative manifestations of the same underlying state form. Indeed, the two abovementioned literatures are generally thought to invoke *opposed* notions of the state (Marcus 2008; Steinmetz 1999). One might go so far as to say that there is a rift in the social sciences and humanities between scholars who view the state as a real institutional structure and those who regard it in nonrealist terms (see Krupa and Nugent 2015).[2]

The fact that existing conceptual frameworks do not allow us to understand developments such as those outlined in this book—in which a single state is seen to wear multiple and seemingly contradictory masks of rule—prompts a reconsideration of state theory. As I have shown in previous chapters, while institutions (governmental and non) were clearly involved in state formation in the Chachapoyas region, in no sense was the state an institution that monopolized the use of force (legitimate or otherwise), and that taxed and conscripted, across the regional territory (Tilly 1985). While cultural meaning was centrally involved in state formation, by no means is the state to be understood as a predominantly cultural construction (Geertz 1980; Steinmetz 1999). While delusion and fantasy informed state activities in fundamental ways, it is highly misleading to characterize the state as an essentially magical projection (Coronil 1997; Taussig 1997).

As I have shown, none of these frameworks allow us to understand how the same state may appear under more than one guise. For most scholars of the state analyze contexts in which political subjection has been more or less accomplished. They focus on "functioning" polities, and seek to understand what lends consistency, potency, order, or effectiveness (or the illusion thereof) to political domination. The investigation of order as a fait accompli makes it difficult to understand instability and disorder, except as processes that are external to the state—as exceptional processes that threaten what it is and does. It is worth noting that this is precisely the way that virtually all governing regimes represent the state and its relation to instability and disorder. It is a commonplace that those in power represent disorder as an aberration that is profoundly dangerous and threatening. Indeed, it is the claim of the state to maintain order that is fundamental to its assertion to the right to rule.

This is not to say that scholars are unaware of the ways that processes of rule may generate disorder, fear, paranoia, and irrationality in everyday encounters—whether with subject populations (Laszczkowski and Reeves 2017) or among state bureaucrats (Gupta 2012). Nor is it to argue that the ordering effects of state are totalizing, or that "creative" crosscurrents (Das and Poole 2004) do not emerge as vulnerable groups assimilate processes of rule. Nor is it to deny that such groups draw upon the language of state to make morally grounded claims for entitlements (Nielson 2007).

Rather, it is to make two points. First, most scholars seek to understand how a sense of the state as an overarching, defining, ordinary presence is maintained despite the everyday production of disorder, fear, paranoia, and irrationality. Such an approach suggests that the reproduction of rule is an inevitable rather a highly contingent phenomenon. Second, in most studies it is the state, or those who act in its name, who set the terms within which people seek to define alternatives, make claims, find spaces of autonomy or engagement, etc. In other words, most scholarship to date has explored contexts in which the state and its agents define the parameters or limits of interaction and engagement.

In the present study, however, conditions of political crisis—in which government officials lose faith in their ability to carry out even the most basic of state functions—make it possible to explore a different question.

I ask what transpires when those who act in the name of the state are unable to define the terms of engagement with vulnerable populations. And I explore the processes that lead to the breakdown in their ability to do this.

The present work thus asks a different set of questions about order and disorder, rationality and irrationality, the routine and the remarkable. Having been confronted with a state form that initially seems quite ordinary and rational but quickly descends into a kind of "madness," I seek to move beyond the simple opposition between order and disorder to examine how each emerges out of the other. In the preceding chapters I do not treat either rationality or paranoia as the "real" form of the state, or as separate states. Neither is regarded as the rule, and the other as the exception. Rather, drawing inspiration from classical anthropological works that view structure and antistructure as mutually co-constitutive, and in constant dialectical tension (Turner 1969), I view these two manifestations of domination as different aspects of a single process, as different "moments" of a single political project. Putting the state in motion, I argue, and also in tension, and viewing it as something that is in continual motion and tension, changes our understanding of what the state is and does.

I have asserted that the government's paranoia about APRA—its obsession with the party as a dangerous evil that had to be eradicated—reflects deeper contradictions in twentieth-century Peruvian state formation. The crisis of the Odría regime, I show, had its roots in earlier state efforts to effect broad social transformation. Beginning around 1920, the national government had undertaken a project even more massive (and more delusional!) than Odría's efforts to eliminate APRA. Central planners had sought to mobilize the collective resources of virtually the entire state apparatus to bring about the redemption of the country's vast mountainous interior—which was regarded as backward and feudal.

In so doing, the government employed a logic that I have referred to as "sacropolitical." As an assertion of the sovereign right to rule, sacropolitics differs in important ways from related concepts discussed in the scholarly literature. It differs from biopolitics (Foucault 2003) in the sense that it is not about the management of life. It differs from necropolitics (Mbembe 2003) in that it is not about the subjugation of life to death. Sacropolitics is about neither managing nor taking life but rather *animating* it. It is about bringing to life dead, dying, or moribund populations and social formations. Sacropolitics seeks to do so by means of a particular form of sacrifice—one that involves broadening the boundaries of political community in an effort to involve the entire population in processes of social transformation. Sacropolitics is based not on a state of exception but rather a state redemption—in which the nation as a whole is to be redeemed from its current state through generalized, public mass sacrifice.

Government officials drew upon the logic of sacropolitics in an effort to accelerate a temporal process that they believed had been stalled in Peru due to the lingering influence of premodern attitudes and institutions. Toward that end, officials employed the personnel of multiple branches of government and the conscripted labor of hundreds of thousands of its citizens. They did so in order to build a material, bureaucratic, and discursive infrastructure that would overcome the dead weight of Peru's past—a past that was seen as preventing the country from entering the modern world era. At stake in government attempts at social transformation was nothing less than the ability to redeem Peru from the profane state into which it had fallen—to overcome the conditions of historical exception in which the country found itself. Today, we would refer to this as a state of underdevelopment.

The concrete expression of the government's (sacropolitical) plans to bring to life a moribund, stagnant social formation consisted of a series of grandiose modernization schemes. Based as they were on forced labor, these schemes provoked novel forms of conflict and resistance that frustrated the designs of central planners. In the preceding chapters I analyze these responses and their role in disordering the operation of government. Attending to these dynamics of disorder, I argue, is essential to reconstructing the genealogy of state crisis that culminated in the government's paranoid fears about APRA. But of equal importance is understanding the official language that state officials were compelled to employ in (mis-) representing the disorder they themselves had done so much to provoke.

Just as was the case with the Odría regime's encounter with APRA circa 1950, in decades prior government officials were compelled to generate ongoing, daily accounts of their efforts to modernize. As one might anticipate, the explanations they produced of their failures and frustrations were filled with elisions and distortions. But there was a logic to these distortions, a logic whose origins can be traced to Peru's foundations as an independent polity in the 1820s.

As was the case with the majority of the nation-states that emerged on both sides of the Atlantic during the "age of democratic revolution" (Palmer 1959–64), elements of a transnational language of political legitimacy figured prominently in the founding charter of the Peruvian republic. In Peru as elsewhere, this new language of state was based on assertions of citizenship, equality, and the common good that systematically masked or distorted extant social relationships—making them unspeakable, unrecognizable, and unrepresentable.[3] In other words, as was true more generally, in Peru state discourse *invented* rather than represented the social world it purported to describe (Ferguson 1990; O'Gorman 1972).

Having imagined the countryside and its inhabitants into being—in ways that rendered it an obstacle to the consolidation of the imagined nation-state—government officials encountered a whole range of difficulties when they attempted to intervene with their modernization projects. The explanations they generated to account for their problems had much in common with state discourse more generally. Official accounts of the frustrations the government experienced in seeking to modernize the highlands misconstrued or masked existing social ties, in ways that made them unrecognizable.

At the same time, government officials conjured into being an entire series of quasi-phantom problems and pseudoimaginary concerns.[4] It was these pseudoimaginary problems, I show, that became the focus of government efforts at surveillance and control. In other words, the delusions in which the Odría regime indulged circa 1950—of a dark and dangerous counterstate that was thwarting official efforts to rule—were but the most recent (and extreme) expression of a process that had characterized the era of modernization as a whole.

*   *   *

The Encrypted State traces the process by which the remarkable emerges out of the routine in everyday state formation, and the role that antiepistemological mechanisms play in that process. The volume challenges conceptions of the state that regard it as a bureaucratic institution as well as those that view it as a magical projection. In the present work "the state" is revealed to be neither an institution nor an illusion. Rather, it is a conflict-ridden and ultimately futile effort to transform the most violent, delusional, and coercive of practices into ordinary, unremarkable acts of administration.

Notes

Introduction

1. APRA is the acronym for the Alianza Popular Revolucionaria Americana (the Popular American Revolutionary Alliance). APRA was formed in Mexico City in 1924 by Víctor Raúl Haya de la Torre, a university student who had been exiled from Peru because of his role in uniting the labor movement and the movement for university reform (Stein 1980; see also García-Bryce 2010, 2014). Haya de la Torre established APRA in the ferment of postrevolutionary Mexico (Flores 2014; Spenser 1999). He called for the nationalization of land and industry, affirmed solidarity with all the oppressed people and classes of the world, and gave great emphasis to anti-imperialism (Haya de la Torre 1973).

Aprista cells formed spontaneously in highland urban centers (see, for example, Glave and Urrutia 2000; Heilman 2006, 2010; Nugent 1997; and Taylor 2000) in 1930–31, as Haya made plans to return from exile to participate in the presidential elections of 1931. The party continued to be very influential in the decades that followed.

2. For a fascinating analysis of an episode of panic from the colonial period, see Silverblatt 2015. See also the classic social science literature on moral panics, especially Cohen 1973; Hall et al. 1978; McCluhan 1964; and Young 1971.

3. I show that government officials communicated and acted as if they were fearful and distrustful of those around them, and I document regularities in the process by which they communicated and acted on the basis of unfounded fear and distrust. The irrationality of the government's response to APRA is reflected in the following: during some periods officials ignored real threats that confronted them, while in other periods they imagined into being threats that were not actually there. They also operated with an ever-expanding radius of doubt about who they could and could not trust. During periods of maximum suspicion, officials communicated and acted as if they had doubts about virtually everyone— even (or especially) those who professed the deepest commitment to the regime. I make no claims about the inner feelings of government officials. What is clear, however, is that

these officials acted and communicated as if they were fearful, distrustful, and ultimately paranoid. My interest is in how they acted and communicated rather than in how they felt.

4. The official fears of APRA discussed in Chapter 2 of this volume unfolded in a broader Cold War context of fears of international communism. Indeed, the regime of General Manuel Odría, which led the assault on the Party of the People, referred to members of the party as APRA-Comunistas. This is ironic considering the longstanding and bitter animosity between the Peruvian Communist Party and APRA (for important treatments of this broader Cold War context, see Grandin and Joseph 2010 and Joseph and Spencer 2007). But the conflict between Odría and APRA is not the focus of this volume.

5. Scholars of early modern Europe (Naphy 1997; Ruiz 2011) have examined the role of affective forces (in particular, fear) in governing processes. As interesting as this work is, however, it tends to reproduce a binary between early modern states, whose irrationality is not exceptional, and modern states, which are irrational only when ruled by despots (whether "Oriental," "sultanistic," etc.).

6. See Mbembe (2003) and Polanyi (1944) for insightful discussions of the more or less obligatory use of liberal discourse in official representations of state activity.

7. See Chapter 9 for a discussion of works on state formation that engage with phenomena such as disorder, fear, and paranoia in everyday encounters with government officials.

8. There is of course an alternative literature on state-related issues—one that views the state as an institution, or series of institutions—and seeks to understand how the state-as-institution came into being. The literature is vast, but influential works include Evans, Rueschemeyer, and Skocpol (1985); Fried (1967); Mann (1986); Miliband (1969); Poulantzas (1975); and Tilly (1985, 1990).

9. See Ferguson (2004) for a similarly subtle and fascinating argument, one that suggests that academics have been complicit in reproducing this vertical geography by accepting the state's claims to be above society. Ferguson's critique of the notion of "levels" resonates strongly with the work of the Manchester School (Vincent 1990).

10. Navaro-Yashin makes it clear that she is referring specifically to Western European statecraft, or alternatively to "the Euro-American paradigm" (2007, 84). Other important work on state documentary practices includes Clanchy (1979), Goody (1986), Hull (2012); Messick (1993) and Navaro-Yashin (2002, 2006).

11. Gordillo (2006) provides an insightful discussion of the role of documents as state fetishes among indigenous people in the Argentinean Chaco.

12. Several of the papers in Laszczkowski and Reeves (2017) and Das and Poole (2004) explore related questions. They focus on the ways in which the arbitrary, unpredictable actions of armed state agents produce powerful affective responses in encounters with subject groups.

13. "Sr. Gallardo" is a pseudonym.

14. An even worse fate almost befell the Municipal Archive. In 2013 a decision was made that the room where much of the archive was being stored was needed for another purpose. As a result, all the documents in the entire archive thrown into plastic garbage

bags and placed on the street to be collected as garbage. Fortunately, action was taken to save them, but not before the documentary record had become extensively disorganized.

15. I prefer *madness* to terms that have a more precise meaning because I am not using this term in a technical or clinical sense. Nor do I use terms like *delusion, fantasy, hysteria,* and *displacement* in a technical or clinical sense. Rather, I am using them to convey the affective dimensions to the mid-twentieth-century crisis of rule.

16. In her 2013 book, Janet Roitman also explores the relationship between times of crisis and normalcy. Roitman is concerned with the political uses of crisis claims—with who articulates such claims, when they do so, and toward what ends.

17. I would like to thank in particular the late Dr. Carlos Torres Mas, who in his role as departmental head of the National Cultural Institute facilitated my access to regional archives.

18. As the discussion in the text should make clear, I find the weak state literature unhelpful in understanding the dynamics of state formation in Chachapoyas.

19. During this period, Peru was divided into a nested hierarchy of territorial-administrative units, from district to province to department to nation. Chachapoyas was the capitol of the department of Amazonas.

20. See Chapter 6 and 7 for an explanation of how these calculations were made.

21. During this period, the Catholic Church receiving a monthly stipend from the government, and in this sense, was part of "the state."

22. See Collins (1988) for an insightful discussion of official assumptions about the underutilization of peasant labor.

23. Government officials' inability to recruit the (fictive) workforce needed for modernization had powerful affective dimensions. See Chapter 2 for a discussion of affect and state formation.

24. Philip Corrigan makes a related point about the state itself. He says "that the state is both illusory and there—indeed, its 'there-ness' is how the illusion is sustained." The state is "an illusion in the sense that its claim to be what it appeared to be is invalid; it is not illusory in the sense that it is not a logical error, a problem with our vision, or a conjuring trick that sustains it but precisely those powers and relations which its claim . . . conceals" (see Abrams 1988: 86).

25. My argument differs somewhat from that of other scholars who have dealt with the similar problems. Especially relevant in this regard is the work of James C. Scott on "state simplifcations" (Scott 1998; see also Ollman 1971). I refer to official objects of surveillance and control as phantoms in order to emphasize the extraordinary powers that are attributed to what are characterized as the most ordinary and mundane of phenomena. In this sense, the identification and construction of official objects of surveillance is integral to the process of displacement. For related analysis of the attribution of agency to inanimate objects and entities see Durkheim (1915); Marx (1967); Shipton (1989); and Taussig (1980).

26. According to the Ley de Conscripción Vial (Law 4113), men between the ages of 18 and 21, and between 50 and 60, were to provide six days of labor per year. Men in the intermediate age category (21 to 50) would be compelled to work for twelve days a

year—six days each semester. Even so, the Ley de Conscripción Vial was worded to ensure that Peru's indigenous groups would provide corvée labor for the project. According to the law, all citizens had the option of meeting their obligation with a cash payment. Since relatively few indigenous cultivators had the cash reserves necessary to take advantage of this option, they ended up providing the vast majority of the conscripted labor for Leguía's highways.

27. I am not even remotely suggesting that some states are irrational and others rational, or that some states are pathological and others not. Nor do I mean to imply that the state is a unitary actor. My point is rather that *all* states fail to live up to their own claims. Beyond that, my interest is not so much *if* state practices do this (which we know, even if we do not appreciate the full extent of it) but *how* they do it—and how they deal with the contradiction between practice and discourse. I devote much of *The Encrypted State* to identifying mechanisms that seek to mask delusion. I am also interested in exploring why it proves so difficult for most people to see past the mask of the state. I also try to identify mechanisms that produce the idea of the state as a unitary, integrated phenomenon despite behaviors on the part of government officials that are chaotic, irrational, etc.

Chapter 1: Sacropolitics

1. Even so, the ability of the sovereign to declare a state of exception, and to reduce any citizen to a condition of bare life, according to Agamben, defines the very essence of the position of the sovereign. Bare life is thus the dark underside of what Agamben calls political life (bios), a specter that can be invoked at any time. Bare life is the negative condition that defines the very possibility of what Agamben calls political life.

2. Foucault was concerned with managing threats to population, which came in several different forms. These included what he called the "endemics, or in other words the form, nature, extension, duration, and intensity of the illnesses prevalent in a population . . . that were difficult to eradicate and that were not regarded as epidemics that caused more frequent deaths, but as permanent factors which—and that is how they were dealt with—sapped the population's strength, shortened the working week, wasted energy, and cost money" (Foucault 2003, Lecture of 17 March 1976, 243–44). They also included, however, human groups that were regarded as a threat to the well-being of population. These groups, which Foucault generally glossed in terms of race, could be subject to a quite brutal thanatopolitics (Foucault 2003, Lecture of 17 March 1976, 243–44).

3. For insightful assessments of Agamben's work see Berlant 2011; Das and Poole 2004; Derrida 2009; Gupta 2012; Hansen and Stepputat 2005.

4. I understand sovereignty as a claim rather than an established fact or a social condition—or rather, as a claim that masquerades as a social condition. It is the conflation of claim and fact that compromises Agamben's theory of sovereignty. To take but one example, was it simply the sovereign's decree that resulted in the concentration camps in World War II? Hardly. Much ink has been spilled in an effort to make sense of the complex processes that resulted in this particular sovereign ban being implemented. To conflate claim/ban and imposition of ban is to presume what must be explained.

5. It is of course the case that not all the regimes of the first half of the twentieth century were equally or exclusively sacropolitical.

6. Peru was regarded as an exception not in Agamben's sense of a state of emergency but rather in being an anomaly or deviation from a norm.

7. Akhil Gupta (2012) is among the few scholars to examine a context (contemporary India) in which, contra Agamben, sovereigns use the law to include rather exclude marginalized groups—many of whom suffer terribly nonetheless.

8. These zones of exception include—concentration camps (Agamben 1998), detention centers (Heidbrink 2018), prisons (Cunha 2014), border checkpoints (Murphy and Maguire 2015), resettlement colonies (Das 2007), sterilization clinics (Molina Serra 2017) and development camps (Gupta 2012).

9. As noted above, this preoccupation with being behind the more industrialized world (as exemplified by Euro-America) was anything but unique to Peru, but rather was common throughout the postcolonial (and communist) worlds. It should be emphasized that the "everyone" who was called upon to sacrifice for the good of the country was discursive rather than actual. While it is true that the law studiously avoided identifying or naming specific subgroups who would be expected to sacrifice, the law was written in such a way as to allow some groups a way of buying out of having to labor. Even so, the sovereign decree was universal and inclusive in nature.

10. This concern with recovering what has been lost so as to restore a healthy state can be seen in the example of the Nazi final solution. While the Jews had become an important part of German society, their (partial) integration was a recent phenomenon and one that was the cause of much concern. Nazi ideology clearly had a future orientation, but that future was predicated on recuperating a lost past—on transforming the (fallen) present into a purer one by ridding society of those elements that were degrading the nation.

11. Mbembe (2003, 13) makes the important point that modernity "was at the origin of multiple concepts of sovereignty."

12. A contrast with the features of other forms of sovereignty will help bring out the distinctiveness of sacropolitics. In speaking of contemporary zones of exception, and the necropolitics that are associated with them, Mbembe (2003, 18) writes about the "perception of the existence of the Other as an attempt on my life, as a mortal threat or absolute danger whose biophysical elimination would strengthen my potential to life and security." In sacropolitics it is not the Other whose existence is regarded as threat to existence—and therefore in need of elimination—but rather the Self, in the form of the past-in-the-present.

13. Gupta (2012, 42) makes a similar point about Foucault and biopolitics: "Foucault's argument for the rise of biopolitics depends on the convergence of diverse institutions in different settings around a particular way of conceptualizing a problem."

14. The notion of affect is a highly contested one (see, for example, the important but contrasting formulations of Massumi 1995 and Sedgwick and Frank 1995). I use the term *affect* to refer "to those forces—visceral forces beneath, alongside, or generally other than conscious knowing . . . that serve [variously] to drive us toward [or away from] movement . . . thought and extension" (Gregg and Seigworth 2010, 1). I am particularly interested in the

contingent and context-specific nature of affective regimes. In this regard, I have found Raymond Williams's work on 'Structures of Feeling' (Williams 1977) to be especially useful.

15. In the present work an affective regime of nonaffect will be regarded as one in which emotions are regarded as clouding rational judgment, and therefore have no legitimate place in the normal activities of state. Conventional liberalism is regarded as having this view of affect (Banerjee and Bercuson 2015). Most studies of the relationship between the state and affect focus on the ways in which processes of rule generate affect among the governed, or alternatively how the state becomes the object of emotional investment by those who are governed (see the papers in Laszczkowski and Reeves 2017). In the present volume I explore a different question. I examine shifting affective regimes among government officials as they seek but ultimately fail to sustain the illusion of their own sovereignty.

16. For a fascinating, original, and insightful discussion of displacement that has much in common with my own, see Alvey (2014).

17. A more in-depth discussion of how government documents overstate, and the affective tone they adopt in the process, is beyond the scope of the present work (however, see Nugent n.d.). For a related discussion, which explores the relationship between the form of documents and the logic of rule, see Boyer and Yurchak (2010), Gupta (2012) and Yurchak (2003; 2006, chapter 2).

18. The following section of the chapter draws on Nugent (2014).

19. I have borrowed the idea of *the awkward classes* from Teodor Shanin (1972), who coined the term *the awkward class* to refer to the peasantry. As will be clear from the discussion in the present chapter, my use of the term has little in common with his.

20. See Nugent (2014) for a more in-depth discussion of the concept of standard deviations. As should be clear from the text, my use of this term has nothing in common with the meaning it carries in statistics.

21. For example, APRA had conspired to overthrow the government in December 1931, had been involved in a large-scale armed uprising intended to do the same in July 1932, and attempted a similar seizure of power in November 1934 (see *Dark Fantasies of State: Discipline, Dissent and Democracy in the Northern Peruvian Andes* [Nugent n.d.], the companion volume to the present work).

Chapter 2: The Descent into Madness

1. For purposes of clarity, I have presented standard deviations as unfolding sequentially in time. In actuality, the processes in question were not always so regular in character. Rather, tendencies in multiple directions often took place simultaneously in different parts of the regional space or reversed themselves.

2. The following sections of the chapter are based on the materials found in five document files: ASC3, ASC9, ASC16, ASC23, ASC29, ASC44. I encountered these files during the summers of 2002–2005, while working in the archive of the Subprefecture of Chachapoyas (formerly, the archive of the Prefecture). I would like to express my deep appreciation to the personnel of the Subprefecture, without whom my work would not have been possible.

3. See Nugent n.d., chapter 6.

4. The Caja de Depósitos y Consignaciones, and the Junta de Obras Públicas.

5. See Nugent n.d., chapter 6.

6. When large numbers of people who had been accused of being Apristas by government functionaries wrote to the prefect swearing their innocence, the Guardia Civil was assigned the task of discovering who was telling the truth. The prefect's subsequent conclusion that most members of the Guardia Civil were actually Apristas appears to have made him question the extent to which he could trust what they had told him about who did and did not belong to the Party of the People.

7. ASC3, 5 February 1949, 11 March 1949, 22 April 1949.

8. ASC3, 10 February 1949, 27 February 1949, 15 March 1949, 22 March 1949, 5 April 1949, 16 April 1949.

9. ASC3, 6 February 1949, 11 March 1949.

10. Nugent n.d., chapter 6.

11. ASC3, 6 February 1949, 11 March 1949.

12. During the period discussed in this chapter, Peru was divided into a nested hierarchy of administrative units. In ascending order, these were: districts (presided over by a governor, justice of the peace, and mayor), provinces (administered by a subprefect, provincial judge, and provincial mayor) and departments (overseen by a prefect and a superior court).

13. ASC3, 8 February 1949, 4 March 1949, 13 March 1949, 3 April 1949, 9 April 1949; ASC 5, 16 January, 25 January, 4 February, 12 February, 19 February, 2 March, 3 March, 7 March, 9 March, 18 March, 21 March, 5 April, 9 April, 12 April, 17 April, 27 April, 4 May, 7 May, 12 May, 19 May, 26 May.

14. Examples include ASC3, 14 February 1949, 20 February 1949, 2 March 1949, 10 March 1949, 19 March 1949, 4 April 1949, 7 April 1949, 16 April 1949; ASC5, 25 January (oficios from the districts of San Pedro, Leimebamba, Pizuquia, and Limabamba), 19 February (oficios from La Jalca, Colcamar, Jumbilla, San Nicolás, and Luya), 2 March (oficios from Huancas, Santo Tomas, Chuquibamba, Luya Viejo, Copallín, San Carlos, and Milpuc), 3 March (oficios from Florida, Valera, Cochamal, Santa Rosa, Camporredondo, Ocalli, and Levanto).

15. Government officials also attributed to APRA a party structure that spanned the entire country.

16. ASC3, 28 January 1949, 16 February 1949, 5 March 1949. See also Nugent n.d., chapters 4–6.

17. Both ASC3 and ASC44 are filled with correspondence showing that government officials that come to suspect even most seemingly innocent and innocuous groups of subversive activity or inclination.

18. ASC44, 22 March 1950.

19. As should be apparent, my use of "the relative autonomy of the state" has nothing in common with state theorists like Theda Skocpol (see Evans, Rueschemeyer, and Skocpol 1985).

20. Government officials' insecurity about their ability to construct a privileged sphere of communication by means of coded messages sent by telegram was heightened by the fact that secret information leaked out of the telegraph office on a regular basis—a situation

undoubtedly related to the fact that the head of the telegraph office was a prominent Aprista and party leader.

21. The document in Figures 2.1 and 2.2 (see ASC44, 8 July 1949) concerns the resignation of the subprefect as head of the Cáclic-Lámud Highway Committee—a group charged with the construction of an important road in the subprefect's province. The subprefect claimed that he had resigned when he had discovered that Apristas were among those on the committee. The prefect discovered, however, that the subprefect had always known that there were subversives on the Cáclic-Lámud Highway Committee. The subprefect had only resigned, however, and had only revealed the existence of the Apristas, when they would no longer side with him when the committee as a whole voted on such weighty matters as what route the highway would follow, who would be given contracts to build it, etc.

22. Žižek's concerns in *A Plague of Fantasies* (1997) have little to do with the argument developed in this chapter. Nonetheless, the brief discussion in his Introduction is unusually thought provoking, and highly relevant to the issues discussed in the present work.

23. See Silverblatt (2015, 176) for a parallel case, from colonial Peru.

24. The prefect suspected that many justices of the peace, who worked alongside the governors in the rural districts, were in fact Apristas. This may explain why he did not have the "Organización Vertical" document sent to them.

25. Apart from its secretariats and subsecretariats, APRA also had separate administrative sections devoted to Youth (FAJ, or APRA Youth Federation), Education, Popular Education, Unions, Cooperatives, and Statistics. As a number of authors have noted, Victor Raúl Haya de la Torre, who had founded the party and was responsible for its organization, had been heavily influenced by the discipline and order of fascist and communist parties during his trip to Europe in the 1920s.

26. See ASC44, 5 February 1949, 15 February 1949, 22 February 1949, 23 February 1949, 26 February 1949, 23 March 1949, 20 August 1949, 22 March 1950.

Chapter 3: The Consolidation of Casta Rule

1. The conditions that variously promote or undermine the unity of action of elite groups was of course a major concern of writers associated with the dependency school (Cardoso and Faletto 1979). For historical/sociological and ethnographic accounts that explore the issue of elite unity in Latin America, see Lewin 1987; Lomnitz 1987; Paige 1998.

2. See AMC1, ASC17.

3. See Nugent 1997, chapters 3–5, for a more in-depth discussion of the contradictions of *casta* rule.

4. This assumes that Leguía would remain in the presidency until 1934. Galarza based this estimate on figures he compiled from the *Balance y Cuenta General*, 1920–1929.

5. According to the Ley de Conscripción Vial of May 10, 1920 (also called the Ley de Caminos), all adult males between the ages of 18 and 60 were obliged to work between 6–12 days per year on the construction or repair of roads within the provinces where they lived. In practice, it was almost exclusively the indigenous population that was subject to the provisions of this law. The abuses of the Conscripción Vial, as it was known, were notorious (see Mallon 1983; Manrique 1987; Meza Bazán 1999, 2003, 2009; Pereyra Chávez 2002).

6. During the *oncenio* funds for highway construction were provided to provincial highway committees (or *juntas viales provinciales*). These were made up of the provincial mayor (who was the president), the judge (of the First Instance), and the military chief (who was responsible for overseeing military conscription). Basadre notes that in many cases, the juntas came under control of the provincial subprefect, and that the mayors often acted as labor contractors for coastal estates (thereby creating a conflict of interest with respect to their role on the junta). Furthermore, the juntas not uncommonly struggled with the highway engineer (one appointed for each department) over such issues as which sections of highway should be prioritized, who would be hired as foremen, and the provisioning of supplies and equipment (Basadre 1968–69, XIII, 255). As we will see in Chapters 6 and 7, after 1930 competition between political officials for control of the labor supply becomes an extremely divisive force.

7. The dynamics of intraelite competition and violence during the *oncenio* are explored with great insight by Mallon (1983), Meza Bazán (2009), and Taylor (1986). See also Nugent (1997), and Chapter 5 of the present volume.

8. Opposing *castas* mounted challenges to the ruling *casta* at election time because the ruling regime in Lima was preoccupied with problems of its own and could not offer the usual level of support to its regional client (Nugent 1997).

9. See ASC2.

10. The Pizarro-Rubio enjoyed unusually close relations with President Leguía. The president was godfather to Victor Pizarro, eldest son of Pablo Pizarro (the president's *compadre*), senator for the state of Amazonas and one of the leaders of the Pizarro-Rubio *casta*.

11. The documentation regarding the increasingly aggressive behavior of the Burga-Hurtado in the months leading up to the elections of 1919, their expected attack on the Pizarro-Rubio at the time of the elections, and the Pizarro-Rubio's punishment of the Burga-Hurtado after the elections, can be found in the following sources: ASC1, ASC4, ASC12, ASC13, ASC32, ASC43, ASC52, ASC54, ASC55, ASC56, ASC57.

12. The Pizarro-Rubio attempted but failed to capture the leading members of adversarial families, who they hoped to make an example of through public displays of humiliation and abuse. The Pizarro-Rubio were unable to do so because the leading opposition families retreated into their fortified hacienda homes, where they and their numerous clients could defend themselves from armed attacks by the ruling coalition.

13. The documentation regarding the efforts of the Pizarro-Rubio to use the judicial apparatus to drive elite members of the Burga-Hurtado out of the region is extensive. It can be found in the document files listed in note 11.

14. See ASC11, Decreto No. 82, 21 de Abril.

15. See ASC11, Decreto No. 86. 26 de Abril.

Chapter 4: Being (and Seeing) Like a State

1. I have borrowed the chapter title from *Seeing Like a State: How Certain Schemes to Improve the Human Condition Have Failed*, James C. Scott's pathbreaking 1998 volume on the dynamics of political rule.

2. There were between twenty-three and twenty-seven gendarmes stationed in Chachapoyas, the capital of the department of Amazonas (and also capital of the province

of Chachapoyas), five men stationed in Lámud, capital of the province of Luya and four men stationed in Jumbilla, capital of the province of Bongará (ASC15).

3. After providing their required days of work under the provisions of this Conscripción Vial law (the number of days varying between six and twelve, depending on the age of the conscript), these individuals could, if they chose, continue to work as day laborers. Their compensation for doing so varied between S/. 50–.80 centavos a day. *Very* few individuals chose to stay on as day laborers after they had served their time as conscripts.

4. As sizeable as were the funds provided to support highway construction, they were dwarfed by additional monies made available to the ruling coalition by the central government. These subventions were provided to help the region recover from the devastating earthquake of May 14–18, 1928. This catastrophic event leveled much of the city of Chachapoyas, and destroyed public buildings, schoolhouses, roadways, and hospitals throughout the region. It damaged marketplaces, water systems, and the rudimentary electric light infrastructure. Several hundred thousand soles were provided to help the region rebuild after the earthquake. It appears that the majority of these funds were not used for their intended purposes (see Nugent 1997, 271–77).

5. The ruling *casta's* violation of the law concerning labor conscription during the *oncenio* is most clearly reflected in the marginal role of the military officers on the *juntas de conscripción vial*, where they were clearly figures of little importance. As a result, military conscription was of only marginal importance during the *oncenio*. Military officers were for the most part ignored, and were unable to influence the goals of the ruling *casta*—which were focused on highway conscription. *Casta* leaders may have been under little pressure to recruit for the military because of President Leguía's hostility to and suspicion of the army. Leguía was skeptical of the loyalty of the army, and in order to protect himself from possible betrayal created an entirely new, national police force—the Guardia Civil. Founded in 1922, the national police grew quickly in size to become nearly equal in number to the army. As we will see, with the end of the *oncenio* military conscription takes on renewed importance.

6. Basadre (1968–69, XIII, 255) also observes that the provincial conscription committees often fell under the control of the subprefect of the province in question.

7. The notion of transparency has been the subject of considerable critical appraisal (see, for example, Sharma 2014). The meaning I attribute to this term will emerge as the discussion proceeds.

8. Men between the ages of 18 and 21 were expected to contribute six days of labor per year, as were men between the ages of 50 and 60. Men between the ages of 21 and 50 were called up to provide twelve days of labor per year.

9. The most common strategy utilized by those seeking to evade their corvée labor obligations was to leave the district in which they were registered and take up residence in a different one, where they would be more difficult to track. This is a time-honored practice in the Andes.

10. By the time this *oficio* was written the prefect had received written permission from the Dirección de Vías de Comunicación in Lima to use highway conscripts for public works projects more generally, as the prefect saw fit (see ASC40, 28 de Abril de 1930).

11. For example, see ASC40, 31 de Mayo de 1930.

12. For example, see "Relación de omisos . . ." (ASC40, 28 de Mayo de 1930; and "Conscriptos viales omisos . . ." (ASC40, 21 de Agosto de 1929).

13. Informants report that clients of the Pizarro-Rubio were not forced to provide this cash payment—and thus that the ruling coalition used this provision of the Ley Vial to demonstrate its ability to violate the precept of "equal treatment under the law," and the precepts of popular sovereignty in general. In other words, the law applied only to those who lacked powerful patrons.

14. For information about the *omisos* from this period, see ASC38 and ASC40.

15. See ASC50.

16. Indeed, after 1930 progress on the highway should have been easy, as by this point it was being built in and along the relatively level flood plain of the Utcubamba River.

17. There was one exception to this pattern that actually proved the rule that the Pizarro-Rubio coalition did indeed exercise virtually total control over public discussion and debate, as well as over the mechanisms of justice. In its various issues, the populist newspaper *Amazonas* did indeed raise concerns about the misappropriation of funds and about the abuses of the Pizarro-Rubio more generally. This newspaper was not published in Chachapoyas, however, but rather in Lima.

Chapter 5: Divided Elite and Disordered State

1. These were the positions associated with the old administrative/territorial divisions (district, province, and department).

2. See the correspondence in ASC22, ASC35, ASC45.

3. See ASC18, ASC26, ASC49.

4. See ASC14, ASC19, ASC24.

5. See ASC31, ASC35, ASC37.

6. The trip involved a combination of ocean steamer, followed by travel by rail and highway. The final week to ten days of the journey, however, had to be done by mule, over exceptionally rugged terrain (through the canyon of the upper Marañon river, which is over 10,000 feet deep).

7. The same was true of individuals from Lima who were appointed to important political posts in the Chachapoyas region. For relevant documentation see: ASC26, ASC27, ASC35, ASC46.

8. See ASC36.

9. See ASC51.

10. See ASC37, ASC48.

11. See Chapter 6 and 7.

12. See Chapter 6 and 7. Thiranagama and Kelly (2010) provide an insightful discussion of the contradictory position of the individuals who are asked to mediate between multiple projects of rule, pointing out that they are often vulnerable to being accused of being "traitors."

13. The *juntas de conscripción vial*, which were associated with the hated regime of Augusto Leguía, were disbanded after the *oncenio*.

14. Not all of the new demands on the regional population associated with the modernization process involved conscription. The activities of the provincial courts (which were located in the provincial capitals) and also the Superior Court (which was located in the departmental capital) placed a different kind of pressure on rural cultivators. As the courts pursued the various cases that were entrusted to them, they called upon a large number of individuals to make the journey from the countryside to participate in court proceedings, both as witnesses and as the accused. These demands were greatly resented, as they required those called to absent themselves from their homes and their farms for many days at a time. It was not at all uncommon for these individuals to travel to the court by the appointed date to discover that the court proceedings were behind schedule or had been delayed. Regardless, the courts were unable to provide these individuals with anything to subsidize the cost of food, travel, or lodging. As a result, in addition to requiring that rural cultivators neglect their farms, the trips could also represent a considerable cash expense for those who were called to appear.

15. See ASC42. Those who chose permanent dislocation appear to have moved away from the districts located in the main catchment area of the Grand Chachapoyas-Pimentel Highway and toward more outlying districts. As suggested by the example quoted in the text, the trend also appears to have been for rural cultivators to leave not only their district but also their province of origin, and to take up residence in a new province (see also ASC18, 13 de Febrero de 1936; ASC25, 20 de Noviembre de 1939; ASC33, 6 de Marzo de 1943). Flight from one province to another made it less likely that the authorities would be able to track those in flight to their new location. Doing so would have required a degree of cooperation among government officials across multiple administrative scales. It was precisely this kind of cooperation that was increasingly rare after the fall of the *castas* (the strategy adopted by rural cultivators to evade conscription by abandoning the site of their official residence and moving to another is an old one in the Andes. It goes back to the colonial period, when people who chose this strategy were referred to as *forasteros* [Wightman 1990]).

16. In the early 1930s, the military persisted in posting public notices, well in advance of conscription, about who was to serve in the armed forces. The result was widespread evasion (ASC47, Capitán Comandante de la Guardia Civil al Sr. Subprefecto de la Provincia, 14 de Octubre de 1933).

17. There was enormous resistance to these labor exactions across the country, which contributed in no small part to the downfall of the Leguía regime. The labor demands of the post-*casta* era in Chachapoyas, however, were far greater than those of the *oncenio*. According to the conscription plans developed by the Office of Highways, men living in villages located in the catchment area of the Grand Chachapoyas-Pimentel Highway (see Chapter 6 and 7) were to provide a fortnight of labor every three months. As explained in the text, in practice, the rural population was subject to even heavier demands.

18. The documentary record is literally overflowing with examples of projects that are planned but never begun, are begun are never finished, drag on over very long periods of time, and seem to be completed but subsequently must be undone or redone.

Chapter 6: The Sacropolitics of Military Conscription

1. Information about the characteristics of the regional population was available in the form of municipal records and census materials.

2. The expansion of the courts and the reorganization of the collection of excise taxes also had a major impact on the rural cultivating population. A consideration of these forces is beyond the scope of the present work.

3. As noted in Chapter 5, Leguía's growing suspicion of the army as a potential threat to his position may have meant that there was less pressure to conscript during the *oncenio* that there would come to be later.

4. The French military mission that President Nicolas de Piérola (1895–1900) invited to Peru in 1896 to reorganize and professionalize the armed forces helped design a law requiring universal military service (see Cobas 1982 and Nunn 1983 for insightful discussions of the nationalizing influence of this professionalized military). In the Chachapoyas region, however, prior to 1930 this law was implemented by the ruling *casta*. As a result, it was predominantly rural clients of out-of-power *castas* that were forced to serve in the military.

5. Conscription was thus one method by means of which the forces of order sought to construct an official topography of rule that would do away with obstacles to the modernization process. As noted in the Introduction, the peasantry was regarded as one such obstacle. In order to effect a topography of rule that would help transform the peasantry from an obstacle into a vital contributing force, the authorities felt compelled to bring them close—to integrate them directly into state projects and plans. Conscription, which would force the peasantry to learn new disciplines of the mind, body, and behavior, was considered indispensable to this process.

6. See in particular ASC5, ASC6, ASC8, ASC18.

7. The previous year, in 1932, the Ministry of War had appealed to the Ministry of Government to instruct municipalities across the country to provide to the chief conscription officer of their respective province with updated lists, every month, of all births, deaths, and changes in residence that had occurred in their districts (according to the provisions of article 24 of the Obligatory Military Service Law #1569 (ASC30, Circular #62. 8 de Marzo de 1932). The rural population was fully cognizant of the role played by the municipal birth and death registers in enabling military recruitment. As a result, they resisted municipal efforts to record these vital statistics—much to the frustration of the municipal authorities, as well as of the military officials who relied on this information in order to identify conscripts. The military did indeed seek to consult with municipal authorities in the course of conscription. As noted in Chapter 5, however, as the post-*casta* period wore on it became increasingly difficult to know with any certainty who lived where. This was because the rural populace had such a powerful incentive to try to disappear from official scrutiny. And with the breakdown of the region-wide structure of surveillance established the Pizarro-Rubio coalition, the rural population had not only the incentive but also the opportunity to disappear. Thus, the fact that a particular individual of draftable age should

have been living in the district of Levanto, for example, did not mean that he actually lived there. He could have fled to another district, where he would have sought out the protection of a patron. It was equally likely, however, that he continued to have his primary residence in Levanto but had temporarily gone into hiding. There was simply no way to know. As a result, chief conscription officers abandoned efforts to locate specific individuals. Instead, they focused on satisfying the conscription quotas for the relevant administrative unit (district or province). Furthermore, they did so regardless of how many men were actually to be found in those units.

8. Although the head of the gendarmes and the prefect seem not to have been aware of it, Julio Abel Qurioz was a prominent Aprista. Landed elites were most likely to engage in open defiance of the central government's new conscription procedures between 1931 and 1934. During this period, civil-war-like conditions obtained in much of the country (see Nugent n.d.).

9. As noted in the text, the figure of 2,125 men per province assumes that men pressed into military service were gone for an average of five years. There are no figures available concerning how many conscripts actually returned home after completing their military service. Because men were obligated to serve in the military only a single time, however, once they had done so they had to be stricken from the draft rolls permanently.

10. These figures should be considered little more than estimates that are useful for illustrative purposes. I have tried to err on the side of caution. There were probably fewer households than I have indicated in each of the department's four provinces.

11. To calculate these figures, I have subtracted the adult men who lived in the city of Chachapoyas, and also those who resided in the large towns of Luya and Lámud, who were registered to vote. In general, they were able to avoid the draft. Men who lived in the towns of the other three provinces were also able to escape having to serve in the army. Due to the difficulties of calculating their numbers from the available information, however, I have elected to include them all. As a result, the figures in the text overestimate the number of men who were available to fill the conscription quotas.

12. In Rodriguez de Mendoza, there were 710 fewer adult men than the number required by the military. The province of Bongará lacked 684 adult men in order to fulfill its draft quota.

13. In calculating these figures, I have followed the procedure outlined above, in note 11.

14. The *oficio* quoted in the text was sent by the Prefect to the head of the Guardia Civil and to the Chief Conscription Officer for the province of Chachapoyas (see also ASC34, Oficio # 256, 19 de Julio de 1935).

15. In general, governors were responsible for maintaining roads, trails, and bridges. Mayors were expected to maintain public buildings and facilities.

16. As this *oficio* suggests, in the context of the increased pressure on the rural labor supply resulting from military conscription, district functionaries found it more and more difficult to carry out their administrative duties. As the region's infrastructure fell into a state of disrepair, the district personnel who were responsible for its maintenance became vulnerable to criticism from competing functionaries, and from members of competing

political networks. The latter would not hesitate to denounce "negligent" personnel to the prefect, subprefects, and provincial mayors, who were compelled to write to their subalterns, reminding them of their obligations and threatening them with punishment if they failed to comply.

17. See Fitzpatrick and Gellately (1997) for a fascinating discussion of denunciation in modern European history.

18. See in particular ASC5, ASC8, ASC18.

Chapter 7: The Sacropolitics of Labor Conscription

1. The twelve districts in the province of Chachapoyas that were included in the catchment area for the highway project were Quinjalca, Olleros, Sonche, Soloco, Leimebamba, La Jalca, Levanto, San Pedro, San Ildefonso, Granada, Huancas and Chuquibamba. The twelve districts in the province of Luya were Luya, Lámud, Conila, Cuechán, Olto, Paclas, Chosgón, San Jerónimo, Luya Viejo, Tingo, Colcamar, and Santo Tomás.

2. The *Oficina de Caminos* experimented with a series of labor recruitment strategies. I have selected the most important to avoid unnecessary confusion.

3. See ASC18, 3 de Julio de 1942.

4. In Chachapoyas province, the three districts were San Pedro, San Ildefonso (Montevideo), and La Jalca. In Luya province, the districts were Conila, Tingo, and Lonya Grande (ASC18, 30 de Diciembre de 1943).

5. See ASC18, 3 de Julio de 1942.

6. To calculate the figure for Chachapoyas province, I have subtracted men in the 19–60 age category who lived in the city of Chachapoyas, as they were able to avoid the draft. Men who lived in the towns of the other three provinces were also able to escape having to serve. Due to the difficulties of calculating their numbers from the census, however, I have elected to include all men in the 19–60 age category. As a result, the figures in the text overestimate the number of men who were available to fill the labor conscription quotas.

7. It is interesting to compare these demands with those of Leguía's infamous *conscripción vial*. The latter called upon the rural cultivating population to provide 6–12 days of labor per year for public works. The Oficina de Caminos in Chachapoyas called upon the peasantry to contribute 15–20 days of labor four times a year (every three months). Even in its most benign form, this labor tax was far more onerous than Augusto Leguía's despised program.

8. The definitive analysis of this issue with respect to the Peruvian Andes is Jane Collins's *Unseasonal Migrations* (1988).

9. Labor recruitment for the Chachapoyas-Cajamarca Highway bore an uncanny resemblance to military recruitment into the armed services—a fact commonly remarked upon by observers. The local population resented both very deeply.

10. The most common way for rural cultivators to earn cash was by involving themselves in the manufacture, transport, and/or sale of cane liquor (*aguardiente*) or brown sugar

(*chancaca*). There was an active regional market for both products, and earning income in this way was vastly preferred over working for wages.

11. While pressures of this kind had always been present, during the *casta* era competing demands for labor had been coordinated by *casta* leaders. During the post-*casta* period this was no longer possible. Furthermore, because the region's old elite families were experiencing a rapid decline in status, they were more desperate than ever for labor. As a result, district functionaries were under constant pressure to divert workers to elite estates.

12. The project referred to in the previous *oficio*—which was focused on improving the sewage system of the city of Chachapoyas—differed from conscription for the military and for highway construction in an important way. It was not a recurrent, regularly occurring phenomenon, but rather took place only once. This made it more difficult for rural cultivators to anticipate and to avoid. There were a large number of these single-occurrence projects during the post-*casta* period. The fact that there were as many as there were, and that they were so difficult to evade, may have encouraged rural cultivators to seek to disappear from official scrutiny by moving to a new district (see Chapter 5).

13. It wasn't until the mid-1950s that the government finally devised a solution to the problem of labor recruitment for the Chachapoyas-Cajamarca-Bagua Highway project. They did so by merging military conscription with conscription for the highway project. In 1956, the army—which was made up of peasant conscripts from all around the country—was given the task of completing the remaining sections of the highway.

Chapter 8: Glimpses of Danger and Subversion

1. The individuals who were forced to labor for the government, of course, were under no illusions about whether or not state activities were based on force.

2. This entire document file, and the quotes selected from it, come from AGN1, 6 de Julio de 1936. It is highly unusual that such a high-ranking officer made these arrests, for officers did not normally patrol the streets, as Collantes appeared to have been doing in the early morning hours of July 4, 1936.

3. This was not surprising. During its brief periods of legality, APRA was quite open about its organizational structure.

4. This last clause actually comes from a subsequent part of the transcript of the interrogation. I include it here because it is important to Muñoz's account.

5. In the transcript of the interrogation of Cabañas, there appears to be some confusion regarding the precise amount of money that is entered opposite the pseudonym, "M. Gordo." The police refer at one point in their report to "5 soles," as they did in their questioning of Muñoz. At a different point, however, they refer to "70 soles" instead of "5 soles." This discrepancy may reflect the fact that the *guardias* had great difficulty deciphering the notebook at all—an issue taken up in greater detail in the text below.

6. See ASC34, 17 de Julio de 1935.

7. Lieutenant Collantes was incorrect about the position that Nicolás Muñoz occupied in the Departmental Command. He was actually the Secretary of Discipline (see Nugent n.d.).

8. Lieutenant Collantes was also incorrect about Torres's position in the APRA hierarchy, for he did not occupy any of the secretariats of which the Departmental Command was composed (see Nugent n.d.).

9. For an illustration of APRA's use of coded messages in the early 1930s, see Santillán Bernuy 2003.

10. See ASC51, 18 Julio, 19 Julio de 1936.

11. See ASC51, 19 Julio de 1936.

12. See ASC51, 20 Julio, 21 Julio, 22 Julio, 23 Julio de 1936.

13. See ASC51, 27 de Julio de 1936.

14. The correspondence concerning the investigations into the political leanings of the Sport-Culture Clubs continued throughout the second half of 1936. The relevant correspondence is to be found in ASC51.

15. The documentary record is silent about what happened to Subprefect Villavicencia in the aftermath of the revelations about his role in warning prominent Apristas about the plans of the police to arrest them. Within several years, however, Villavicencia reappears, and goes on to become the subprefect of several provinces in the department of Amazonas.

16. The Benavides regime had not realized this. The fact that the regime had assumed that it could engineer the results of the elections of October 1936 showed just how out of touch with the Peruvian electorate the government actually was. Furthermore, it showed this publicly, to one and all, in the most humiliating of manners. The fact that Benavides annulled the elections was of course a serious blow to APRA. But the fact that he had allowed them to proceed in the first place showed that it was the Party of the People, rather than the government, that had captured the hearts and minds of a very large number of Peruvians.

Conclusion

1. For influential scholarship that focuses on issues of fantasy, fear, anxiety, and delusion in state formation see Aretxaga 2003; Navaro-Yashin 2007; Taussig 1997; Taylor 1997. For influential scholarship in the utilitarian tradition see Mann 1986, 1993; Scott 1998, 2009; and Tilly 1985; 1990.

2. See Sharma and Gupta (2006) for an insightful treatment of the distinction between functional and cultural approaches to the state.

3. For a perceptive discussion of Roman law as a new language of legitimacy in early modern European state formation, see Abrams (1988).

4. Larson (2004) provides a fascinating account of the role of semi-imaginary fictions in the process of state making. She does so in her analysis of the rise of the "Indian question" in the Andean republics in the late nineteenth century, and its relation to elite efforts to modernize the region.

Bibliography

Primary Sources

Archivo General de la Nación (Lima, Peru)
AGN1. Documentos de Correspondencia de la Prefectura del Departamento de Amazonas. 1936.

Archivo Municipal de Chachapoyas (Chachapoyas, Peru)
AMC1. Contribuciones Rurales, Provincia del Cercado, 1920. Actuación de Matrículas de la Contribución Rural.

Archivo Subprefectural de Chachapoyas (Chachapoyas, Peru)
ASC 1. Colección de Artículos. 1922. "Colección de artículos sobre el movimiento revolucionario del 5 de Agosto de 1921." *El Oriente* [periódico], del 1 de Abril de 1922 [no publisher listed].
ASC2. Compañía Recaudadora de Impuestos, 1913.
ASC3. Continuación [of Oficios Remitidos. Personal y Secretos. Años 1947–48–49–50–51–52 y 53)].
ASC4. Copiador de Oficios a la Prefectura del Departamento de Amazonas, 27 de Abril al 3 de Diciembre, 1920.
ASC5. Copiador Oficios. En Completo Desorden. Departamento. República. Años 1934–36–35 [*sic*!].
ASC6. Copiador. Oficios Varios [República]. Dpto. Junio 1933–Junio 1934.
ASC7. Copiador Oficios. Departamento. República. Año 1935.
ASC8. Copiador. Oficios Varios de la Prefectura a Varios Autoridades Departamentales. Mayo 1937–Agosto 1944.
ASC9. Cuaderno de Manifestaciones sobre antecedentes Políticos 1949.
ASC10. Decretos y Resoluciones de la Prefectura del Departamento de Amazonas, 1924.

ASC11. Decretos y Resoluciones de la Prefectura del Departamento de Amazonas, 15 de Enero de 1924 al 8 de Julio de 1924.

ASC12. Decretos y Resoluciones de la Prefectura del Departamento de Amazonas, 10 de Julio de 1924 al 30 de Noviembre de 1924.

ASC13. Diversos Años del 1849 al 1924. Varias Reparticiones Administrativas.

ASC14. Documentos Varios. Prefectura. 1943.

ASC15. Gendarmería—Chachapoyas. 1926–1927–1928.

ASC16. Gobernadores al Prefecto del Departamento. 1949.

ASC17. Haciendas, [Sus] Propietarios i Producciones, 1889.

ASC18. Hojas Sueltas. Oficios Diversos. 1929–1945.

ASC19. Hojas Sueltas. Oficios Diversos. 1930–1949.

ASC20. Jefatura Departamental [de la Circunscripción Territorial]. 1932.

ASC21. Legajo de Oficios. Juzgado de Primera Instancia. Cercado. 1920.

ASC22. Legajo de Oficios, Oficinas Locales, Correspondiente al Año de 1942.

ASC23. Legajo de Oficios. Prefectura de Departamento de Amazonas. 1949.

ASC24. Legajo de Oficios. Subprefectura del Cercado, Correspondiente al Año de 1939.

ASC25. Legajo de Oficios Varios, Subprefectura del Cercado a la Prefectura. 1939.

ASC26. Legajo de Oficios. Subprefectura de Luya. 1942.

ASC27. Legajo de Oficios. Subprefectura del Cercado, Correspondiente al Año de 1941.

ASC28. Legajo de Oficios Varios. Año 1938.

ASC29. Legajo de Oficios de la Subprefectura de la Provincia de Luya-Lamud, Correspondiente al Año de 1949.

ASC30. Oficios. Dirección de Gobierno. 1932.

ASC31. Oficios. Dirección de Gobierno. 1933.

ASC32. Oficios. Gobernadores al Prefecto. 1921.

ASC33. Oficios. Gobernadores del Departamento. 1943.

ASC34. Oficios. Prefectura. Departamento. 1935.

ASC35. Oficios. Prefectura. Departamento. 1936.

ASC36. Oficios. Prefectura. Departamento. 1938.

ASC37. Oficios. Prefectura. Departamento. 1944.

ASC38. Oficios. Varias Dependencias del Departamento. 1928–1932.

ASC39. Oficios de la Subprefectura del Cercado. 1934.

ASC40. Oficios de las Diversas Autoridades del Departamento. 1929. Ramo de Vías de Comunicación.

ASC41. Oficios de los Gobernadores. Año 1936.

ASC42. Oficios de los Gobernadores. 1941.

ASC43. Oficios Dirigidos a la Prefectura y Demas Autoridades del Departamento por la Subprefectura del Cercado, Marzo 12, 1919. Terminado el 31 de octubre de 1919.

ASC44. Oficios Remitidos. Personal y Secretos. Años 1947–48–49–50–51–52 y 53.

ASC45. Oficios Varios [Departamento]. 1933–1934.

ASC46. Oficios Varios [República]. Departamento. Año de 1935.

ASC47. Oficios Varios. Prefectura del Departamento de Amazonas. 1933.

ASC48. Oficios Varios. Prefectura del Departamento de Amazonas. 1934.

ASC49. Oficios Varios de la Prefectura a Varios Autoridades. 1939.

ASC50. Planillas, Carretera Chachapoyas-Pimentel, Junta Provincial Vial de Chachapoyas. 1927, 1928.

ASC51. Prefectura del Departamento de Amazonas a Diversas Dependencias. 1936.

ASC52. Subprefectura del Cercado a la Prefectura del Departamento. 2 de Febrero al 14 de Agosto de 1920.

ASC53. Toma de Razón y Decretos y Reso[luciones], 1923–24.

ASC54. Un Legajo de Oficios del Juzgado de Primera Instancia. Año de 1919.

ASC55. Un Legajo de Oficios del Juzgado de Primera Instancia. Cercado. 1920

ASC56. Un Legajo de oficios de las Gobernaciones del Departamento. Año de 1920.

ASC57. Un Legajo de Oficios del Juzgado de Primera Instancia. 1921.

Other Primary Sources

Amazonas (newspaper, Chachapoyas, Peru).

El Comercio (newspaper, Lima, Peru).

La Ortiga (newspaper, Chachapoyas, Peru).

Secondary Sources

Abrams, Philip. 1988. "Notes on the Difficulty of Studying the State." *Journal of Historical Sociology* 1 (1): 58–89.

Agamben, Giorgio. 1998. *Sovereign Power, Bare Life and the State of Exception*. Stanford, CA: Stanford University Press.

———. 2000. *Means Without Ends. Notes on Politics*. Translated by Vincenzo Binetti and Cesare Casarino. Minneapolis: University of Minnesota Press.

Alvey, Jennifer. 2014. "Contested Boundaries: Border Disputes, Administrative Disorder and State Representational Practices in Nicaragua (1935–1956)." *Focaal* 2014 (68): 105–23.

Anderson, Benedict. 1991. *Imagined Communities: Reflections on the Origin and Spread of Nationalism*. London; New York: Verso.

Aretxaga, Begona. 2000. "Playing Terrorist: Ghastly Plots and the Ghostly State." *Journal of Spanish Cultural Studies* 1 (1): 43–58.

———. 2003. "Maddening States." *Annual Review of Anthropology* 32: 393–410.

Banerjee, Kiran, and Jeffrey Bercuson. 2015. "Rawls on the Embedded Self: Liberalism as an Affective Regime." *European Journal of Political Theory* 14 (2): 209–28.

Basadre, Jorge. 1980. *Elecciones y centralismo en el Perú*. Lima: Centro de Investigación de la Universidad del Pacífico.

———. 1968–89. *Historia de la República del Peru. 1822–1933*. Sexta edición. Lima: Editorial universitaria.

Bataille, Georges. 1985. *Visions of Excess: Selected Writings, 1927–1939*. Minneapolis: University of Minnesota Press.

Ben David, Lior. 2018. "Modernización y colonialismo en la 'Patria Nueva': La perspectiva de los delincuentes indígenas 'semi-civilizados.'" In *La Patria Nueva: Economía, sociedad y cultura en el Perú 1919–1930*, edited by Paulo Drinot, 115–38. Raleigh, NC: Editorial A Contracorriente.

Berlant, Lauren. 2011. *Cruel Optimism*. Durham, NC: Duke University Press.

Birmingham, Peg. 2014. "Law's Violent Judgment: Does Agamben Have a Political Aesthetics?" *New Centennial Review* 14 (2): 99–110.

Blanco, Maria del Pilar, and Esther Peeren, eds. 2013. *The Spectralities Reader: Ghosts and Haunting in Contemporary Cultural Theory*. London: Bloomsbury.

Bourdieu, Pierre. 1999. "Rethinking the State: Genesis and Structure of the Bureaucratic Field." In *State/Culture: State Formation after the Cultural Turn*, edited by George Steinmetz, 53–75. Ithaca, NY: Cornell University Press.

Boyer, Dominic, and Alexi Yurchak. 2010. "American Stiob: Or, What Late-Socialist Aesthetics of Parody Reveal about Contemporary Political Culture in the West." *Cultural Anthropology* 25 (2): 179–221.

Brenneis, Don. 2000. "Reforming Promise." In *Documents: Artifacts of Modern Knowledge*, edited by Annalise Riles, 41–70. Ann Arbor: University of Michigan Press.

Cardoso, Fernando Henrique, and Enzo Faletto. 1979. *Dependency and Development in Latin America*. Translated by Marjory Mattingly Urquidi. Berkeley: University of California Press.

Centeno, Miguel Angel. 2002. *Blood and Debt: War and Taxation in Nineteenth-Century Latin America*. Princeton, NJ: Princeton University Press.

Chouliaraki, Lilie. 2010. "Post-Humanitarianism: Humanitarian Communication Beyond a Politics of Pity." *International Journal of Cultural Studies* 13 (2): 37–51.

Clanchy, Michael T. 1979. *From Memory to Written Record, England, 1066–1307*. Cambridge, MA: Harvard University Press.

Cobas, Efraín. 1982. *Fuerza armada: Misiones militares y dependencia en el Peru*. Lima: Editorial horizonte.

Cohen, Stanley. 1973. *Folk Devils and Moral Panics*. St Albans: Paladin.

Collins, Jane L. 1988. *Unseasonal Migrations: Rural Labor Scarcity in Peru*. Princeton, NJ: Princeton University Press.

Coronil, Fernando. 1997. *The Magical State: Nature, Money, and Modernity in Venezuela*. Chicago: University of Chicago Press.

Corrigan, Philip. 1981. "On Moral Regulation." *Sociological Review* 29 (2): 313–37.

Corrigan, Philip, and Derek Sayer. 1985. *The Great Arch: English State Formation as Cultural Revolution*. Oxford: Oxford University Press.

Cumings, Bruce. 1999. "Webs with No Spiders, Spiders with No Webs: The Genealogy of the Developmental State." In *The Developmental State*, edited by Meredith Woo-Cummings, 61–92. Ithaca, NY: Cornell University Press.

Cunha, Manuela. 2014. "The Ethnography of Prisons and Penal Confinement." *Annual Review of Anthropology* 43: 217–33.

Dagicour, Ombeline. 2014. "Political Invention in the Andes: The Peruvian Case. An Essay on President Augusto B. Leguía's Strategies and Practices of Power during the Oncenio, 1919–1930." *Jahrbuch für Geschichte Lateinamerikas* 51: 59–86.

Das, Veena. 2007. *Life and Worlds: Violence and the Descent into the Ordinary*. Berkeley: University of California Press.

Das, Veena, and Deborah Poole, eds. 2004. *Anthropology in the Margins of the State*. Santa Fe, NM: SAR Press.

Deere, Carmen Diana. 1990. *Household and Class Relations: Peasants and Landlords in Northern Peru*. Berkeley: University of California Press.

de la Cadena, Marisol. 2000. *Indigenous Mestizos: The Politics of Race and Culture in Cuzco, Peru*. Durham, NC: Duke University Press.

Derrida, Jacques. 2009. *The Beast and the Sovereign*, Volume I. Translated by Geoffrey Bennington. Chicago: University of Chicago Press.

Douglass, Mary. 1966. *Purity and Danger: An Analysis of Concepts of Pollution and Taboo*. London: Routledge.

Drinot, Paulo. 2000. "Peru, 1884–1930: A Beggar Sitting on a Bench of Gold?" In *An Economic History of Twentieth-Century Latin America. Volume I: The Export Age: The Latin American Economies in the Late Nineteenth and Early Twentieth Centuries*, edited by Enrique Cardenas, José Antonio Ocampo, and Rosemary Thorp, 152–87. Basingstoke: Palgrave.

———. 2011. *The Allure of Labor: Workers, Race, and the Making of the Peruvian State*. Durham, NC: Duke University Press.

———. 2018. "Introducción: La Patria Nueva de Leguía a través del siglo XX." In *La Patria Nueva: Economía, sociedad y cultura en el Perú 1919–1930*, edited by Paulo Drinot, 1–34. Raleigh, NC: Editorial A Contracorriente.

Durkheim, Emile. 1915. *The Elementary Forms of the Religious Life: A Study in Religious Sociology*. New York: MacMillan.

Evans, Peter B., Dietrich Rueschemeyer, and Theda Skocpol, eds. 1985. *Bringing the State Back In*. Cambridge: Cambridge University Press.

Ferguson, James. 1990. *The Anti-Politics Machine. "Development," Depoliticization, and Bureaucratic Power in Lesotho*. Cambridge: Cambridge University Press.

———. 2004. "Power Topographies." In *A Companion to the Anthropology of Politics*, edited by David Nugent and Joan Vincent, 383–99. Malden, MA, and Oxford, UK: Blackwell.

Ferguson, James, and Akhil Gupta. 2002. "Spatializing States: Toward an Ethnography of Neoliberal Governmentality." *American Ethnologist* 29 (4): 981–1002.

Fitzpatrick, Sheila, and Robert Gellately. 1997. "Introduction to the Practices of Denunciation in Modern European History." In *Denunciation in Modern European History, 1789–1989*, edited by Sheila Fitzpatrick and Robert Gellatly, 1–21. Chicago: University of Chicago Press.

Flores, Tatiana. 2014. "Dialogues Along a North-South Axis. Avant-Gardists in 1920s Mexico and Peru." *Third Text* 28 (3): 297–310.

Foucault, Michel. 1980. *Power/Knowledge: Selected Interviews and Other Writings, 1972–1977*, edited by Colin Gordon. New York: Pantheon.

———. 2003. *Society Must Be Defended: Lectures at the College de France, 1975–76*, edited by Mauro Bertani et al. New York: Picador.

Frazer, James G. 1922. *The Golden Bough: A Study of Magic and Religion*. New York: Macmillan.

Fried, Morton. 1967. *The Evolution of Political Society: An Essay in Political Anthropology*. New York: Random House.

Galarza, Ernesto. 1931. *Debts, Dictatorship and Revolution in Bolivia and Peru*. New York: Foreign Policy Association.

Galison, Peter. 2004. "Removing Knowledge." *Critical Enquiry* 31 (1): 229–43.

García-Bryce, Iñigo. 2010. "A Revolution Remembered, a Revolution Forgotten: The 1932 Aprista Insurrection in Trujillo, Peru." *A Contracorriente* 7 (3): 277–322.

————. 2014. "Haya de la Torre and the Pursuit of Power in Peru, 1926–1948: The Seven Paradoxes of APRA." *Jahrbuch für Geschichte Lateinamerikas* 51: 87–111.

Geertz, Clifford. 1980. *Negara: The Theatre State in Nineteenth-Century Bali*. Princeton, NJ: Princeton University Press.

Glave, Luis Miguel, and Jaime Urrutia. 2000. "Radicalismo político y élites regionales: Ayacucho 1930–1956." *Debate Agrario* 31: 1–37.

Goody, Jack. 1986. *The Logic of Writing and the Organization of Society*. New York: Cambridge University Press.

Gordillo, Gaston. 2006. "The Crucible of Citizenship: ID-Paper Fetishism in the Argentinean Chaco." *American Ethnologist* 33 (2): 162–76.

Gordon, Avery. 2008. *Ghostly Matters: Haunting and the Sociological Imagination*. Minneapolis: University of Minnesota Press.

Gorman, Stephen. 1979. "The State, Elite and Export in Nineteenth Century Peru." *Journal of Interamerican Studies and World Affairs* 21 (3): 395–418.

Gramsci, Antonio. 1971. *Selections from the Prison Notebooks*, edited and translated by Quintin Hoare and Geoffrey Nowell Smith. New York: International Publishers.

Grandin, Greg, and Gilbert M. Joseph, eds. 2010. *A Century of Revolution: Insurgent and Counterinsurgent Violence During Latin America's Long Cold War*. Durham, NC: Duke University Press.

Gregg, M., and G. Seigworth. 2010. "An Inventory of Shimmers." In *The Affect Theory Reader*, edited by M. Gregg and G. Seigworth, 1–25. Durham, NC: Duke University Press.

Gupta, Akhil. 2012. *Red Tape: Bureaucracy, Structural Violence and Poverty in India*. Durham, NC: Duke University Press.

Hall, Stuart., et al. 1978. *Policing the Crisis. Mugging, the State and Law and Order*. London: Macmillan.

Hansen, Thomas Blom, and Finn Stepputat, eds. 2001. *States of Imagination: Ethnographic Explorations of the Postcolonial State*. Durham, NC: Duke University Press.

————. 2005. *Sovereign Bodies: Citizens, Migrants and States in the Postcolonial World*. Princeton, NJ: Princeton University Press.

Haya de la Torre, Víctor Raúl. 1973. "What Is APRA?" In *APRISMO: The Ideas and Doctrines of Víctor Raúl Haya de la Torre*, edited by Robert J., Alexander. Kent, OH: Kent State University Press.

Heidbrink, Lauren. 2018. "Care in Contexts of Child Detention." Hot Spots, Cultural Anthropology website, January 31. https://culanth.org/fieldsights/1298-care-in-contexts -of-child-detention.

Heilman, Jaymie Patricia. 2006. "We Will No Longer Be Servile: Aprismo in 1930s Ayacucho." *Journal of Latin American Studies* 38 (3): 491–518.

———. 2010. *Before Shining Path: Politics in Rural Ayacucho, 1895–1980*. Stanford, CA: Stanford University Press.

Herbold, Carl R. Jr. 1973. "Developments in the Peruvian Administrative System, 1919–1930: Modern and Traditional Qualities of Government Under Authoritarian Regimes." PhD diss., Yale University.

Herzfeld, Michael. 1992. *The Social Production of Indifference: Exploring the Symbolic Roots of Western Bureaucracy*. New York: Berg.

Hirsch, Steven Jay. 1997. "The Anarcho-Syndicalist Roots of a Multi-Class Alliance: Organized Labor and the Peruvian Aprista Party, 1900–1933." PhD diss., George Washington University.

Hobbes, Thomas. 1964. *Leviathan*. New York: Washington Square Press.

Hubert, Henri, and Marcel Mauss. 1899. *Essai sur la nature et la fonction du sacrifice*. Travaux de *l'Année sociologique*. Paris: Librairie Félix Alcan.

Hull, Matthew S. 2012. *Government of Paper: The Materiality of Bureaucracy in Urban Pakistan*. Berkeley: University of California Press.

Joseph, Gilbert M., and Daniela Spenser, eds. 2007. *In From the Cold: Latin America's New Encounter with the Cold War*. Durham, NC: Duke University Press.

Joseph, Gilbert M., and Daniel Nugent, eds. 1994. *Everyday Forms of State Formation: Revolution and the Negotiation of Rule in Modern Mexico*. Durham, NC: Duke University Press.

Kapferer, Bruce. 1988. *Legends of People, Myths of State: Violence, Intolerance, and Political Culture in Sri Lanka and Australia*. Washington, DC: Smithsonian Institution Press.

Krupa, Christopher, and David Nugent. 2015. "Off-Centered States: Re-Thinking State Theory through an Andean Lens." In *State Theory and Andean Politics: New Approaches to the Study of Rule*, edited by Christopher Krupa and David Nugent, 1–31. Philadelphia: University of Pennsylvania Press.

Larson, Brooke. 2004. *Trials of Nation Making: Liberalism, Race and Ethnicity in the Andes, 1810–1910*. Cambridge; New York: Cambridge University Press.

Laszczkowski, Mateusz, and Madeleine Reeves, eds. 2017. *Affective State: Entanglements, Suspensions, Suspicions*. Oxford: Berghahn.

Lewin, Linda. 1987. *Politics and Parentela in Paraíba. A Case Study of Family-Based Oligarchy in Brazil*. Princeton, NJ: Princeton University Press.

Li, Tania Murray. 2007. *The Will to Improve: Governmentality, Development and the Practice of Politics*. Durham, NC: Duke University Press.

Lomnitz, Larissa Adler. 1987. *A Mexican Elite Family, 1820–1980: Kinship, Class and Culture*. Chapel Hill: University of North Carolina Press.

Lopez-Alvez, Fernando. 2000. *State Formation and Democracy in Latin America, 1810–1900*. Durham, NC: Duke University Press.

Mallon, Florencia. 1983. *The Defense of Community in Peru's Central Highlands*. Princeton, NJ: Princeton University Press.

Mann, Michael. 1986. *The Sources of Social Power: Volume 1, A History of Power from the Beginning to AD 1760*. Cambridge: Cambridge University Press.

————. 1993. *The Sources of Social Power: Volume 2, The Rise of Classes and Nation-States, 1760–1914*. Cambridge: Cambridge University Press.

Manrique, Nelson. 1987. *Mercado interno y region. La sierra central 1820–1930*. Lima: DESCO, Centro de Estudios y Promoción del Desarrollo.

————. 2009. ¡Usted Fue Aprista! Bases para una historia crítica del APRA. Lima: Fondo Editorial, Pontificia Universidad Católica del Perú.

Marcus, Anthony. 2008. "Interrogating the Neo-Pluralist Orthodoxy in American Anthropology." *Dialectical Anthropology* 32 (1–2): 59–86.

Marten, Kimberly. 2012. *Warlords: Strong-Arm Brokers in Weak States*. Ithaca, NY: Cornell University Press.

Marx, Karl. 1898. *The Eighteenth Brumaire of Louis Bonaparte*, translated by Daniel De Leon. New York: International Publishers.

————. 1967 [1867]. *Capital*. Vol. 1. New York: International Publishers.

Masco, Joseph P. 2010. "Sensitive but Unclassified: Secrecy and the Counter-Terrorist State." *Public Culture* 22 (3): 433–63.

Massumi, B. 1995. "The Autonomy of Affect." *Cultural Critique* 31: 83–109.

Matto de Turner, Clorinda. 1948. *Aves sin nido*. Cuzco: Universidad Nacional de Cuzco.

Mauss, Marcel. 2000. *The Gift: The Form and Reason for Exchange in Archaic Societies*, translated by W. D. Hall. New York: Norton.

Mayer, Enrique. 1991. "Peru in Deep Trouble: Mario Vargas Llosa's 'Inquest in the Andes' Reexamined." *Cultural Anthropology* 6 (4): 466–504.

Mbembe, Achile. 2003. "Necropolitics." *Public Culture* 15 (1): 11–40.

McLuhan, Marshall. 1964. *Understanding Media: The Extensions of Man*. New York: Signet.

Messick, Brinkley. 1993. *The Calligraphic State: Textual Domination and History in a Muslim Society*. Berkeley: University of California Press.

Meza Bazán, Mario Miguel. 1999. "Caminos al Progreso. Política vial y movilización laboral. La Ley de Conscripción Vial en el Perú. 1920–1930." Tesis de licenciatura en Historia- UNMSM. Lima.

————. 2003. "Los caminos de la modernidad. La Ley de Conscripción Vial." *Énfasis. Revista de reflexión y debate*, no. 1: 42–49.

————. 2009. "Estado, modernización y la Ley de Conscripción Vial en Perú." *Revista Andina* 49: 165–86.

————. 2011. "Caminos, campesinos y modernización vial en el Perú: Debate político y aplicación de la Ley de Conscripción Vial, 1900–1930." In *Trabajos de historia. Religión, culture y política en el Perú, siglos XVII–XX*, edited by Dino León Fernáandez, Alex Loayza Pérez and Marcos Garfias Dávila, 302–34. Lima: Fondo Editorial, Universidad Nacional Mayor de San Marcos.

MHC (Ministerio de Hacienda y Comercio). 1940. *Extracto estadístico del Perú*. Lima: Dirección de Estadística, Ministerio de Hacienda y Comercio, República del Perú.

————. 1942. *Censo nacional de población de 1940, Tomos III, IX*. Lima: Dirección Nacional de Estadística, República del Perú.

Migdal, Joel S. 1988. *Strong Societies and Weak States: State-Society Relations and State Capabilities in the Third World*. Princeton, NJ: Princeton University Press.

Miliband, Ralph. 1969. *The State in Capitalist Society*. New York: Basic Books.

Miller, Rory. 1982. "The Coastal Elite and Peruvian Politics, 1895–1919." *Journal of Latin American Studies* 14 (1): 97–120.

———. 1987. "Introduction." In *Region and Class in Modern Peruvian History*, edited by Rory Miller, 7–20. Institute of Latin American Studies Monograph No. 14. Liverpool: University of Liverpool.

Mitchell, Timothy. 1991. "The Limits of the State: Beyond Statist Approaches and Their Critics." *American Political Science Review* 85 (1): 77–96.

———. 1999. "Society, Economy and the State Effect." In *State/Culture: State-Formation after the Cultural Turn*, edited by George Steinmetz, 76–97. Ithaca, NY; London, UK: Cornell University Press.

Molina Serra, Ainhoa. 2017. "(Forced) Sterilization in Peru: Power and Narrative Configurations." *Revista de Antropología Iberoamericana* 12 (1): 31–52.

Moore, Barrington Jr. 1966. *Social Origins of Dictatorship and Democracy: Lord and Peasant in the Making of the Modern World*. Boston: Beacon.

Murphy, Eileen, and Mark Maguire. 2015. "Speed, Time and Security: Anthropological Perspectives on Automated Border Control." *Etnofoor* 27 (2): 157–77.

Naphy, William G. 1997. *Fear in Early Modern Society*. Manchester: Manchester University Press.

Navaro-Yashin, Yael. 2002. *Faces of the State: Secularism and Public Life in Turkey*. Princeton, NJ: Princeton University Press.

———. 2006. "Affect in the Civil Service: A Study of a Modern State-System." *Postcolonial Studies* 9 (3): 281–94.

———. 2007. "Make-Believe Papers, Legal Forms and the Counterfeit." *Anthropological Theory* 7 (1): 79–98.

Nettl, J. P. 1968. "The State as a Conceptual Variable." *World Politics* 20 (4): 559–92.

Nielson, Morten. 2007. "The Potency of Fragmented Imaginaries of the State." *Review of African Political Economy* 34 (114): 695–708.

Nugent, David. 1997. *Modernity at the Edge of Empire: State, Individual and Nation in the Northern Peruvian Andes*. Stanford, CA: Stanford University Press.

———. 1999. "State and Shadow State in Turn-of-the-Century Peru: Illegal Political Networks and the Problem of State Boundaries." In *States and Illegal Practices*, edited by Josiah Heyman, 63–98. London: Berg.

———. 2010. "States, Secrecy, Subversives: APRA and Political Fantasy in Mid-20th Century Peru." *American Ethnologist* 37 (4): 681–702.

———. 2014. "Standard Deviations: On Archiving the Awkward Classes in the Northern Peruvian Andes." In *Unarchived Histories: The 'Mad' and the 'Trifling' in the Colonial and Postcolonial World*, edited by Gyanendra Pandey, 58–72. London: Routledge.

———. n.d. "Dark Fantasies of State: Discipline, Dissent and Democracy in the Northern Peruvian Andes." Unpublished, in files of the author.

Nugent, David, and Adeem Suhail. 2018. "State Formation: The Anthropology of Politics, Law, Power and Identity." In *The International Encyclopedia of Anthropology*, edited by Carol Greenhouse, 1–9. Hoboken, NJ: Wiley.

Nunn, Frederick M. 1983. *Yesterday's Soldiers: European Military Professionalism in South America, 1890–1940*. Lincoln: University of Nebraska Press.

O'Gorman, Edmundo. 1972. *The Invention of America: An Inquiry into the Historical Nature of the New World and the Meaning of Its History*. Westport, CT: Greenwood Press.

Ollman, Bertell. 1971. *Alienation: Marx's Conception of Man in Capitalist Society*. Cambridge: Cambridge University Press.

Paige, Jeffrey M. 1998. *Coffee and Power: Revolution and the Rise of Democracy in Central America*. Cambridge, MA: Harvard University Press.

Palmer, Robert R. 1959–1964. *The Age of the Democratic Revolution: A History of Europe and America, 1760–1800*. Princeton, NJ: Princeton University Press.

Pereyra Chávez, Nelson E. 2002. "Los campesinos y la conscripción vial: aproximaciones al studio de las relaciones estado-indígenas y las relaciones de Mercado en Ayacucho (1919–1930)." In *Estado y Mercado en la Historia del Perú*, edited by Carlos Contreras y Manuel Glave, 334–50. Lima: Pontificia Universidad Católica del Perú.

Pietz, William. 1985. "The Problem of the Fetish I." *RES: Anthropology and Aesthetics* 9: 5–17.

Polanyi, Karl. 1944. *The Great Transformation: The Political and Economic Origins of Our Time*. New York: Farrar and Rinehart.

Poulantzas, Nicos. 1975. *Political Power and Social Classes*, edited and translated by Timothy O'Hagen. London: New Left Books.

Rice, Susan E., Corinne Graff, and Carlos Pascual, eds. 2010. *Confronting Poverty: Weak States and U.S. National Security*. Washington, DC: Brookings Institution Press.

Sedgwick, E. Kosofsky, and A. Frank. 1995. "Shame in the Cybernetic Fold: Reading Silvan Tomkins." In *Shame and Its Sisters: A Silvan Tomkins Reader*, edited by E. Kosofky Sedgwick and A. Frank, 1–28. Durham, NC: Duke University Press.

Smith, W. Robertson. 1927. *Lectures on the Religion of the Semites: The Fundamental Institutions*. 3rd ed. New York: Macmillan.

Roitman, Janet. 2013. *Anti-Crisis*. Durham, NC: Duke University Press.

Roseberry, William. 1994. "Hegemony and the Language of Contention." In *Everyday Forms of State Formation: Revolution and the Negotiation of Rule in Modern Mexico*, edited by Gilbert M. Joseph and Daniel Nugent, 355–77. Durham, NC: Duke University Press.

Rowe, John Howland. 1957. "The Incas Under Spanish Colonial Institutions." *Hispanic American Historical Review* 37 (2): 155–99.

Ruiz, Teófilo F. 2011. *The Terror of History: On the Uncertainties of Life in Western Civilization*. Princeton, NJ: Princeton University Press.

Santillán Bernuy, Germán. 2003. *Apuntes Para La Historia del Apra en Amazonas. Chávez Vargas. Chachapoyas 1930*, edited by Eduardo Pelaez Bardales. Lima: n.p.

Sayer, Derek. 1994. "Everyday Forms of State Formation: Some Dissident Remarks on 'Hegemony.'" In *Everyday Forms of State Formation: Revolution and the Negotiation of Rule in Modern Mexico*, edited by Gilbert M. Joseph and Daniel Nugent, 367–77. Durham, NC: Duke University Press.

Scott, James C. 1985. *Weapons of the Weak: Everyday Forms of Peasant Resistance*. New Haven, CT: Yale University Press.

———. 1998. *Seeing Like a State: How Certain Schemes to Improve the Human Condition Have Failed*. New Haven, CT: Yale University Press.

———. 2009. *The Art of Not Being Governed: An Anarchist History of Upland Southeast Asia*. New Haven, CT: Yale University Press.

Shanin, Teodor. 1972. *The Awkward Class. Political Sociology of Peasantry in a Developing Society: Russia, 1910–1925*. Oxford: Clarendon.

Sharma, Aradhana. 2014. *Democracy and Transparency in the Indian State: The Making of the Right to Information Act*. New York: Routledge.

Sharma, Aradhana, and Akhil Gupta. 2006. "Introduction: Rethinking Theories of the State in an Age of Globalization." In *The Anthropology of the State: A Reader*, edited by Aradhana Sharma and Akhil Gupta, 1–43. Malden, MA; Oxford, UK: Blackwell.

Shipton, Parker. 1989. *Bitter Money: Cultural Economy and Some African Meanings of Forbidden Commodities*. American Ethnological Society Monograph Series, 1. Washington, DC: American Anthropological Association.

Silverblatt, Irene. 2015. "Haunting the Modern Andean State: Colonial Legacies of Race and Civilization." In *State Theory and Andean Politics: New Approaches to the Study of Rule*, edited by Christopher Krupa and David Nugent, 167–85. Philadelphia: University of Pennsylvania Press.

Skidmore, Monique. 2004. *Karaoke Fascism: Burma and the Politics of Fear*. Philadelphia: University of Pennsylvania Press.

Spalding, Karen. 1984. *Huarochirí: An Andean Society Under Inca and Spanish Rule*. Stanford, CA: Stanford University Press.

Spenser, Daniela. 1999. *The Impossible Triangle: Mexico, Soviet Russia and the United States in the 1920s*. Durham, NC: Duke University Press.

Stein, Steve. 1980. *Populism in Peru: The Emergence of the Masses and the Politics of Social Control*. Madison: University of Wisconsin Press.

———. 1986. "Popular Culture and Politics in Early Twentieth-Century Lima." *New World* 1 (2): 65–91.

Steinmetz, George, ed. 1999. *State/Culture: State Formation After the Cultural Turn*. Ithaca, NY: Cornell University Press.

Stoler, Anne L. 1995. *Race and the Education of Desire: Foucault's History of Sexuality and the Colonial Order of Things*. Durham, NC: Duke University Press.

———. 2002. *Carnal Knowledge and Imperial Power: Race and the Intimate in Colonial Rule*. Berkeley: University of California Press.

Taussig, Michael. 1980. *The Devil and Commodity Fetishism in South America*. Chapel Hill: University of North Carolina Press.

———. 1997. *The Magic of the State*. New York: Routledge.

———. 2003. *Law in a Lawless Land: Diary of a Limpieza in Colombia*. Chicago: University of Chicago Press.

Taylor, Diana. 1997. *Disappearing Acts: Spectacles of Gender and Nationalism in Argentina's Dirty War*. Durham, NC: Duke University Press.

Taylor, Lewis. 1986. *Bandits and Politics in Peru: Landlord and Peasant Violence in Hualgayoc 1900–30*. Cambridge Latin American Miniatures, No. 2. Centre of Latin American Studies. Cambridge: Cambridge University.

———. 2000. "The Origins of APRA in Cajamarca, 1928–1935." *Bulletin of Latin American Research* 19 (4): 437–59.

Thiranagama, Sharika, and Tobias Kelly. 2010. "Introduction: Specters of Treason." In *Traitors: Suspicion, Intimacy, and the Ethics of State-Building*, edited by Sharika Thiranagama and Tobias Kelly, 1–23. Philadelphia: University of Pennsylvania Press.

Thompson, E. P. 1963. *The Making of the English Working Class*. New York: Vintage.

Tilly, Charles. 1985. "War Making and State Making as Organized Crime." In *Bringing the State Back In*, edited by Peter B Evans, Dietrich Rueschemeyer, and Theda Skocpol, 169–91. Cambridge: Cambridge University Press.

———. 1990. *Coercion, Capital and European States: AD 990–1992*. Malden, MA; Oxford, UK: Wiley-Blackwell.

Trouillot, Michel-Rolph. 2001. "The Anthropology of the State in the Age of Globalization: Close Encounters of the Deceptive Kind." *Current Anthropology* 42 (1): 125–38.

Turner, Victor W. 1969. *The Ritual Process: Structure and Anti-Structure*. Ithaca, NY: Cornell University Press.

Tylor, Edward B. 1871. *Primitive Culture: Researches into the Development of Mythology, Philosophy, Religion, Art, and Custom*. London: John Murray.

Vega-Centeno B., Imelda. 1991. *Aprismo popular. Cultura, religión y política*. Lima: Tarea.

Vincent, Joan. 1990. *Anthropology and Politics: Visions, Traditions, and Trends*. Tucson: University of Arizona Press.

Weber, Max. 1980. "Politics as a Vocation." In *From Max Weber: Essays in Sociology*, translated and edited by H. H. Gerth and C. Wright Mills, 77–128. New York: Oxford University Press.

Wightman, Ann M. 1990. *Indigenous Migration and Social Change: The Forasteros of Cuzco, 1570–1720*. Durham, NC: Duke University Press.

Williams, Raymond. 1977. *Marxism and Literature*. Oxford: Oxford University Press.

Wilson, Fiona. 2013. *Citizenship and Political Violence in Peru. An Andean Town, 1870s–1970s*. New York: Palgrave/MacMillan.

Wolf, Eric R. 1969. *Peasant Wars of the Twentieth Century*. New York: Harper & Row.

———. 1982. *Europe and the People Without History*. Berkeley: University of California Press.

Young, Jock. 1971. *The Drugtakers: The Social Meaning of Drug Use*. London: Judson, McGibbon and Kee.

Yurchak, Alexi. 2003. "Soviet Hegemony of Form." *Comparative Studies in Society and History* 45 (3): 480–510.

———. 2006. *Everything Was Forever Until It Was No More: The Last Soviet Generation*. Princeton, NJ: Princeton University Press.

Žižek, Slavoj. 1997. *The Plague of Fantasies*. London; New York: Verso.

Index